LOUIS PHILIPPE D'ORLÉANS
KING OF THE FRENCH
1773–1850

LOUIS PHILIPPE D'ORLÉANS
1773–1850
KING OF THE FRENCH 1830

UNSUNG HERO

Ann Allestree

Ann Allestree (signature)

Book Guild Publishing
Sussex, England

July 2012 (handwritten)

First published in Great Britain in 2012 by
The Book Guild Ltd
Pavilion View
19 New Road
Brighton, BN1 1UF

Typesetting in Garamond by
YHT Ltd, London

Printed in Great Britain by
CPI Antony Rowe

A catalogue record for this book is available from
The British Library.

ISBN 978 1 84624 717 0

For
Prince Jean D'Orléans
Duc d'Vendôme

and

Tom, my husband

Allestrey
C·33—C·34—

Right: family tree reproduced from
Bourbon-Orléans: A Family Album,
Prince Michael of Greece

LOUIS PHILIPPE I
King of the French 1830-1848
1773-1850 m1809
MARIE AMÉLIE THÉRÈSE
Princess of The Two Sicilies 1782-1866

Ferdinand, Duke of Orleans
1810-1842 m1837 **Hélène**
of Mecklenburg-Schwerin 1814-1858

> **Philippe, Count of Paris**
> 1838-1894 m1864
> **Isabella, Infanta of Spain 1848-1919**
>
> **Robert, Duke of Chartres**
> 1840-1910 m1863
> **Francois of Orléans 1844-1925**

Louise
1812-1850 m1832 **Léopold I,**
King of the Belgians 1790-1865

> **Léopold of Belgium 1833-1834**
>
> **Léopold II of Belgium 1835-1909 m1853**
> **Marie Henriette of Austria 1836-1902**
>
> **Philippe, Count of Flanders 1837-1905**
> m1867 **Marie of Hohenzollern 1845-1912**
>
> **Charlotte of Belgium 1840-1927 m1857**
> **Maximilian I of Mexico 1832-1867**

Marie
1813-1850 m1832 **Alexander**
of Württemberg 1804-1881

> **Philipp of Württemberg**
> 1838-1917 m1865
> **Maria Theresia of Austria**
> 1845-1927

Louis, Duke of Nemours
1814-1896 m1840 **Victoire of**
Saxe-Coburg and Gotha 1822-1857

> **Gaston, Comte d'Eu**
> 1842-1922 m1864 **Isabel,**
> **Princess Imperial of Brazil 1846-1921**
>
> **Ferdinand, Duke of Alencon**
> 1844-1910 m1868
> **Sophie, Duchess in Bavaria 1847-1897**
>
> **Marguerite of Orléans 1846-1893**
> m1872 **Wladyslaw Czartoryski 1828-1894**
>
> **Blanche of Orléans 1857-1943**

Francoise, Prince of Joinville
1818-1900 m1843 **Francoise**
of Brazil 1824-1898

> **Francoise of Orléans**
> 1844-1925 m1863
> **Robert, Duke of Chartres**
> 1840-1910
>
> **Pierre, Duke of Penthièvre**
> 1845-1919
>
> son 1849

Charles
1820-1828

Henri, Duke of Aumale
1822-1897 m1844 **Marie Caroline**
of The Two Sicilies 1822-1869

> **Louis Philippe, Prince of Condé**
> 1846-1866
>
> **Henri, Duke of Guise 1847-1847**
>
> **Francois, Duke of Guise 1852-1852**
>
> **Francois Louis, Duke of Guise**
> 1854-1872

Antoine, Duke of Montpensier
1824-1890 m1846 **Luisa Fernanda,**
Infanta of Spain 1832-1897

> **Infanta Isabella 1848-1919 m1864**
> **Philippe, Count of Paris 1838-1894**
>
> **Infanta Maria Amélia 1851-1870**
>
> **Infanta Maria Christina 1852-1879**
>
> **Infanta Maria dela Regla 1856-1861**
>
> **Infante Fernando 1859-1873**
>
> **Infanta Maria de las Mercedes 1860-1878**
> m1878 **Alfonso XII, King of Spain**
>
> **Infante Felipe 1862-1864**
>
> **Infante Antonio 1866-1930 m1886**
> **Infanta Eulalia of Spain 1864-1958**

Francoise
1816-1818

Clémentine
1817-1907 m1843 **August**
of Saxe-Coburg 1818-1881

> **Philipp of Saxe-Coburg 1844-1921**
> m1875 **Louise of Belgium 1858-1924**
>
> **August of Saxe-Coburg 1845-1907**
> m1864 **Leopoldina of Brazil 1847-1871**
>
> **Clotilde of Saxe-Coburg 1846-1927**
> m1864 **Joseph of Austria 1833-1905**
>
> **Amalie of Saxe-Coburg 1848-1894 m1875**
> **Max Emanuel, Duke in Bavaria 1849-1893**
>
> **Ferdinand, King of Bulgaria 1861-1848**
> m1893 **Marie Louise of Parma 1870-1899**
> m1908 **Eleonore of Reuss 1860-1917**

PHILIPPE, Duc d'Orléans,
younger son of King Louis XIII (ob. 1701)
m 1. **HENRIETTA MARIA**, d. of Charles I of England
m 2. **CHARLOTTE ELIZABETH**, d. of Charles, Elector Palatine

1. Maria Louisa
m **Charles II, King of Spain**

2. Philippe,
Duc d'Orléans, **Regent of France** (ob. 1723)

Philippe Louis (ob. 1752)

Louis Philippe (ob. 1785)
m Louisa Henrietta, d. of Armand, Prince de Conti

Louis Philippe Joseph, Duc d'Orléans, ("Egalité") (b. 1747; ob. 1793)
m Louise Marie Adélaïde of Bourbon, d. of Duc de Penthièvre

Louis Philippe, Duc d'Orléans King of the French, 1830-48
(b. 6 Oct. 1773; ob. 26 Aug. 1850)
m **Marie Amélie**, d. of Ferdinand IV of Naples
(b. 26 April 1782)

Adélaïde, **Mademoiselle d'Orléans**

Antoine, **Duc de Montpensier**
(ob. 1807)

Alphonse, **Comte de Beaujolais,**
(ob. 1808)

Ferdinand, Duc d'Orléans (b. 1810; ob. 1842)
m Hélène Louise, Duchess of Mecklenburg Schwerin

Louise Marie Thérèse, Queen of the Belgians (b. 1812; ob. 1850)

Louis Charles, Duc de Nemours (b. 1814; ob. 1859)
m Victoire Princess of Saxe-Coburg

Marie Christine, (b. 1813; ob. 1839)
m **Prince Frederick of Würtemberg**

Marie Clementine, (b. 1817; ob. 1907)
m **Augustus Prince of Saxe-Coburg-Gotha**

François, Prince de Joinville (b. 1818; ob. 1906)
m **Françoise Princess of Braganza**

Henri, Duc d'Aumale (b. 1822; ob. 1897)
m **Caroline Princess of Naples**

Antoine, Duc de Montpensier (b. 1824; ob. 1890)
m **Maria Luisa Infanta of Spain**

Louis Philippe Comte de Paris (b. 24 Aug. 1838)
Robert Duc de Chartres (b. 9 Nov. 1840)

Louis Comte d'Eu (b. 28 April 1842)
Ferdinand Duc d'Alençon (b. 12 July 1844)
Two daughters

1. **Pierre Duc de Penthièvre** (b. 4 Nov. 1845)
2. A daughter

Louis Philippe Prince de Condé (b. 15 Nov. 1845)
François Duc de Guise (b. 5 Jan. 1854)

1. **Ferdinand** (b. 30 May 1859)
2. Four daughters

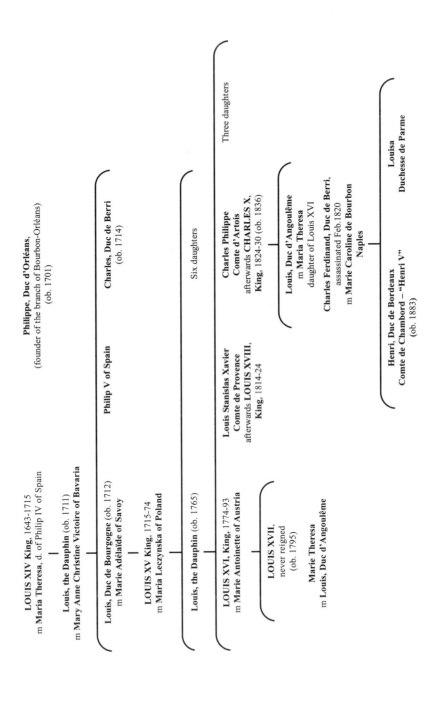

LOUIS XIV King, 1643-1715
m **Maria Theresa,** d. of Philip IV of Spain
|
Louis, the Dauphin (ob. 1711)
m **Mary Anne Christine Victoire of Bavaria**

Philippe, Duc d'Orléans,
(founder of the branch of Bourbon-Orléans)
(ob. 1701)

Louis, Duc de Bourgogne (ob. 1712)
m **Marie Adélaïde of Savoy**

Philip V of Spain

Charles, Duc de Berri
(ob. 1714)

LOUIS XV King, 1715-74
m **Maria Leczynska of Poland**

Louis, the Dauphin (ob. 1765)

Six daughters

LOUIS XVI, King, 1774-93
m **Marie Antoinette of Austria**

Louis Stanislas Xavier
Comte de Provence
afterwards **LOUIS XVIII,**
King, 1814-24

Charles Philippe
Comte d'Artois
afterwards **CHARLES X,**
King, 1824-30 (ob. 1836)

Three daughters

LOUIS XVII,
never reigned
(ob. 1795)

Marie Theresa
m **Louis, Duc d'Angoulême**

Louis, Duc d'Angoulême
m **Maria Theresa**
daughter of Louis XVI

Charles Ferdinand, Duc de Berri,
assassinated Feb.1820
m **Marie Caroline de Bourbon**
Naples

Henri, Duc de Bordeaux
Comte de Chambord – "Henri V"
(ob. 1883)

Louisa
Duchesse de Parme

ix

Acknowledgements

My acknowledgements and thanks to the Musée Louis Philippe at Château d'Eu; and to the curator, Mme Martine Bailleux.

To Mr Christopher Forbes, for his photographs from the Louis Philippe collection at his Château de Balleroy.

To Georges Lenoir, Conservateur at Château de Balleroy.

To Penelope Hatfield, archivist at Eton College Library, who led me to the etching by Pingret, of Louis Philippe's visit.

To Howard Farrar FRICS, Development Director of Claremont, now a school. He gave me an evocative tour of the handsome rooms where the Orleáns family dined & prayed & slept.

To Douglas Matthews for the incomparable index.

To Yvonne Saltoun for her accuracy through all the drafts of the manuscript.

Lastly, to William Drummond, for his photograph of Monsieur de Perthuis' house, set high above Honfleur, where the Royal couple hid in fear and cold before their escape by steamer to Newhaven.

Preface

Who led me to Louis Philippe? For thirty years the portrait of a young woman has hung on our drawing-room wall. She has a pleasant face, luxuriously decked in an upswept crown of fair hair and ringlets. An intelligent and thoughtful face, with a hint of melancholy. Her enviable waist is caught in a dress of old gold taffeta, lavishly adorned with turquoise ribbons; the majestic frame has vestiges of Versailles. She was indeed a lady-in-waiting to Marie Antoinette. She was the Duchesse de Chartres; to become the Duchesse d'Orléans. I knew that one day I would write of her. To cheer her chronic doldrums I would slip flowers between the gilded cartouches of her frame. When I discovered that she had been the mother of four surviving children; that her eldest son was to become Louis Philippe the first, King of the French ... I switched courses.

Delving through Adolphe Thiers' *History of the French Revolution* and other contemporary reflections, Louis Philippe's arresting existence spilled out before me. Buffeted by revolution and army campaigns; a Général at nineteen years, and forcibly exiled to save his neck. Hounded for his arrest; alone, penniless and footsore, he had tramped the Alps. Finally, he found a few months' respite; above the Rhine, at Reichenau, he was offered a post at a boys' college; he taught Geography and Mathematics; and the pretty Italian cook, on how to fall in love with him. It was all a tough initiation for an incognito Prince; a struggle for survival. So young, so sensible, he had soon become a good judge of men and flexible to pressures.

In this biography of Louis Philippe, I have chosen to discard bias and I confess to an outrageous attraction for the man. I can appreciate calumnious argument to provoke political jibe; but was he avaricious? Did he steer his children into positions of marital advantage for himself and his country? Was he not determined that his own youthful experiences of appalling violence would never be vented on them?

Could Louis Philippe now be judged as a man for our time? A dedicated family man; with his irresistible sense of humour, his humanity and compassion? His assiduous reading from early life lent him a sharp intuition for the men around him; it gave a cultural energy to his restoration of France's Palaces and Monuments. His readiness to throw himself into the fray of battle, riots and attempted assassination was legendary.

There were two damaging traits in Louis Philippe's character. He was an unmitigated pacifist and ... he liked to be liked. For both, he was unfairly reproached and derided.

1

The young Colonel leapt on to a small bench beside the inn. He yelled for calm as the mounting crowd surged before him. It paused to ogle this authoritative adventurer in his dark green military uniform with silver buttons. And then more shrill abuse shattered the lush folds of the Loire valley – and threats of death. The two terrified non-juring priests who had provoked this fury had darted into the inn for their very survival. They had been seen pulling faces at the newly appointed 'Constitutional' curé as he had carried the Holy Sacrament in the Fête-Dieu's morning procession.

It was Friday June 24th, 1791 and the Mayor of Vendôme had agreed to the astute Colonel's offer that his 14th Regiment of Dragoons should stand by on horseback throughout the parade. The venerable occasion had passed without incident and by two o'clock the Colonel and his officers had disbanded for lunch. Suddenly, at table, they had been shocked by a breathless messenger warning of riots in the main street.

The Mayor was now seriously alarmed at the plight of the lone Colonel holding his own with this menacing crowd. The two priests clearly had to be removed from the inn before the door was forced in. He sent for a carriage. 'They are lawbreakers; they must be hanged; string them up from the lamp posts!' The Colonel calmed and cajoled from his stance on the bench. He waited in trepidation for the carriage and slowly claimed the morbid rabble's attention. He was a good patriot, it finally conceded, and out of respect for his courage and humanity, it would spare the priests. 'Do you promise me?' urged the Colonel. 'Yes, yes, yes, yes!' The carriage arrived and the wretched men were hustled out of the inn, half fearful of being lynched and torn to shreds. But they were denied the expedience of a carriage. 'Let them walk, so that we can hiss at them at our leisure!' The Colonel was quick to remind the surly mob of its promise and that the priests would be escorted out of town by himself, the Mayor and two officers. A river lay a mile beyond, with a little bridge and no handrail. A horde of alerted and armed peasants had raced down a hill to meet the party. They were clearly intent on throwing the terrified prey into the water and were already aiming sticks between their legs to trip them up.

'The rotten bastards must be hanged!' And cries of 'Death! Death!' heralded their hideous advance. The Colonel grabbed one of the priests around the waist and the other by the arm, while the Mayor was borne off bodily into the crowd. These evil ruffians had made no pledge to spare the two men. Next, a purposeful rogue sprang out and levelled his carbine at their hearts. But the Colonel braced himself flat before his two charges. 'You kill me first!' he shouted and his unexpected and imperious command rang out to all. He continued, 'They must be tried; to the prison, take them to the prison.' 'Prison! Prison!' echoed the brawling mob and had the satisfaction of seeing the two unfortunates delivered to the jailer at his gate.

A few weeks later, the intrepid Colonel had another opportunity to demonstrate his courage. On August 3rd, after a tiring day at the barracks disciplining his men and horses, he had taken a bath. Putting on his clothes, he heard frantic screams from the river close by. 'Help! Help! I am drowning!' He jumped, fully dressed, into the water crying 'Courage, my friend. I am coming to you fast.' The Colonel reached the exhausted man as his hands slid under the water. The victim clung desperately to his rescuer while the two men were close to being engulfed by the current. Mercifully, the Colonel's domestic, a virile negro named Edouard Noir, had also heard the shouts for help and swam vigorously towards the two men. Disentangling them, he managed with pain and difficulty to deliver them to the bank. It transpired that the man near death was Monsieur Siret, the invaluable sub-engineer to the bridges and embankment of Vendôme.

Two such feats of brave initiative had not escaped the notice of the municipality and the Colonel was presented with a civic crown; painted on toile with oak leaves and entwined ribbon, to encircle the words 'A l'humanite et au courage; décernée par la ville de Vendôme.' In mid-August, when the 14th Regiment of the Dragoons set off for the garrison at Valenciennes, they were given an effusive farewell. Wrote the Colonel in his diary: 'A lovely day. Long live the Dragoons! There's no regiment like them in France; with such men, we'll give a fine reception to any beggar who has the audacity to set foot on French soil and the country will be free or we will perish with her...' To his good friend, Monsieur de Musset-Pathay, he had given the Vendômin trophy for safekeeping. In years to come, their two sons would be exact contemporaries at the Lycée Henri IV in Paris: namely, the future poet Alfred de Musset and the Duc de Chartres.

But before resuming the command of his Regiment on the North Frontier, the Colonel, who should now be identified as the Duc de Chartres, the future Louis Philippe, the King of the French, had disturbing private matters to assimilate.

On June 23rd news had been sent to him from Madame de Genlis, his former cloying preceptress, of the Royal flight to Varennes. Félicité de Genlis was proving an avid correspondent. The previous week she had urged him to develop his seat in the saddle, to practise pistol-shooting, to assume a noble air of poise and to avoid milk foods, salt-meat and pastry. As ever, she had ended on an effusive note ... 'Farewell, then, dear child, I embrace you from the depths of my heart.'

Her timely report of the King and Queen and family mysteriously leaving the Tuileries at 23.50 hours on Monday June 20th had arrived at Vendôme two days later. The gates of Paris had been locked when the king's escape had been discovered and dispatches were forbidden. The Duc de Chartres, now nearing eighteen years, read Félicité de Genlis' letter with shock and considerable alarm.

June 21

My friend,
   The King and all the Royal Family have escaped in the night. All Paris is in turmoil ... the people and all good patriots are behaving perfectly.
   He escaped along the subterranean passages of the Tuileries kitchen. My son, summon up all your prudence, all your courage; I have no anxieties as to your conduct ... You will shed, if need be, the last drop of your blood for the cause of liberty...!

On the morning of June 22nd she had written again describing 'an admirable state of order throughout Paris'. In the evening, she continued: 'I have just learned the King has been stopped at Varennes, five leagues from the frontier, this is positive ... Goodnight, dear friend. I await news of you

3

with extreme impatience...' By midnight on June 24th, she was coasting along with her familiar defiance at the *Ancien Régime*.

Oh, my son!

Thanks to the Revolution, we live in a century when the man himself and not his rank makes his reputation.

She next unleashed her republican relish on the scenario of the King and Queen quavering before the officious Monsieur Sausse, procurator and sometime grocer, of Varennes, and begging for his help.

News of the King's flight to Varennes and his summary arrest was calamity of the first order. As the Duc de Chartres and a Prince of the Blood, our military fledgling was aghast. He had been received as a member of the left-wing Jacobin Club on November 1st, 1790. The Marquis de Sillery, Mme de Genlis' husband, had presented him at the headquarters of the former Convent of the Jacobin Order, in Paris. He had already attended the Vendôme local branch where he had made a zestful speech. His bombastic assurance was applauded as he swore to renounce his titles and privileges (this new decree just issued by the National Assembly at Versailles). He vowed to his bemused audience that courage and patriotism were to be his only values. But, confronted with the clash and conflict of his loyalty to the King and his newly founded social inclinations, he now felt soundly toppled.

He noted in his diary: 'Although the King's flight and his arrest at Varennes had absolutely nothing to do with me ... it is necessary to know the facts about them to be in a position to understand the consequences arising from them.' He resolved to visit Varennes and in September 1792, under the charge of Général Dumouriez, the Commander-in-Chief of the armies on the North Frontier and in Belgium, the army camp was installed just five leagues away. In the hamlet of Braux-Sainte-Cohière, the quadrilateral château, with its moats and turrets and ample stabling, reigned in feudal seclusion behind a screen of chestnut trees. The château was re-christened Braux-sous-Valmy in deference to the revolutionary authorities. The owner, Le Seigneur Origny, and his two daughters had been allowed to stay, on condition they tended the sheep, the piggery and the horses. The Seigneur had promptly emigrated. And so the pigeons fluttered around the fortress as the military prepared and pined for the nearby battle on the hill and their proverbial victory at Valmy.

Louis Philippe knew that the berline had passed through this hamlet around 21h.30 on June 21st, 1791. They had been one hour and a half away from their fateful entry into Varennes. A frisson ran through him as the timbered houses and barns, the church and the château with gates fast shut, crowded in on the narrow road to haunt the autumn dusk.

Taking the long straight road from Clermont, the berline, hung with lanterns, had forged its way on to Varennes. The valley, and hills and darkening forests of the Argonne had enveloped it in halcyon calm. The children, Marie Thérèse, aged thirteen years and the six-year-old dauphin, Louis Charles, dozed fitfully, cuddled against their mother and their aunt Elisabeth, the sister of the King. In her memoirs, Marie Thérèse – to become the Duchesse d'Angoulême – recalled the savage jolt of the berline as it was stopped before the entrance to a dark vaulted archway that served as the town gate.

Of his own arrival at Varennes, some eighteen months later, Louis Philippe wrote: 'I took good note of its landmarks, so I can speak with certainty.' He described the arch, humped on the steep hill that led down to the narrow bridge over the river Aire. It was a typical country town of the Argonne: red roofs and slate steeples, the church, the convent, the mill and the Auberge au Bras d'Or; more a republican venue. The recherché Hôtel du Grand Monarque was sited on the lower right bank by the bridge. It was at this vantage point that a detachment of Hussars, under the command of Officer Délon, was ready and vigilant for the berline's arrival. Stationed on the immediate opposite bank was a fresh relay of horses and a considerable escort of Cavalry. The last lap of the King's escape had been amply provided for; he and his family would have been free, as they were raced across the Meuse, through the Lorraine to Metz and to the loyal guard of Général de Bouillé beyond. Alas! By overwhelming negligence, the arrival of the berline on the hill had not been noted by the Hussars far below. Officer Délon had blundered; the Royal party had reckoned on fresh horses at the top arch entrance.

In his own account of the escalating dilemma, Louis Philippe made the sanguine observation: "It seems that a lash of the whip administered to the horses at this point would have saved the King." No horses! No escort! And a devastated king, who shouted in vain to the postilions to charge down the hill in search of cavalry. But the horses were now spent and their riders dismounting. Marie Antoinette's last-ditch bribe of fifty louis to each man – of no avail.

Still the berline creaked and swayed through the gaping black arch. A clattering of hooves as it emerged, slow as a snail, to the rasping command '*Halte-là!*' and '*Au feu!*'. Mme de Tourzel, the children's governess, peeping from her carriage window, saw men with muskets, together with an authoritative figure holding a lantern. Monsieur Jean-Baptiste Sausse, the town procurator and candle maker, made his peremptory enquiries. Where were they going? To Frankfurt? It would seem they had lost their way ... The passport? He would have to examine it overnight. Would they care to step down and accept accommodation in his house close by? The time was 23.30. The tocsin shrilled throughout the town. An agitated crowd was swarming up the hill. The movement of troops and the cavalry beside the river below had panicked them; the blocking of the bridge with a tipped-up wagonload of furniture and dung disturbed them. Above all, the rumour that Général de Bouillé and his troops would massacre the citizens of Varennes if the berline had not been released on their arrival had swept them into waves of hysteria and mayhem. The Royal Family accepted the grocer's offer with alacrity.

Meanwhile, Drouet, the young postmaster from Sainte-Ménehould, had galloped through the forest of Argonne and alerted Sausse of the identity of the travellers. And it was Drouet who had tipped the blockade over the bridge and was now alerting the crowd that their King and Queen and two children were bent on fleeing to a foreign land.

Ensconced in the homely setting of a grocer's shop, with its waxy aroma of tallow and sausage meat, the two exhausted children were put to bed. A bottle of burgundy momentarily calmed Mme Sausse's distinguished visitors. The King, weeping with relief and fatigue, explained to his modest audience of municipal officers that he had come to the provinces to find the peace and freedom such as they enjoyed; if he had stayed in Paris, he would have been murdered. Marie Antoinette, observing her husband's surprise performance with due *froideur*, tried Mme Sausse for sympathy. 'Oh! Madame! You have children, a husband, a family!'

'I would like to help you, certainly; but as you think of the King, I myself think of Monsieur Sausse,' was the tart reply.

The night was continuously buffeted by the shrieks and turmoil of the swelling crowd. '*A* Paris! *A* Paris!' was the hysterical demand. The king had abandoned all hope of Général de Bouillé's rescue arrival. At 7.30am, the party descended Sausse's narrow back staircase and stepped into their berline for their ignominious return to Paris. (At 9am, Bouillé's cavalry had Varennes in its sights.)

At the time of Louis Philippe's visit to Varennes, he would have seen Sausse's timber-framed and cob house. The Sausses themselves had been incriminated for the timely aid given to their King, and had emigrated to Saint-Mihiel, a prosperous Benedictine town on the banks of the Meuse. But when on September 3rd, 1792 this ancient stronghold was invaded by the Prussian army, Mme Sausse, in her escape, fell down a hole breaking both legs. She died days later. By 1793, an inscription marked the strategic clock tower on the hill:

Le 21 Juin 1791
entre 11 heures et minuit
en cet endroit
furent arrêtés Louis XVI
et la Famille Royale ...

And Mme Sausse had not been denied her parting shot at the King. As he set off on the gruelling return to Paris, she had reminded him that the Nation paid him **24 million**. Worth keeping, she felt; he must be queer in the head if he wanted to give that up.

The valley of the Marne was hung with haze and rising heat. The morning sun added to the stifling temperature. Streams of villagers ready to revile the disgraced family lined the narrow roads. One man leaned into the carriage window and spat in the King's face. Another, at variance with the tone of the day, made a gesture of respect to the Queen; he was shot and decapitated. These fiendish crowds were rehearsing for a full-blown revolution.

Alexandre Dumas, in his own account sixty years later, assured his readers that no event of the French Revolution was invested with more drama than the flight of the Royal Family towards the East Frontiers. Across the Channel, Lord Beaconsfield later voted the Siege of Troy and the French Revolution the only two events in history.

2

On June 14th, 1791, when Louis Philippe had rejoined his regiment at Vendôme, he had first taken his leave of the King and Queen at the Tuileries. He had been given a markedly cold reception. Certainly, he had appreciated their dire troubles and vulnerability; the emigration of the nobility and the ultra-Royalist aristocracy was an incalculable threat to their very existence. The King's youngest brother, the Comte d'Artois, and the Orléans Princes of Condé and Conti had already fled to the Rheinland. His heir presumptive, the Comte de Provence, with his alcohol-prone wife, the daughter of the King of Sardinia, were to quit France the same night as his own planned escape; they subsequently settled in Koblenz.

The young Louis Philippe, standing before the King and Queen, and mindful that they were his godparents, recalled a glorious gold morning at Versailles in 1785. He had been twelve years old and the occasion was his Christening. The massive and lustrous Palace façade had captivated him with its phalanx of pillars and soaring arched windows. He had watched the arrival of the fine équipages from his father's carriage, with its Orléans livery; next the parade of magnificent gowns and uniforms thronging the candlelit chapel. How the trumpets had swelled as the King and Queen arrived! They had each taken his hands and led him to the font. Marie Antoinette! With her cloud of fair curls mounted high with nodding plumes. Her dress and train drowned in diamonds. How ravishing she was that day and how young.

But eight years on, in the sombre confines of the Tuileries, he now pitied her fatigue and distress. The neck and chin had thickened and her hair was whitening too fast for a thirty-six-year-old woman. But still the young Duc inwardly applauded her allure and fine deportment as she swayed towards him. The silent King had sat like stone throughout; his pasty features fallen, his manner irresolute.

Louis Philippe noted the meeting in his memoirs: 'I had constantly gone to the Tuileries to discharge my duties towards Their Majesties since they had been installed there, and this was the last time that I had the honour of paying them my court.' A coolness and distrust had pervaded relations between the Bourbon kings and the legitimized Orléans family down the centuries. The legacy of Louis XIV, through his obliging ladies and progeny, had fuzzed the lineage; the descendants of his younger brother, Philippe d'Orléans had excelled in either piety or profligacy. Despite this detrimental balance, both dynasties had harboured a mutual suspicion. But the proximity of the Orléans to the throne posed a perennial threat; their superior brain power, their fast accumulated wealth and their alarming rapport with the populace was now all too apparent.

Louis Philippe had also fitted in a rapid journey to Normandy, to see his mother, now living at Château d'Eu with her father the Duc de Penthièvre. On this favourite family estate, the Duchesse d'Orléans, alone with her thoughts, walking the long lime avenues, high above the sea coast, felt secure and comforted. She led her son in from the great cobbled yard, towered over by the robust hauteur and turrets of the Château. They sat in the Duc de Penthièvre's customary 'golden chamber', where the gilded panelling and murals and gleaming marquetry floor were not immediately conducive to intimate talk.

Bewildered by his parents' separation in April, Louis Philippe had long sensed an inkling of the trouble; it was Mme de Genlis. He recalled his mother's recent letter describing her to him as an interloper, stealing the love of her children, which should be their mother's right. Félicité de Genlis was generally considered exceedingly pretty, witty and clever. Elisabeth Vigée-Le Brun painted a more reserved portrait in her memoirs: 'Mme de Genlis was never really pretty, she was very tall and quite plump with a very expressive face; though her eyes and smile were very fine, I do not think her face would have adapted easily to an expression of kindness ...' The daughter of the Marquis de St Aubin could nevertheless be assured that her questioning eyes and the cascade of thick, dark curls that lapped her pretty shoulders were set to cry havoc.

The Duchesse d'Orléans, her reddened eyes welling up in tears, observed her dutiful son. She thanked him for the correct and affectionate letters sent by himself and by his brother Montpensier. But she had found their tone constrained and understandably distant. Only her little Beaujolais, aged twelve years, wrote in abundant love for his mother (although his writing, according to Mme de Genlis, was virtually illegible). With added verve, the Duchesse had next reprimanded her son for now signing his letters to her 'Le republicain L-P'. And she made no secret of her agitation at the changing scene of moral and social mores: the relapse of 'Court Etiquette', the growing swell of democracy, the revolutionary attitudes. And she had cared even less for Mme de Genlis' addiction to Rousseau and his 'discourses in equality' and her abysmal liking for wooden eating spoons. In fact, she had long despaired of her precious children's education under the questionable training methods of 'that woman'.

Her saddened son was aware that his mother knew of his father's indelible lust for Félicité de Genlis; and that his fourteen-year-old sister, the Princesse Adélaïde, even looked on the charismatic governess as her 'tendre mère'. In order to alleviate this dirge of gloom, Louis Philippe reminded his mother of the loving and poignant letter he had written her in January. Indeed, he had truly opened his heart to her:

For about a year now my youth has caused me almost continuous struggles. I suffer greatly. But there is nothing bitter about this pain. On the contrary, it makes me envisage a happy future. I think of the happiness I will enjoy when I have a kind and pretty wife who will afford me the legitimate means of satisfying these ardent desires by which I am devoured ... Oh, my mother, how I bless you for having preserved me from all those evils by inspiring in me the religious feelings which give me strength!

And he again remembered all too vividly his own infatuation for Félicité de Genlis. She had urged him to keep a day-to-day diary, in which he had taken pains to refer to letters from his 'amie'; her expressions of tenderness had overwhelmed him. A mere six months ago, on a cold January night, he had inscribed: 'Je suis rentré chez mon "amie"; j'y suis resté jusqu' à minuit ... et quelques minutes ... en verité, je ne sais pas ce que je deviendrai quand je ne serai plus avec elle.'

His mother gazed on her son; she remembered uneasily how stretched he had recently become with his newly gained interests and pressures: the exigencies of 'amour-bébé'; his regular morning attendances at the Assembly debates at Versailles; his revolutionary evenings with the Jacobins – they had all taken a toll. In March he had told her that he could dine at Palais-Royal, *en famille*, twice a week only. Oh! She had assured him she was happy with whatever suited him. She had felt sure he would always dine with her when he could; she did not want to cramp his life. And when one evening he was seized with a feverish headache, on his way to the Jacobin Club, and had chosen to seek comfort from his '*amie*' rather than his mother, she had made no bitter remonstrance. For twenty-four hours he had swung between shivering and sweating; he had then slept for ten more. She had visited him several times, and his father had sat with him one full half-hour. But it was the "*amie*" who did the final honours with soup, baked apple, ices and mousses, a choice of tea, and the time-honoured wooden spoons. Touched immeasurably with such attentions, he had attended midnight mass at Saint-Eustache for a whole week, his happiness overflowing at such Gothic glory and the renowned organ music.

On April 3rd, he had again written to his mother. Had she remembered? Indeed it was a warm and touching letter, she now assured him.

For a long time I have wanted to tell you about my morals, as I particularly want you to know how I am behaving. I can say without hesitation that they are in every respect as pure as they possibly could be, in fact completely intact. My dear Mama has perhaps been imagining that I have been getting into bad habits … However, I won't conceal from you that I have not succeeded in keeping myself pure without struggles and suffering and even my health has sometimes been affected … I have opened my heart to you and hidden nothing.

Mother and son sat in brief silence as dusk filtered through the gilded room. A gentleman-in-waiting lit the ormolu oil lamps and the flames glowed low through the crystal globes. The Duchesse d'Orléans leaned forward in her chair and talked earnestly to her son. She explained briefly the other salient reason for his parents' separation. His father, she assured him, had led a life of sheer profligacy and dangerous self-gratification. She had hoped to regulate his excessive spending and *louche* behaviour, but now feared that he would die insolvent; his finances were in a shambolic state.

Her main aim in separating from their father was to secure her fortune in the favour of her precious children.

Louis Philippe was well aware of his mother's fortune. Her father, the Duc de Penthièvre, was the last descendant of the legitimized branch of Louis XIV and the Marquise de Montespan. As his only surviving child, the Duchesse stood to inherit the estates of Dreux, Blois, Anet, Aumale, Bizy and several more. The death of his son, the Prince de Lamballe, in 1768, from syphilis was loosely attributed by some to the then Duc de Chartres; his reprehensible moral conduct had led the young Prince astray. And prompted by his father, Louis Philippe le Gros, and the scent of a fortune, the Duc had next made advances to the Duc de Penthièvre for his daughter's hand. The marriage took place a year later; the sixteen-year-old bride, Louise Marie Adélaïde, had barely been released from her training with the nuns of Montmartre.

Louis Philippe, seeing his mother's head sway sideways and her eyes droop, had stolen from the chamber. He was fond and respectful of her; her natural beauty, her quiet charm and touching melancholy had always inspired his constancy. He walked through the dark corridors; the familiar uneven wood flooring undulated like waves. Reaching the main mahogany staircase, he crept up to the first floor to the Guise Gallery. In 1578, Henri le Duc de Guise, together with his wife, Catherine de Clèves, had founded the Château d'Eu with the Jesuit Chapel and College alongside. de Guise, liberally scarred from his combats for Catholicism, and his wife, notorious for her indiscriminate '*galanteries*', had nevertheless shared fervent religious beliefs. Portraits of their descendants decked the gallery walls. The Ducs, Duchesses, Princesses, Abbesses and demoiselles rejoiced in such picaresque names as le Duc de Joyeuse, d'Aiguillon (a prick or thorn), la Duchesse de Chèvreuse (a she-goat), les Ducs d'Armagnac, Montmartre, Monaco...

Louis Philippe cast a cursory glance at his towering ancestors. With their ample thighs swathed in pale hose and the fitted doublets with bulky padded sleeves, they had a predatory stance. The long gallery with its high-coffered ceiling and low-hung chandeliers was intimidating. There was a movement in a far corner wing chair. His grandfather raised a hand and beckoned him to come and sit. Diminished and weakened with old age and anxieties, the Duc de Penthièvre sat bowed and saddened. He had been appalled at his son-in-law's callous behaviour. Fancy throwing his daughter out of Palais Royal with nothing but the clothes she was wearing! He was proud of her resolute refusal to share her children with that infamous Mme de Genlis and he applauded his daughter's strong decisions. She had become her own woman and had defined her rightful powers and character; she was the traditional and loving mother and daughter who stood tall and without fuss.

He rested a frail hand on his grandson's knee. 'I fear this upheaval and the effect on you children. Your mother has always been tenderly disposed to the Duc d'Orléans and has only lived for him and her children. I see myself as a shelter in this catastrophe and will offer my daughter the resources and sympathy which she would expect from a father.' He next confided in a hoarse whisper his fears for France and for the King and Queen. He was alarmed at the growing turbulence at court, and had been shocked by the provocative emigration of the Comte d'Artois with his courtier friends.

His grandson kept silent. How could this distinguished old advocate of the *Ancien Régime* ever condone the new tricolore cockade and the laws of a radical constitution? The Duc de Penthièvre had more troubles to divulge. His daughter-in-law, the Princesse de Lamballe, through her exclusive association with Marie Antoinette, was in danger. They were inseparable and open to avid calumny. Louis Philippe had few recollections of his aunt. She seldom visited Palais Royal. He was once told that she was allergic to lobster and violets; this had induced his sympathy as he himself, at the time, had nursed a fear and disgust for dogs and vinegar. He had often heard Mme de Genlis speak of her disparagingly: that the Princesse was 'destitute of talent'; that she would sit in on serious discussion, with an assumed inattention and suddenly repeat the content word for word. She affected astonishment when her repetitive résumé was revealed to her. Seen by the populace and the nobility as a remarkably pretty blonde with milky skin, there was also the general assertion, *de haut en bas*, that she had lesbian tendencies.

The Duc de Penthièvre continued his soliloquy: his daughter-in-law was morbidly highly strung, ate little and swooned regularly. She now warned of Paris threatened with mounting horrors and massacres. She planned to flee the Tuileries and join the Queen in an unknown destination. The old man did not approve of such unseemly haste and hysteria; he would stay with his country. The thought of ordering carriages from Tréport to transport his

14

most precious objects, and making any arrangements for his own departure, was anathema to him. 'I am happy in my home – the Eudois people like me and will look after me. I prefer to live with the risk.'

Louis Philippe rose early the next morning and at eight o'clock set off for Paris. Journeying over narrow rough roads through the Forest of Eu, and following the Bresle River, they reached the fertile cattle-farming country and cider orchards of Neufchâtel. Timber-framed farmsteads scattered the open plains approaching Evreux and on to Dreux. They would gain Paris in five hours, the coachman told him, as they clattered through the shuttered streets before the hillside in which vaulted cellars of the Duc de Penthièvre's family were dug deep. As they passed through the lush Eure valley, Louis Philippe pondered deeply on his mother and father. The gentle green slopes and riverbanks soothed his mood; but angst gnawed at his heart.

His father born 1747, the young Louis Philippe-Joseph later to become the Duc d'Orléans had been debonair and handsome. He had danced gracefully, fenced with finesse, had been adept at field sports and had enchanted all with his élan; he dressed fastidiously and had an air of command. He had thrown open his salons at Palais Royal and had welcomed the vociferous theories of political reform and encouraged literary luminaries and avant-garde scientists. In 1784 he even dabbled in aeronautics and the renowned Robert brothers constructed for him a balloon for pleasure rides. Launching it from the park at St Cloud, where a mass of spectators had collected, the two brothers and the Duc d'Orléans rose majestically into a cloud and to disastrous upper air turbulence. With the balloon perilously out of control, the intrepid Duc had shinned up the suspension ropes and pierced it with his knife. The gas released, the entire balloon apparatus dived to the ground; a stupendous event of dubious achievement, in which nobody had been injured.

Louis Philippe shuddered as he remembered that day; he had been eleven years old. But the anticipation, exultation and horror had been eclipsed by his overwhelming love and pride for his father. He sat disconsolate in his carriage as it rumbled on to Paris. Any happiness derived from his parents' marriage had been short-lived. The call of the brothels and the gaming tables had soon obsessed his father; his handsome face and his fast balding head had become studded with festering carbuncles. His mother became withdrawn and depressed and wept alone. But he now liked to recall that portrayal of fleeting happiness, hanging in his mother's old study at Palais Royal: an engraving by Augustin de Saint-Aubin. His younger brother Montpensier, a babe in his mother's lap, and he himself with outstretched little arm and fingers welcoming home their father, elegantly dressed, silk top hat in hand. His mother in her yellow taffeta gown with its wide blue bow caught at the bodice. And he had loved her massed golden hair, coiled in silky ringlets to her shoulders. And he would stand close to her as she sat on the velvet *canapé* with the plump and tasselled cushions, nudging his little body into her skirt and nodding his toy feathered headdress at his father. But this cherished image, now rekindled fifteen years on, had long since perished in bad blood and bitterness.

Having taken leave of his family, Louis Philippe next left Paris on June 14th for the start of his military career at Vendôme. There had been no suspicion then of the Sovereign drama that, a week later, would strike France savagely at her roots.

3

At the end of August 1791, bolstered by his exemplary command of the Dragoons at Vendôme, Louis Philippe and his brother, the Duc de Montpensier, barely sixteen years and an officer, were admitted to the frontier garrison at Valenciennes. They were accompanied by their valets and a groom. Their father, the Duc d'Orléans, had been anxious to get his younger son out of Paris and knew that the renowned garrison would prove an incomparable training ground. The vicissitudes of their disturbed childhood had firmly bonded the two brothers and, as Louis Philippe kept a proprietorial eye on the fledgling officer, he was reminded of his own jubilant jottings on reaching seventeen... 'The day I reached that age, I became *my own master*, that is to say that I was no longer subject to any tutor, that I was no longer bound to do anything except of my own free will, and that I could even do anything I liked.'

The young Ducs were to serve under Maréchal, the Comte de Rochambeau, who, together with Général Lafayette and Maréchal Lückner, was defending the French borders, in three divisions, from Dunkirk to Bitche, by the Rheinland. The brothers were eager for active service. Preparations for frontier attacks were underway and rumours of war were rife. But why no mobilisation of troops? Louis Philippe appreciated that the distinguished Maréchal had only served in the infantry and had no experience in a regiment of mounted troops ... but might not the Maréchal be persuaded to assemble a cavalry unit? A show of warlike manoeuvres along the borders might even encourage the anxious patriots. The Maréchal looked askance at the young man and his impetuous manner. He suggested that Louis Philippe should cool off and mind his own business; he should command his regiment and not concern himself with matters above his station. The Maréchal further asserted his superiority by reminding his two princely charges that the Rochambeau family had been in service to the Orléans for generations; he himself had been ADC to their grandfather Philippe le Gros. The arrogant Maréchal's antagonism to Louis Philippe's zeal for action was apparent; he adopted a cold and unsympathetic manner towards the two brothers. Indeed he was distinctly embarrassed to have them under his command with their leanings towards revolutionary change; he feared to be seen patronising the provocative 'Orléaniste faction'.

In a further attempt to quell this attitude of entrenched inertia, Louis Philippe next suggested to Maréchal, Comte de Rochambeau, that he procure officers to inject urgency and discipline in the troops . . . and by autumn 1791, Rochambeau had set up manoeuvres on the plains, lying between the garrisons at Valenciennes and Quesnoy. Maréchal de Chalus soon took over as the Maréchal de Camp. He was much admired and depended on by Maréchal Rochambeau, until one morning when he approached Louis Philippe and asked if he might be introduced to the Jacobin Club in Valenciennes. It was agreed that de Chalus and his aide-de-camp could be admitted by Louis Philippe the same day; indeed it was considered a ploy for Générals and officers to fraternise local clubs and inspire a front of patriotism. In the event, having had their entry confirmed, de Chalus and his ADC, to Rochambeau's wrath, scarpered the next morning.

The two brothers were assigned Commandants to the Castle. Continuous inspections ensued, day and night; tours of the prisons, hospitals, stores, arsenals and visits to the watches. Rochambeau would expect Louis Philippe to intervene in any quarrels in the garrison, usually between the French and German regiments. The Maréchal also required that he visit the local brothels and arrest any soldiers inside – on the spot. Louis Philippe refused and retorted that it was the duty of police officers. On this matter Rochambeau concurred.

The Ducs had taken a house near the citadel with their respective valets; the senior, Monsieur Pieyre, long attached to the Orléans Household, was especially appreciated for his music making in the evenings. Officers would come to dinner; some evenings were spent at Maréchal Rochambeau's quarters, playing whist, or at the modest theatre, when open. Although shielded from the rigours of the barracks, Louis Philippe was concerned over the costs of their comparative comfort. Their father's income had been dramatically reduced and with the young Duc's salary of a Colonel, at 4,000 francs a month, finances were depleted further.

Life at Valenciennes was monotonous and the Ducs' attendance at the stables and the daily parade was punctilious. The dilapidation of the barracks was execrable; some were even left empty, deemed unfit for troops. Louis Philippe failed to persuade Maréchal Rochambeau to view the atrocious quarters; as a Commander-in-Chief he had judged the suggestion beneath his dignity. Louis Philippe's spirited altercations with the Maréchal were reminiscent of his sparring with his Lieutenant-Colonel, Lagondie, at Vendôme. Sweeping out the stables at dawn and checking his officers at their posts, he had taken his duties seriously.

One pouring wet morning, emerging from the yard, he had met Lagondie who questioned him. Why did he work so hard and so early? Better if his officers saw less of him. They should be kept in awe of him. He should keep his distance and not risk his men getting bored of him. Seeing so much of their Colonel could only lead to familiarity. Louis Philippe remonstrated that his own discipline and zeal could only enhance the respect of his men. The Colonel and his brother officer were to spend seven months at Valenciennes.

Repercussions still rumbled from the King's flight to Varennes, setting the European powers in ferment. His two younger brothers, les Comtes de Provence and Artois, had nimbly persuaded the Prussian and Austrian armies to establish a collective defence around France, which was now deemed of ubiquitous concern for surrounding Monarchs. The Declaration of Pillnitz (August 27th, 1791) had even induced Léopold II, Emperor of Austria, and King Fredrick William II of Prussia, to mount a military front to restore the French Monarchy. Reports grew of a counter-revolutionary French army streaming across the borders, preparing for a formidable about-turn with the added force of the foreign allies. The Prussian Commander had even hinted at the demolition of Paris in the event of harm to the Royal Family; an unfortunate gibe to denote clearly Louis XVI's own alliance with the invaders.

Mme de Genlis still had a contaminating hold on Louis Philippe and in July 1791 had written to him of the Princesse de Lamballe's descent on the Duc de Penthièvre and his mother, at Aumale, the previous month. Her copious letter writing was interesting and well informed. Aumale, an old market town set in rolling downland and thick woods, was a favourite estate of the old Duc. He and his daughter liked to retreat to its peace and commune with the restored and cherished churches and chapels.

While they were staying in the Bailli's Mediaeval house that commanded the centre of town, the old man and his daughter, returning from evening service, saw a sizeable postchaise at the gate. The Princesse de Lamballe stumbled from her carriage and threw herself into the arms of her father-in-law and the Duchesse. She and her troop of servants had been thirteen hours on the road. They were dead tired, famished. At Passy, she had seized her jewellery but no food. Her maids and valets staggered from the coach.

The Duchesse seated them at a table. They were urged to tear at hunks of bread and half frozen meat. 'Eat as much as you can!' shrilled the Princesse. 'Hurry!' In fifteen minutes they had to be '*en voiture!*' The Duchesse sobbed bitterly as she rushed about in her good-hearted way, searching for what she considered bare necessities for the continued journey. She slipped into their pockets an assortment of hats and handkerchiefs and stockings. The Princesse had come and gone like a demented whirlwind. She was heading for England. She was fated to flee Paris, she told them; to join the Queen.

Mme de Genlis also wrote to Louis Philippe of his mother's American admirer, Governor Morris, visiting Eu. He had described a sad scene, full of constraints. However, the esteemed old Duc de Penthièvre had been in command and the lunch excellent. At the end of July 1791, the Duc and his daughter were put under polite house arrest, with the proviso they leave their château at their convenience and go wherever they chose. No Bourbons could have been treated more leniently, wrote Mme de Genlis to Louis Philippe and his brother, Montpensier. Their mother and grandfather were made welcome on the estate of the Marquis de Radepont, a Maréchal of the King's army. Here they were lapped in comfort and peace, in a valley of villages, ancient trees, streams and sheep. In September they were to take up residence at Anet, another favourite château owned by the Duc de Penthièvre; founded on historical romance and much restoration, with renowned hunting country. Here again he was respected and held in affection by the people. He and his daughter would be secure in the face of the mounting revolution.

In April 1792 Louis Philippe was appointed a Maréchal-de-Camp. Tension was reaching fever pitch on the North Frontiers. The Austrian and Prussian forces were as strong and disciplined as the ill-assorted French troops were in disorder; the mix of the old Royal Garde with national volunteers was proving a parlous union. But the King was secretly heartened that the foreign allies were of such determined calibre; he had declared war on the Emperor of Austria on April 20th 1792 with the hope that a Royal Family rescue was in the offing.

Through the winter months Louis Philippe had exchanged more splats with Maréchal Rochambeau. The two brothers were denied leave in Paris and their Regiment was withdrawn from the frontier. It was re-installed at Laon. Rochambeau knew how fervently Louis Philippe wished his men close to the action; with hostilities breaking out on the Flemish border, they would now be excluded. Louis Philippe pumped Rochambeau for alternatives. In vain he asked for Lille, Maubeuge or even to return to Valenciennes. The Maréchal, thoroughly irritated, retorted: 'I cannot have the troops sent hither and thither in this way like valets.' First this insolent youth had complained about the barracks at Valenciennes, and now, still complaining, he was off to one of the finest barracks in France!

Two dynamic Générals next stepped in to relieve the fledgling Maréchal-de-Camp from this petulant martinet. The first was Général Charles-François Dumouriez, a soldier in his fifties who could already boast of twenty-two battle wounds and an imprisonment in the Bastille, for espionage. The second was the debonair Duc de Biron, a long-standing companion of Dumouriez, who was now giving the orders. Maréchal Rochambeau had unexpectedly and implacably refused to continue in the campaign to march the three Armies of the North to Mons. He confessed he could not involve himself in anything pertaining to an offensive war ... but had grudgingly given permission, under the aegis of the Minister of War, le Comte deGrave, for the return of Louis Philippe, and his 14th Regiment of Dragoons to Valenciennes. Général Biron was a devoted friend of his father, Duc d'Orléans; they had shared many gregarious and amatory adventures. With his characteristic audacity and zest, he now took charge.

Louis Philippe next noted that 'on April 28th our small detachment set off at daybreak ... along the Ronelle River separating French and Austrian territory, where we met an Austrian officer stationed by a bridge. Général Biron ordered a trumpeter to notify the Austrians of France's declaration of war. No withdrawal from the Austrians and Biron sent a skirmish to the fore and occupied the village of Quiévrain where we spent the night.' The next morning, Biron's troops marched along the main road to the village of Boussu, said to be under Tyrolean influence. Shots were fired. Lieutenant-Général Cazenove's horse was killed and he himself taken prisoner. Biron ordered the 74th Regiment of Grenadiers to form up and the Austrian riflemen were driven back. Continuing on to Mons, they found Austrians had taken up position at Quaregnon, along with three-pounder cannons. With a few injuries sustained the enemy was dislodged. The troops, to include Grenadiers, Cavalry and Dragoons, bivouacked that night of April 29th beside a stream. It was effectively the front line and Gardes were despatched to surrounding villages. Biron had seized a deserted house nearby, with the distant hills of Jemappes beyond. He ordered the horses to be kept saddled. The young Ducs slept in a hayloft, fully dressed, with the officers, including Lieutenant-Colonel Alexandre de Beauharnais (married briefly to the Empress Josephine, until his death in the Terror). At ten o'clock, pistol shots rang out. 'To horse! To horse!' the cry went up. Everyone mounted and no one, not least Général Biron, knew what was happening. All followed him to the road; like all roads in Flanders, it was narrow, muddied and edged with deep ditches. The Cavalry was at once trapped and swept along, caught up in a relentless force. The Ducs stayed up front behind Biron, who was enraged and baffled by the events. It was impossible to turn a horse round. Finally – 'Attention! Slow march!' he yelled, and his riders plunged into a field, extricating themselves and their mounts from the remorseless scrimmage. The scare was later believed to be a prank orchestrated by devious officers.

The next morning there was news from Lille of turmoil and carnage under Général Dillon. His advance Garde had been sent to attack enemy outposts on the Tournay road, but they had suddenly been seized with panic and fled, leaving their horses to tumble over the infantry. Général Biron next chose to fall back from the frontier. Seeing the French withdrawal, the Austrians attacked their rearguard but were repulsed by Hussars and infantry. Again Biron took up position by the Ronelle. All appeared quiet until two battalions guarding the Mons road hurtled down to the river, with 300 Uhlan Cavalry advancing on Quiévrain. Louis Philippe took up the tale: ' "We are betrayed! Every man for himself!" screamed our battalions, fleeing to the right and left of the villages. The Uhlans charged into the town, sabering any fugitive they could catch. They came within thirty paces of the Biron camping site. An order to fire a few volleys along the road drove them off.' But this confounded mêlée had obscured the arrival of Colonel, the Marquis de Flers, who had just crossed over the Ronelle, at Quiévrain, with his column. Seeing rifle fire on the road, he had ordered a quick trot. In the dark and remaining cloud of gun shot, they were mistaken for Austrian Cavalry as they reached Biron's camp. Disorder and misunderstanding broke out as the 6th Regiment of the Dragoons fled at a gallop with the artillery and ammunitions wagons. Biron and his remaining officers attempted to hold back this disbandment as they ran rife through houses with stray sabre blows. Captain Mortier had his horse shot under him, while Biron's valiant ADCs – Messieurs Chartres and Montpensier – distinguished themselves and rallied round some of the deserters.

The Austrians made no attempt to enter the fracas. Général Biron, with his habitual determination, managed to finally engage the one infantry battalion that had not broken up and again headed an attack on the Austrians from Quiévrain. But depleted of arms, the Général was ordered to withdraw from the front, ditching all over the plain pieces of cannon, rifles and camping equipment for 8,000 men. The Austrians descended at 2am and looted all they could transport. On May 1st, Louis Philippe's horse, which he had not changed in three days, died on the point of extreme exhaustion.

In his memoirs, he dealt at length and in detail with these shamefully disordered beginnings of the French Frontier Wars. He had read no accurate accounts of the varying débacles, and the chaotic movements of April 29th had been hushed up. He also wrote of Maréchal Rochambeau's brazen inactivity. From his perch at the nearby windmill of Saint-Sauve, he had gazed coldly through his eyeglass at the littered plains below: 'Your Regiment is here. Put yourself at its head and await my orders without moving,' he had commanded the Duc. He added: 'These gentlemen wanted to go to war, they must get themselves out of it.' The Maréchal was finally shown up in his true, monstrous colours when he snapped his sword and threw its bits at his Regiment, vowing never to conduct them again. Maréchal Lückner, the final commander of Louis Philippe's brigade in the Army of the North, was a formidable septuagenarian of Bavarian origin. He had surprised the Duc by dissolving into tears when given *Carte Blanche* by the Minister of War. Speaking despairingly in bad French, he explained, 'I have never had *Carte Blanche* in my life ... one tells me "advance" and the other "retreat".' Louis Philippe urged him to take full advantage of his *Carte Blanche* and attack the enemy: 'Give it a good thrashing. Have a go!'

The Comte de Grave had also buckled under pressure; a wise man, tolerant of disputes, but his ministry had failed after one month to gain any cohesion. He resigned with Général Biron's praise of the two Ducs ringing in his ears: 'Messieurs Chartres and Montpensier have accompanied me as volunteers and, being exposed for the first time to a brisk fire from the enemy, behaved with the utmost heroism and intrepidity.' On May 7th, 1792, Louis Philippe, the eighteen-year-old Duc de Chartres, was appointed a Brigadier.

He thrived on the anomalous mix of his two Dragoon Regiments; this Prince of the First Blood rubbed shoulders with the volunteers and commanded with ease. His men were happy to have him at their head, with his ready tongue and zeal. The command that he and Montpensier had landed for the looming battle of Valmy was a morale boost to all; their reputation for bravery was an inspiration.

4

Bored and troubled with Paris, Louis Philippe's father had secured permission from the King to accompany the headquarters of the Army of the North as an ordinary volunteer. The Royal blessing was given with a desultory 'you may do as you please'; there was no love lost between the two cousins. The opportunistic Duc d'Orléans wanted to join in on the Frontier fray. He had already been declined employment in the navy in an appropriate rank, and had been declined as a Lieutenant-Géneral in any army. Above all, he wished to be with his war-waging sons and consequently rented a house in Valenciennes. He took along his twelve-year-old son, the Comte de Beaujolais, and was particularly relieved to withdraw himself from Paris. His vociferous *de-haut-en-bas* cajoling of the populace and his bogus defaming of Absolute Monarchy had caused much pain and his own social banishment. On New Year's Day, at the Tuileries, in an effort to appease his cousins, he had been shunned by the Courtiers. Insults and spit had berated him down the Queen's staircase. At a subsequent dinner at the Palace, a cry went up: 'Take care of the dishes!' There had been a suggestion he might have sprinkled them with poison. As he was pushed from the dining-room, his toes were trodden on. The *Ancien Régime* had prevailed, a space.

The Duc d'Orléans' sons, always happy in his company, however reprobate his talk and behaviour, spent their off-duty evenings with him and his good friend Général Biron. Beaujolais gave his elder brothers news of their mother and grandfather, the Duc de Penthièvre, and of the most recent dramas at the Tuileries on June 20th, 1792.

The King had been brave; while waiting for the mob to storm his Palace, he had played backgammon with his sister, Madame Elisabeth. At four o'clock in the afternoon, the rabble tore up the stairs to the private apartments. A few loyal Courtiers and Grenadiers heaped up a barrier of tables and chairs to protect the Queen and her children. 'Down with the veto! No aristocrats! No priests! The *sans-culottes* forever!' Beaujolais told how the King was shoved back into a window recess and taunted with blades and pistols jammed up to his face. There was endless shouting and abuse at their composed prey, but no bloodshed. The King was next proffered a red freedom bonnet on the end of a pike. He put it on obediently to hysterical applause. The ruffians produced wine and insisted the King drink to the health of the populace. Fearing he might be poisoned, he nevertheless drank and was again applauded. After three hours, the excitable crowd moved off into the evening through a garden gate, to the Pont Royal and down the quay.

Beaujolais paused in his account; he then told them how Madame Elisabeth had followed her brother from window to window through all his trials. Everybody thought she was the Queen! 'There's the Austrian!' And all she said was: 'Leave them in their error, and save the Queen.' Beaujolais was slapped on the back for his vivid reportage. 'Oh! *Ça ira, ça ira, ça ira!*' he quipped merrily. Mme de Genlis had launched a true revolutionary patriot in her youngest Orléans charge; the junior Comte already delighted in his corporate label: 'Beaujolais, the Citizen Alphonse Léodgard Egalité'.

Referring to that early aperçu of the Revolution, the formidable diarist Bourrienne includes the figure of the young Bonaparte. Advancing his military career in Paris at the outbreak of the Revolution, Bonaparte and an army companion were in the rue St Honoré on June 20th. They were in a coffee house when a clamorous rabble, armed with hatchets and bayonets, loped past them towards the Tuileries. Bonaparte insisted they follow. They walked through the gardens on the terrace beside the Seine. Finally, they saw the King in a window, wearing the red cap. Bonaparte seethed with anger. He could not understand the King's weak appeasement. 'What madness!' he exclaimed. 'How could they allow these scoundrels to enter? They ought to have blown four or five hundred of them into the air with cannon. The rest would then have taken to their heels.'

Beaujolais' news of their grandfather, the Duc de Penthièvre, and their mother had proved equally dramatic. Leading a sad and dwindling existence at Anet, the old Duc was plagued with giddiness and breathing difficulty. The château had been surrounded by forces from Paris. Since March, many local people had been interrogated and even arrested. In Paris, there was ongoing torment and upheaval. Beaujolais had also heard from the Comte de Moriolles that the Princesse de Lamballe had now regained her position at the Tuileries. 'Run, Escape!' she had urged him and he had fled to Anet. The old Duc was praying at his prie-Dieu, and noticeably stupefied with exhaustion. He received Moriolles with his customary gentleness and was told of his meeting with the Princesse de Lamballe, his erstwhile daughter-in-law. 'What does it all mean? Is it the end of the world?' Beaujolais told his brothers how, during the week that Moriolles had stayed at Anet, he had never once seen their mother dry-eyed; her 'deluge' of tears and sobbing, her eyes reddened like blood itself, her endless pouring out of misery and despair at the thought of her dying father, of being left with no protection and her children dispersed . . . Beaujolais had more to divulge: on June 19th, 1792, their grandfather and mother had left Anet for Bizy, his home near Vernon. Nestling in the wooded Seine valley, it was formerly a Royal Château with stables to compare with Versailles. Their carriage had overturned at the far end of the garden entrance. The single coachman had had difficulties mastering a sharp downhill turn with eight horses. Nobody was hurt, but the old Duc felt the incident a presage of ill fate.

The Duc d'Orléans' eager initiative to involve himself in the Frontier imbroglio was short-lived. He and Beaujolais accompanied the first stage of the march; but the restless Duc soon became bored with an army moving across France to change location. He took Beaujolais back to Paris, intending to join up again when Metz was reached. But the King forbade Maréchal Lückner to receive him.

From the balconies of Palais Royal, Beaujolais kept a keen watch over the escalating revolutionary activities. The counter-revolutionary forces at home and abroad had swept mayhem through the faubourgs of Paris. By August 10th, 1792, the downfall of the Monarchy was assured. The Porte-Royale – a side entrance to the Tuileries – had been knowingly left unlocked through the afternoon. By evening a torrent of workers from Saint-Antoine, to include market women and their ferocious band of *poissardes*, had burst into the Royal Gardens. Descriptions of the ensuing glut and gore have coloured history pages down the centuries.

'Sire,' said the Queen to her toppling King, 'it is time to show yourself.' With his hair askew, and undressed since the previous night, and wearing a mauve coat, he shuffled on to the balcony. The time-honoured cry of '*Vive le Roi!*' went up from the Grenadiers; their last cry for the last time. The King descended to the Royal court to review his troops. There was a momentary rapport. In defending the King and his family, they were defending their own wives and children, he assured them.

'*Gros Louis! Tremblez tyrans! Voici les sans-culottes!*' screamed the furious crowd, separated by a single tri-coloured ribbon. It was then that Louis XVI saw his battalions and gunners slip away through the gardens. The few who had not yet deserted were now upon him, thrusting fists at his face and yelling gruesome abuse. The Royal Family was urgently persuaded to escape to the Assembly building by the garden terrace. They were given a brisk escort by the remaining Swiss Garde. The distracted Queen was robbed of her watch and purse in this brief transit. The liberated throng ran rife through the Palace and a raving massacre took hold. The Swiss Garde were butchered and their weapons snatched. Any inmates left in the Palace were slashed to death. Fugitives, racing into the gardens, were murdered in the trees and by the fountains. Some, in desperation, shinned up the marble monuments.

In his own prodigious 'Chronicles', the politico Louis-Adolphe Thiers includes a grotesque footnote (from 'Alison's French Revolution. E'.) 'The insurgents refrained from firing lest they should injure the statuary, but pricked them with their bayonets till they came down and then slaughtered them at their feet.' Alison E. continued with fitting sang-froid: '... an instance of taste for art mingled with revolutionary cruelty unparalleled in the history of the world.'

The *poissardes*, squatting in groups in the dark, were excited by the smell of blood. They tore out the hearts from the Swiss Garde and their livers, for frying. Limbs were cut up and cutlets shaped from the flesh. Vast cooking pans of oil steamed and sizzled.

At eleven o'clock, the blasted Royal Family heard from their crushed space in the Assembly Reporter's Box, the eloquent Girondin, Pierre-Victurnien Vergniaud's proposal of the King's suspension from constitutional duty. This was understood as an effective guarantee of the King's pending dethronement. A barrage of jubilation rolled through Paris. The Marseillaise rose up and down in a thousand throats and the pikes and hatchets were propelled with furious joy into the Tuileries. 'The Declaration of the Rights of Man and of the Citizen' (1789) was vindicated! The Monarchy was doomed!

At the end of August, Louis Philippe and Montpensier were ordered to join the Army of the Centre, under the command of the veteran Général Kellermann. As the strapping Alsatian observed the slim, blue-eyed Brigadier, he exclaimed loudly: '*Diable!*' He had never seen so young a Général! By September 11th, Louis Philippe was promoted to Lieutenant Général with Montpensier his aide-de-camp. He was also nominated to the command of Strasbourg. He refused the post, affirming he was too young to be enclosed in a citadel and preferred active service. The battle of Valmy was just nine days ahead. The enemy count of the Frontier armies had now stabilised. The Prussian army under King Frederick William and the Duke of Brunswick was 52,000 strong. The Austrians, under Général Clerfayt, were only 13,000 men. But Clerfayt, always resplendent in his stars and lace as a Knight of the Golden Fleece, was judged the best Général ever opposed to the French, during the Revolutionary wars. The Hessians, the Brunswickers and the Würtembergers amounted to 20,000 men. The French émigrés, headed by Monsieur le Comte de Provence, and by le Comte d'Artois, had raised 14,000. The French army was made up of 50,000 professional soldiers and volunteers, with talk of reinforcement. As the Ducs' bored and agitated battalions kicked their heels in the Camp de Braux, there were rumours of the Prussian army dying of hunger, of rampant dysentery and of dead horses carried off in the hundreds. The French army's health was satisfactory, but delayed bread wagons provoked much bad language from the soldiers. Retorted their rumbustious Général Dumouriez: 'The Prussians you see before you sometimes go four days without bread and eat their dead horses.'

Louis Philippe had developed into a tall, courageous young man with a strong physique. His steady gaze exuded poise and a certain candour, wrested from the circumstances of his life. His blue eyes and shapely lips, the bold Bourbon nose, and his head of thick, wavy hair, had undeniable allure. Voltaire, in 1778, the year of his death, had taken the five-year-old boy on to his knee; he claimed that his childish features had already a striking resemblance to the Orléans pedigree. In his fifties, on the throne, Louis Philippe was to be likened to his ancestor Louis XIV, as he strode purposefully through the restored galleries of Versailles. Charles Greville, the English diarist, similarly remarked '. . . the King has a fine head and closely resembles the pictures of Louis XIV.'

But the young boy of eight years, under the tutelage of Mme de Genlis, had not been judged so favourably. She portrays him as 'completely ignorant with no intention of remedying this defect'. At their first schoolroom meeting she read to him from a history book. He stretched out on the sofa, yawned loudly and rested his feet on the table. Mme de la Tour du Pin, whose renowned beauty compared dangerously with Queen Marie Antoinette's, gives another disenchanted view: 'He was heavily built, very ungraceful and awkward with pale, heavy cheeks and a sly expression, a solemn, shy boy.' His figure and manners improved as he matured. He became clever and good-looking and dressed with care. His poise and breeding and social skills became the envy of the *Ancien Régime* whose heirs, the Duc d'Angoulême and the Duc de Berri were clumsy and awkward in comparison. The Duc de Montpensier exuded more charm and fascination on first encounter; he was a music lover, prone to penning romantic lines to any *amour*, and was a talented artist. The Comte de Beaujolais, six years younger than his eldest brother, was decidedly handsome with the expressive Orléans eyes. He pursued a more hedonistic existence, the fashionable life with every leisured enticement. Dull politics were not of his calling. But the revolutionary excesses had amazed him. Indeed, he had not been satiated by the sights and sounds and smells of the night of August 10th, 1792. The Princesse de Lamballe's head and severed limbs, displayed on pikes in Palais Royal courtyard, below his room, had taken the biscuit. He had heard noises and was horror-struck to see his aunt's head swinging past. He had been doing his lessons at the time. His father had watched her remains pass below from a balcony. He stood with his latest infatuation, the Comtesse de Buffon. The Princesse de Lamballe! Her superb mane of blond hair! Her fresh milky skin! Philippe, Duc d'Orléans was shocked to see her dead and so grievously mutilated. She was his sister-in-law – and had been his mistress.

Citizen Beaujolais dispatched a brief and exaggerated summary to his brothers at the front. It was the day of the September 3rd massacres. 'They say four or five thousand have been killed!' The official figure was later put at 1,400. Fear and uncertainty had fuelled the panic in Paris as the Prussians had invaded France on August 19th. The Duke of Brunswick seized the fortress of Verdun; it had surrendered on September 2nd. Foreseeing massacre and anarchy, the newly appointed Justice Minister, Georges-Jacques Danton, proceeded to have the seven main Paris prisons filled with 'suspects'. Debtors, forgers, counter-revolutionaries and aristocrats were stripped of valuables, and any serviceable clothes; later released for municipal funds. Danton, a pugnacious man, spelt out a vehement plan to save Paris. 'A decree must be passed which shall make it obligatory on every citizen to serve in person or to give up his arms.' (Some bemused prisoners were served lunch that day with no table knives tucked in their napkins.)

As the tocsin wailed out through the early afternoon and the alarm gun boomed, the populace watched twenty-four priests removed in six hackney coaches to the Abbaye prison. They had refused to take the constitutional oath. They were seized and pierced by weapons on their way and slaughtered before the howling mob. Victims through the night were speared, their bodies left writhing and convulsed; laughed at, and then decapitated. The September massacres must be accredited the worst of atrocities. Where were the government authorities? Where was Danton? Late at night the Assembly was alerted of the gratuitous carnage mounting in the prisons. They sent out deputies to appease the crowds and to save the victims. On the Monday morning of September 3rd there was an announcement from the Minister of the Interior, Jean-Marie Roland: '...Yesterday was a day over the events of which we ought perhaps to throw a veil...' The following year, in November 1793, he sat down by a tree on the Paris road and stabbed himself to death. His sword had been concealed in a cane.

5

The battle of Valmy was effectively contained in the space of one day – September 20th, 1792. On a high, undulating plateau, divided by the Argonne Hill forest, with the Meuse and the Aisne streaming each side below, the French Revolutionary Army fought off the Prussians. Any attempt from the Allied armies to tamper with France's new and fragile liberty was decisively defeated. This bizarre battle was orchestrated by batteries of cannonade positioned on the plain, on equal enemy terms.

Louis Philippe noted: 'At 6.30am we heard continuing gunfire and the call to arms was sounded at Camp. Thick mists obscured the body marching down; the whole Prussian army, it was rumoured.' It was a raw and freezing morning. Striking camp and loading packhorses took time. It was eight o'clock before he was at the head of his infantry, up at the windmill, on the crest of the hill. He set up a strong battery position. At ten o'clock the cannonade from the Prussians' vanguard, by the small farm 'La Lune', was deafening. Général Kellermann's horse was killed from under him and men from Louis Philippe's division were badly wounded when a shell landed by the mill, exploding two chests of cartridges. Recorded Louis Philippe after the event: 'The zeal that day of the troops was so loyal and marked that any Cavalryman, Carabinier or Dragoon with killed or wounded horses, ran with recovered rifles to the infantry.' The fog lifted at eleven o'clock and the Prussians deployed. Their entire army was revealed in perfect column on the vast plain. By two o'clock they had divided into two lines for attack.

'*Vive la Nation*! *Vive la France*!' roared the ranks, bemused by the Prussians' taunting display. But the attack never came. Was the Duke of Brunswick, a cautious man, waiting for Général Clerfayt's Austrian contingent to arrive that night? The French continued their cannonade until dusk, when Brunswick, noting the steady efficiency of the French guns, conceded with good grace to questionable defeat. A liberally minded man, he had no firm belief in Counter-Revolutionary forces; the recent Republican surges of August 10th had put paid to all that. He put out the order to his troops: '*Hier schlagen wir nicht*.' His soldiers, subsisting on muddy water, a rough mix of wheat paste and an overdose of grapes, were ravaged by diarrhoea. (Despite the mud and dysentery that plagued the Frontier Wars, James Christie of London asserted in a wine catalogue, 'hogsheads of the 1791 vintage – the best that France has produced for many years.')

Louis Philippe later recorded 1,600 killed on the French side; on questioning the Prussian officers on their losses, he was told 2,000. There were deliberations that evening on what should happen next. The French Générals Kellermann and Dumouriez, Chartres and his ADC Montpensier, met in the dark little hut of Valmy's mill. A Grenadier, sitting in a chair with his back to the door, was thought asleep. Général Dumouriez tapped him on the shoulder. 'Come on, friend, would you mind going and leaving us alone.' But the man was dead and fell to the ground. A cannon ball had ripped open his stomach.

It was decided that Dumouriez' army return to occupy Braux-Saint-Cohière and that Kellermann's army camp on the Dampierre heights. This collective strategy was to raise the level of the river Auve by means of dams, causing it to burst its banks and flood the surrounding plains and villages. The short distance that night to Dampierre was made chaotic by the whole army contingent having to cross the single bridge over the Auve. It gave way again and again under the weight of horses and artillery. A lot of time and effort was expended in mending and rebuilding. The troops, worn out and irritable, broke ranks and became mixed up. Always with a keen eye for shambles, Louis Philippe envisaged the end of their army or, at least, fearful flight if any Prussian Hussars had appeared on the scene. But by 3am, Camp Dampierre was established, the change of position was successfully completed and order restored. Louis Philippe noted, 'The Prussian army made no attempt to intercept our work, of flooding the Auve, from our new entrenched position.' He then added his own observations on the horrific disorder of some army camps; waves of undisciplined volunteers, from the Revolutionary mob, and *sans culottes*, had infiltrated the new forces. No discipline and crime was rife. Officers and Commissioners had been murdered, their heads carried on pikes. Maréchal Lückner himself had nearly become victim to these crazed attacks.

The Valmy windmill was the next casualty. Louis Philippe had it destroyed; made entirely of wood and now riddled with bullet holes, it was in a state of imminent collapse. This emblem has been re-erected four times since its iconic introduction to the First Republic. Today's working model, to replace the one destroyed by the devastating storms of December 26th, 1999, was ensconced on April 1st, 2005. The white canvas sails, hoisted high on the plain still tilt and swing as the wheat grinds below; a salute to that strange bombardment of 1792. Johann Wolfgang von Goethe was fighting in the Prussian army on that conspicuous day. The consummate poet and politician had recently completed his book *Italian Journey* (1786–1788). His deflated companions asked his opinion on the battle's outcome. 'From this day, and in this place, dates a new era in the world's history,' was the succinct reply. But the Royal Family's tentative dream of rescue by the Duke of Brunswick was certainly shattered. Overnight, the National Convention had abolished the Monarchy and the First French Republic was born. Undeterred, on the following evening of September 21st, Kellermann sent a dispatch to *Le Moniteur*, extolling his young aristocratic soldiers for their remarkable courage under sustained fire. In total disregard for the new social mores, he spelt out, and commended Monsieur le Duc de Chartres and his ADC, Monsieur le Duc de Montpensier.

Two hundred years on, the plains and low hills of Valmy ripple with corn and wheat and green pea seed for cattle. There are clumps of forest tunnelled with beech and birch and sycamore. The tangled undergrowth is alive with birds and bees; horses' hooves evoke old battles as they mark the narrow, mud rides. And Kellermann is raised high in bronze and peace after the turbulence of guns; cannon-balls at his feet; his peaked hat raised in his left hand and in the right, his sword. He was appointed Maréchal in 1804 by Bonaparte, and in 1808, the Duc de Valmy. Chartres and Montpensier left for Paris on September 27th, skirting any marauding Prussian army as they rode the highway to Sainte-Ménehould, towards Chalons-sur-Marne. They rested at the camp of Notre-Dame de Pin and arranged a carriage for Paris. By chance, they had met up with Mme de Genlis' nephew, César Ducrest; they had all been taught together by her as children. Ducrest was to become ADC to Louis Philippe in the ensuing war at Jemappes and later joined him in Switzerland at the start of his exile.

The brothers found their father in an agitated state at Palais Royal. He was waiting for them in the Great Chamber. He had just been notified by the local authorities that his inherited title – Duc d'Orléans – was illegal, feudal, defunct. To accord with the new laws of abolished privileges, his title must now comply with a nameless citizen. He had been assigned the label 'Egalité'. He was overjoyed to see his sons, but mortified by this demeaning sobriquet clapped on the family. Louis Philippe rated it a load of nonsense – and to be got rid of. And why had their dear father expressed anxiety over their fighting on the front line? Louis Philippe was determined to return to Kellermann's army, where he knew the troops – 'and I am known by them'. And he was disturbed by an official notification just received that his place in Kellermann's army had been filled. He was to proceed instead to Douai, in defence of Lille from the Austrians. And he knew too well that the discipline of the rough provincial recruits was abysmal. He was furious that his father and military friends – to include the Duc de Biron and Alexandre Beauharnais – had judged him and Montpensier exposed to too much danger. There were fears of their abduction and imprisonment. They should be stationed in 'places of safety'. The next morning, Louis Philippe strode out of Palais Royal to the nearby War Ministry. Général Servan, a brave old patriot, agreed to see the young Brigadier. Sickly, confined to bed and sporting a tasselled nightcap, the Général listened attentively to Louis Philippe's report on Valmy. His side table was heaped with unanswered papers, but he had no intention of giving short shrift to the Duc de Chartres; he had been told of his considerable capabilities and it was now incumbent on him as Minister of War to assure the young hero that it was his father and friends who were insistent on the change of fighting ground.

As Louis Philippe left the room, a massive figure lurched at him from the corner and tapped him on the shoulder. 'A word in your ear.' Danton, the formidable Minister of Justice, led him to the window; the square-jawed, podgy face, gored by a bull in childhood, was savagely scarred. He continued: 'Don't waste your time talking to that imbecile.' He suggested Louis Philippe meet him at eight o'clock the following morning at the Chancellery in the Place Vendôme. Louis Philippe was punctual. He reiterated his wild upset at being withdrawn from Kellermann's army. He wanted to be reinstated. He had served five months. Danton suggested Dumouriez' army.

Louis Philippe accepted. His brother, Montpensier, was to be reappointed his adjutant Général Lieutenant-Colonel. They had hoped again to fight together. He rose to leave, but Danton restrained him. He had something to say: Louis Philippe was very young, an ardent patriot and friend of liberty, who had relinquished without regret the rank bestowed on him by accident of birth. He had opposed the invasion of foreign armies and preserved France from the return of émigrés and the odium of Counter-Revolution. He had the people's confidence and affection. Louis Philippe replied that he had been horrified by the blood and massacres in Paris. Danton warned him not to voice his indignations. It was the émigrés, the Princes of the Blood, his own cousins, who had brought about the murder of those victims without trial; enemies of his father and of Chartres himself. Louis Philippe retorted to the great force towering before him: 'But no atrocity from either argument could justify the September Massacres.'

'Give up this talk,' said Danton. 'You are young and inexperienced – do not censure rightly or wrongly. And it was I who gave the orders for those September Massacres.'

'You!' exclaimed Louis Philippe. 'Monsieur Danton, you make me shudder.'

After a further diatribe on conspirators, treason and rivers of blood between the French army and the émigrés, and a gruesome insight on prisoner abuse from hanging and bodies broken on the wheel, Danton again urged him to keep silent and to voice no political opinions. 'All eyes are focused on you. Try to contain your bursts of indignation.'

'Ah! I cannot undertake to do that – the cry of my conscience.' And how could he ever condone the killing of unarmed civilians?

'It is not a question of your conscience,' Danton assured him and pressed upon him to keep to a military career. Coming from his Bourbon background, it was his only option. 'Now go away, Général, and join Dumouriez' army and beat the Austrians.' He paused; and looking down from his great height, he made an unexpected forecast – of a future democratic Monarchy, and that Chartres, having fought under the 'tricolore' had a good chance of reigning. Forty years on, Louis Philippe loved to recount to his sons his robust interview with the orator Georges-Jacques Danton (who was felled at the scaffold on April 5th, 1794, against a blazing sunset).

Staying on in Paris, Louis Philippe attended two sittings at the newly elected National Convention by the Tuileries Terrace. Seated on the ground floor, in the Recorder's Gallery, he was painfully aware of how crushed and confined the Royal Family had been in the hours spent in that narrow little box: the Dauphin had called for water and the King had asked for food. His overindulgence at table had always been a butt for his critics. By the evening of August 13th, the doomed family was imprisoned in the Mediaeval keep of the Temple Fortress.

Louis Philippe's eye wandered over the new members of the Convention. He noted their worn and dishevelled clothes; a reflection of the new spirit of Republican vulgarity, where good manners and dignity were now banned. 'Grands dieux!' Was this then the Assembly to determine the destiny of France? He searched in vain for his father; always easily distinguished by his understated, careful dress.

The next morning he returned for a debate on that revolt of August 10th against the Monarchy. Suddenly, from the opposite benches, a man screamed for attention; a sickly little fellow in a dirty greatcoat was shaking convulsively. Marat! The owner of the paper *The People's Friend*, which every morning demanded 300,000 heads should roll – 'to have done with the enemies of liberty'. Swiss by birth, Jean-Paul Marat had, until the Revolution, been physician to the Comte d' Artois' bodyguard.

Uproar ensued. 'Marat! Marat! Down with Marat! Don't let him speak! He is an insult to us all – a monster – a disgrace to the Convention. *Monsieur le Président* – you cannot let this man speak. This is shameful! Chase him out!' Président Pétion, an associate of Robespierre, rang his bell and made it clear that as a member of the Convention, Marat could not be refused permission to speak. The clamour redoubled. Marat advanced to the rostrum. Deputies blocked his path as he halted at the foot of the steps. Casting a malevolent glare over the Assembly, he asked for a drink of water. 'Give him a glass of blood – yes, yes, give him blood!' Marat slowly mounted the rostrum and drew a little pistol from his pocket. Putting it to his temple, he was greeted with general derision. Louis Philippe was disgusted with Marat's bloodthirsty theatrics; his stirring up a mob mentality into this crescendo of bad order.

Each evening Louis Philippe and Montpensier dined with their father, and would accompany him to the opera or theatre, where the 'Marseillaise' now roused the audience at the fall of the curtain. Such performances had become an addiction for Philippe Egalité; an escape from his self-imposed anxieties and he would doze through most of the action. There were no more elegant receptions at Palais Royal, which had now been absurdly labelled Palais-Egalité. His sons were demonstrably grieved by the separation from their mother, and looked with shame on the 'wooden tent' erected in the garden, from where harangues could be delivered, protected from wind and rain. Louis Philippe, aware of his father's financial shortcomings, the liberal differences that had alienated him from his friends and his ambiguous attitude to his cousin, the King, now pleaded with him to emigrate. To live in England, the country he admired. Or even America? 'It is impossible,' replied the apathetic Egalité. 'Those plantations – those negroes.' The Duc de Biron had fought in the American War for two years, he reminded his sons. 'No congenial households, society, theatres; everything sad and mournful; a melancholy scene.' In Paris he still had the opera and the lively Comtesse de Buffon. And they should not forget that the trial of the King was only weeks away. And would he be a fatal victim? A hostage in the uncertainty of wars was their father's reply.

6

On October 6th, 1792, his nineteenth birthday, Louis Philippe joined Dumouriez' army, together with Montpensier and César Ducrest as his ADC. After a month of repulsing half-hearted Austrian attacks on Lille, Dumouriez asked the Belgians to make a bigger effort guarding their borders. He next pushed on to Mons. Louis Philippe, commanding an advance guard, captured and upturned an Austrian battery at the mill of Boussu. The familiar narrow roads were still straggled with the retreating Prussian army. He wrote of stinking carcasses and skin peeling off rotting horses. Villages were devastated with severe food shortages. Dumouriez would open up the army wagons for handouts. Along their route were shouts of 'Bravo, bravo! Long live France! Long live our brave troops, long live the army, long live Dumouriez!' On November 5th, in broad daylight, having struggled through heavy ploughed land, Dumouriez reached clear grazing ground below the heights of Jemappes, to the west of Mons. He was immediately confronted by Clerfayt's Austrian army in a formidable position above. Louis Philippe formed his division in densely massed battalions; bivouacked and ready for any attack. Dumouriez feared a night assault and joined him at his watch until daybreak. It later transpired that a nocturnal attack had been mooted at Austrian headquarters. Général Beaulieu, positioned on Mount Panisel, had marked the layout and details of the French positions; but the War Council had refused permission. November 6th was the date for the battle of Jemappes. The town, perched on green hills skirting the city of Mons, looked down on the marshy terrain and boot-clogging clay of the plains below. The Austrian army was comfortably entrenched in the town where a hill in the centre was a natural observation post of the woods and slopes below.

Twelve noon was the agreed hour to open combat, but with the Austrian regiment of Coburg Dragoons fast trotting before time down the hill, Dumouriez ordered his whole army to strike immediately. Louis Philippe, commanding the Centre, marched his division, in battalion column, through stiff, deep soil towards the woods at Flénu. He repulsed the Austrian infantry who were circling the wood, and forced his men through twisted trunks and saplings out to the slopes beyond. But as the heads of his column poked out from the trees, they were shot at by the enemy above. The shaken soldiers streamed back into their cover, with many casualties from musket balls. Général Drouais, the Maréchal de Camp at Quiévrain, had both feet shot away by a cannon-ball; it had swiped across the forest floor. Always exquisitely dressed with powdered curls, a three-cornered hat and a sword with a shagreen scabbard, he had once been the King's Equerry. He passed by Louis Philippe in the arms of four soldiers, carrying him to the hospital tent. 'You will get better, my dear Général, and I shall see you soon.' 'No,' insisted Drouais, 'I will not see you again.' He died the next day.

In another instance, he saw the son of a Prussian Général lying stretched on the ground. The surgeon judged nothing could be done, but Louis Philippe insisted he help dress the shattered hip. Since he was so kind, the young soldier asked if he might be carried to Boussu, to the house of a young lady who loved him and whom he was to marry. Louis Philippe had a stretcher made of branches and sent him off with six soldiers. He was still alive in the evening when he called. The young lady was in tears. He died in the night.

A handful of Austrian cavalry had descended on the wood, but achieved little. Louis Philippe encircled his fief with a picket guard and had any fugitives seized and checked as they broke free. He captured any Austrian guns at bayonet point. Finally, gathering up all the stray units, he formed 'the Battalion of Mons'. Heading his men down the weakened Austrian Centre, this innovative battle cry induced fresh energy and spirit. By nightfall a French victory was acclaimed. On November 7th, Général Dumouriez, flanked by Louis Philippe and Montpensier, trotted up the steep, mediaeval streets of Mons with his triumphant advance guard. The city Alderman and Burgomaster, resplendent in their neck ruffs, made speeches. 'The French Republic has abjured conquests and wants none other than to give freedom to the peoples among whom its victorious army pursues their enemies.' Dumouriez was proudly presented the keys of the town on a silver salver.

But the Belgians, beholden to their saviours, the French, were not entirely-enthralled. They had their own National Independence and reviled against any foreign yoke; if they ever chose revolution or mob rule, it would be under their own powers. For the French, the victory of Jemappes was a surprise. The Republicans were overjoyed, this new faculty of winning great battles was a proud departure. The rising applause of success was soon to be rebuffed; the fall of Liège on November 28th from the grip of the Austrians, and Antwerp on the 29th, were achieved at a cost: reduced cavalry and arms; and a lack of boots, with a distribution of clogs to circumvent the muddy rock paths. Years after his experiences at Jemappes, Louis Philippe recalled his feelings of battle to his young Military Minister, the Comte de Montalivet: 'I was close to the enemy; I could count the Cavaliers; I was struck by their fine military deportment and composure. Suddenly the cannon boomed and I saw falling before me whole lines of men who just moments ago had been full of life. A wave of Austrian Cavalry had fled from my gunfire. First exhilarated by success, I was then hit by a profound sadness for all those families, to whom I had caused a sudden loss of a son or a brother.'

He would always look on war as the most terrible curse of humanity and swore never to inflict such cruelty on the world if it was within his powers. At the end of his eventful reign, on the morning of his desperate abdication, he ordered the withdrawal of troops from Paris, repeating again and again – 'I have seen enough blood.'

At the start of December 1792, Louis Philippe and Montpensier took another short leave in Paris. They found their father at his 'Palais-Egalité', riven with fresh despair. Félicité de Genlis, and their fifteen-year-old sister Adélaïde had extended their stay in England, incurring political exile. His daughter an émigré! De Genlis, savouring a zestful life in London, Bath and Bury St Edmunds, had studiously ignored the evil omens from Paris. They were also startled to hear the continuous street cries of 'Capet to the guillotine!' The faubourgs were seething in anticipation of the trial and head of the King. Aligning their Royal prey with his tenth-century forebear, Hugues Capet*, in the abbot's 'Cappa', was a derogatory dig. Paris was alive with Terror, torment and angry plotting; markets, frantically besieged for

---

* HUGUES CAPET, founder of the Capetienne Dynasty, was elected the King of France in the year 987. He proved a weak ruler; his subsequent successors equally ineffectual. Their reign came to an ignominious collapse in 1328.

dwindling sacks of flour, were cursed for rising prices. A steam of boiling bouillon from dead cow, horse-flesh and donkey, hung in a miasma above the milling crowd. But it was still the spectacular gardens of Palais Royal that drew the most feverish hostilities; and the most vehement Republican protesters. The dazzling arcades of cafés, billiard saloons and gaming houses were open to every rank and persuasion; from orators to prostitutes. The controversial Duc d'Orléans, Philippe Egalité, had generated a forum of vociferous exchange. The coffee houses, reputed to attract the best of furious agitators, were crammed inside and out, with an open-mouthed crowd, as some provocateur, propped on a chair or table, bawled out his own brew of barbarity.

Louis Philippe urged his father again to take no part in the King's trial; but the sly politico could only warn his son of widely held suspicions and collusion: that cousin Louis was in league with enemies of France; that he had carried on communications to overthrow the Constitution and for propagating the counter-revolution. Early on December 3rd, Louis Philippe went to see Jerôme Pétion, the recently deposed Mayor of Paris; he lived close by, off rue de Rivoli. He caught him in his shirtsleeves, shaving from a mirror hooked on the window. A mournful scene, in a mournful period. He repeated to Pétion the dismay and repugnance he would feel if his father voted at the King's trial. 'Kindly tell your father from me to evade and to abstain from the King's trial.' But as Président of the Convention, Pétion knew, and Louis Philippe also well knew, that any one member's authority to talk or to vote was implicit.

That same day, his sister Adélaïde, returned from England, was waiting for him, with Mme de Genlis, at the family château, Le Raincy; an obscure rendezvous just outside Paris. Their time limit in France was about to expire. Louis Philippe dined with them that evening; his exasperated father, also present, refused to eat with Félicité de Genlis. Louis Philippe was the intermediary of angry messages, requests and replies, from one room to another. It was decided that he, Adélaïde and Mme de Genlis should leave early next morning. Avoiding Paris and taking the main Flanders road, they would sleep at Mons and arrive the next evening at Tournay, the Belgian frontier town annexed by the French, where Général Dumouriez had now established his headquarters. It was decided that Montpensier should stay with their father in Paris; to report on events and any perilous decrees served on the Bourbon family.

Departing from Le Raincy, Tuesday 4th December, Félicité de Genlis made a deep bow to the Duc d'Orléans; no word passed between them. He took leave of his son and daughter tenderly; the little party was profoundly moved and sad. Descending the stairs Louis Philippe was called back. 'Adieu, my dear Chartres; if you can think of some way to get me out of this wretched trial, it would be a real comfort to me.' He was not to see his father again. Efforts to undertake his exile to America had failed; and he had not concealed from his father the disgust with all that he saw in Paris; and, more ominously, what he foresaw. He and his two émigrées arrived safely at Tournay and felt the fastness of the ancient bourgeois city close around them. The market square was dominated by the twelfth-century cathedral and its five massive towers; like stern observation posts of the street scenes below. A soaring belfry, built in the pale blue local stone, competed close by.

Adélaïde and Mme de Genlis were greeted by the commander of the town, Général Moran, and were ushered to a rented furnished house in the square, a cobbled, spacious area of rose brick and stone, bordered with the tall, fine façades of Romanesque and Gothic houses. Louis Philippe was comforted that his sister was now under his aegis, and Félicité de Genlis, having heard of Dumouriez' exploits, was looking forward to any like encounters with handsome officers.

Montpensier kept Louis Philippe well briefed on the home front. The news was dire. Despite the advice of friends and counsellors, their father had attended the Convention for the 'Judgement of Capet' on December 11th. The king was questioned for three hours by the Revolutionary Convention; the incisive lawyer, Bertrand Barère, presided. 'Capet' was to be judged as an enemy, not a citizen. He was an enemy of liberty and had broken his word and oath to the nation. He had deployed counter-revolutionary troops against the people.

King Louis had appeared comatose after four uneventful months of family life in the Temple Fortress with three-course meals, and music, and his wife and sister enwrapt in embroidery; he had even enjoyed giving his adoring children a smattering of lessons. Many a Royalist still clung to the reasonable hope that their King Louis would be voted to imprisonment until peace and national order was reinstated.

Montpensier and Beaujolais, stationed at Palais Royal, watched their father with growing despair; the whole Orléans family seemed now set on a hazardous course. At the Convention, on December 16th, a decree was mooted by François Buzot, a confirmed Girondin lawyer, who had turned Republican after Varennes. He proposed, euphemistically, that all Bourbons be banished. Louis Philippe read of this potential death knell in a little evening paper on a street corner in Tournay. It determined him the more to arrange asylum for himself and his siblings in America. He wrote to his father in vain. Montpensier replied from Paris that their father was still pained over any talk of exile. He was becoming critical of Louis Philippe and was full of complaints, reproach and muddied political opinion. The voting day on the King's death flung suspense across Paris. Philippe Egalité had made fervent promises to Montpensier, Beaujolais, the Comtesse de Buffon and other close friends that he would not vote at the Convention, for his cousin's death. Voting began at eight o'clock on the evening of January 16th, 1793. The roll-call lumbered through thirteen hours on an exceptionally cold night. Egalité was called at dawn. Picking a crumpled piece of paper from his pocket, he read out forcibly: 'Uniquely concerned to do my duty and convinced that all those who have conspired or will in future conspire against the sovereignty of the people, deserve death. I vote for death.'

With 361 members and deputies of the Convention, Egalité had voted for death to the King. Three hundred and twenty one had voted for his imprisonment or exile and some had wished to see him harnessed to hard labour. Twenty-eight out of the 749 had abstained.

On January 17th, Montpensier found his father weeping at his desk. He tried to embrace him, but his father turned away. 'No – I am too miserable. I do not understand how they made me do what I have done.' Terror and fear seized Paris; all cowering Royalists lay low. The theatres had filled with triumphant Republicans, with the lowest women of the night in the best boxes. Streets were filthy and disordered and no one dared to stop and speak together. Soldiers entered homes at random for papers and any conspiracies, robbing people on demand. Householders were accused of hiding emigrants; of hoarding flour; of conspiring to deliver Marie Antoinette from the

Temple. Fear hovered in every room of every private home; laughter or weeping could lead to some accusation of political misdemeanour.

On the morning of January 21st, the gates of Paris were closed; to anyone who asked why, the order was to give no reply. Doors and windows were shuttered and the people of Paris waited in numbed disbelief for the killing of a King. In her memoirs of that morning, Madame de la Tour du Pin wrote how she and her husband looked out over Paris from a window of their house. It was eight o'clock. 'We stood there in shocked silence, hardly daring to say a word to one another ... The deepest silence lay like a pall over the regicide city. At half past ten, the gates were opened and the life of the city resumed its course unchanged.'

King Louis had woken at five o'clock. His valet, Cléry, kindled a fire and moved a chest of drawers to form an altar. After receiving Communion from Abbé Edgeworth, the King had asked if he might cut his own hair to save him the humiliation of the executioner's attentions. But he was denied this simple request; the Fortress authorities would not trust him with scissors.

With officers of the *gendarmerie* on the front seat of the carriage, the King and Abbé Edgeworth in the back, the two-hour ride from the Temple to the Place de la Révolution took its place in history. A calm and uneventful journey in which Louis busied himself with the *Abbé*'s breviary on 'prayers for persons at the point of death'. The *gendarmes* were astonished at the deposed sovereign's poise and resignation. The night before had been a welter of family loving, sobbing, embracing and heartbreaking farewells. In the cold clear light of day, Louis decided to avoid any painful renewal of such cruel emotion. Cléry wrote:

In the course of the morning, the King said to me ... 'Tell the Queen, my dear sister and my children, that, although I promised to see them again this morning, I have resolved to spare them the pain of so cruel a separation. Tell them how much it costs me to go away without receiving their embraces once more!' He wiped away some tears; and then added in the most mournful accents, 'I charge you to bear them my last farewell.'

7

Two days after the execution, Général Dumouriez dispatched to the Convention a forceful condemnation from Tournay: 'The catastrophe of January 21st without any doubt makes everyone in Europe our enemy.' Louis Philippe wrote harshly to his father, upbraiding him for the king's death; his letter was promptly burnt. Philippe Egalité, on February 10th, accentuated his shame by insisting before the Convention that he was the bastard son of Monsieur Lefranc, the late Duc d'Orléans' coachman.

Dumouriez next mustered his shrinking forces to conquer the Netherlands before the Austrians came to their aid. His attacks on Dordrecht and Maastricht, two of the strongest cities that had sustained centuries of siege, proved negligible. Early in March, Dumouriez collected his army at Louvain. It was a diminished body, he warned the Convention. He was short of men and money. Many volunteers who had flocked to the call of '*La Patrie en danger*' had deserted; there were no doctors, no field ambulances; his battalions were sorely depleted. And Dumouriez reminded the Convention of the niggardly supplies he and his men had already suffered from the former War Minister, Jean-Nicolas Pache. The son of a Swiss porter had now become Mayor of Paris! Pache! The toady who had carried a piece of bread in his pocket; never to leave his desk for refreshment just to impress his superiors!

In the face of their Général's gloom and anger, Louis Philippe geared up for the attack on the Austrians at Neerwinden. He headed 9,000 men in the Centre, with Général Miranda to the right and the Comte de Valence on the left. He led the charge with renewed dash, until his horse was shot under him; de Valence took ten sabre cuts and Miranda was bamboozled by the wily Archduke Charles. Despite such hazards, they captured the village, then lost it, and again captured and lost it. The Austrians had poured in relays of fresh troops. Dumouriez' army was routed. Louis Philippe's men could only dig into the freezing mud for the night. France and Belgium were astonished by this ignominious defeat at Neerwinden. It was outrageous! The

Convention blamed Dumouriez. They judged him offensive, defiant, a dangerous liability. Dumouriez had also lost respect for the Convention, but his offer of resignation was refused. Louis Philippe wrote in despair to his father: 'Where I formerly saw through rose-coloured spectacles, everything now seems as black as pitch. I see liberty lost; I see the Convention totally destroying France through its neglect of all principle; I see the civil war blazing; I see foreign armies descending from all sides on our unhappy country and I see no army to oppose them.' The letter was seized by the Convention and read out in all its denigration.

Dumouriez knew that any such risky exposure could lead to a definitive order for the execution of the entire Bourbon family. He evolved a daring plan. He would first arrange a truce with the Austrian chief of staff, Baron Karl Mack van Leiberich, and then enlist his aid. On March 25th, Dumouriez, the Baron, Louis Philippe and de Valence met secretly, and a campaign was forged between them. Dumouriez would march his army to Paris, capture members of the Convention and resurrect the previously abolished Constitution of 1791. In the event of failure to overthrow the Government of the Revolution, the Austrians agreed to send reinforcements. Louis Philippe was intrigued to be party to such an intrepid escapade and, when Dumouriez urged him to be discreet and to limit himself to military duties, he was reminded of Danton's similar cautions after the battle of Valmy. But it was Dumouriez who spilt the beans. At Tournay on March 26th, Louis Philippe had finally succumbed to scarlet fever. In a daze of sickness and nursing a sore throat, he lay in a room on the second floor of Mme de Genlis' rented house. Général Dumouriez was dining with Adélaïde and her vivacious governess. The front door was pushed open. Three emissaries from the Jacobin Society had been ordered to seize Dumouriez. He was furious at such an interruption and ordered them to wait for him at headquarters. But they soon returned. Dumouriez, thoroughly stirred up, proclaimed: 'I alone can make peace with Général Coburg and if I don't do so, the Austrians will be in the Tuileries in three weeks.' His select audience was horrified to hear of his plan to abolish the Convention and restore the Monarchy; to save the wholesale destruction of France; to negotiate an honourable peace with the sovereign powers; to banish all revolutionary 'blood-drinkers' and all the counter-revolutionaries; to establish a fundamental '*juste milieu*'. (A later report from the emissaries claimed wrongly that Louis Philippe, the Duc de Chartres was present and implicated at this heated meeting.)

Through his spasmodic pain and dozing, Louis Philippe had in fact been mourning his grandfather, the Duc de Penthièvre; he had only just had news of his death at Bizy, on March 3rd. He felt especially saddened for his mother who had barely recovered from the horrific fate of the Princesse de Lamballe – and then the King's execution ... A few days after that, the Duc de Penthièvre was found to have water on the chest. It swelled his body; he choked perpetually. But his discipline prevailed; he saw to his papers, attended church, took rides in his carriage. His doting daughter, Louise Marie Adélaïde, Duchesse d'Orléans, hovered and fussed and tended him with fear and obsession – 'If only I could vegetate a few minutes and think of nothing – that would do me better than all your drinks and medicines.' On March 3rd, the Duc deteriorated rapidly. His regular confessor, l'Abbé Lambert, was called. Between three o'clock in the morning and four, he died in his armchair, eking out his last words: 'Go out from this world my spirit – leave.' Louis Philippe was thankful the old man had escaped the Terror, a possible death on the scaffold, the demolition of his châteaux. It was the horror of the Revolution, which had shamed and bled his country, that in turn had killed the old Duc.

Scenes of Bizy floated through Louis Philippe's mind: the sheen and tumble of the water cascade; the fountains adorned by the spewing lions and dolphins; the fine stables where gleaming horses snuffled and shuffled for a hunt or a carriage and pair. As he drifted into sleep, the wood-panelled salons mingled before him; the family portraits, tapestries, the chattels of a rich man's castle. The people of Vernon had respected Penthièvre; he had always cared for the poor and responded to and rebuilt any community needs. The *sans-culottes* had saluted him and presented arms. He had lived to his end as a grand Seigneur.

On April 1st, Louis Philippe, together with Adélaïde and Genlis, left Tournay for the nearby village of Boues de Saint Amand. It had the advantage of housing Dumouriez in his modest headquarters and could boast of its thermal mud baths. They lodged with a Monsieur Leblanc. It was Louis Philippe's first day of convalescence.

At four o'clock the next afternoon, the peace of the small community was shattered by the furious Minister of War, Comte Beurnonville, and four commissioners from the Convention beating on Dumouriez' door. Dumouriez was handed a letter from the Convention and ordered back to Paris to explain his erratic behaviour. After some spirited argument, Dumouriez was accosted with a final command: 'Citizen Général, I suspend you from your functions. I forbid anybody to obey your orders and your person will be seized.' Dumouriez rapped out an order in German and forty Austrian Hussars stormed the house, marching off with the Minister of War and his four deputies to the enemy camp. Beurnonville had tried to escape, but was bundled back into the carriage with sabre blows. A report claimed that Louis Philippe was certainly present at this latest fracas and that he would be arrested, through his scheming with Dumouriez. Rumours were rife. But it was clear to Dumouriez that the French army was now indomitably loyal to the Republican camp; any more haranguing of the troops or talk of Armistice with the Austrian Générals was now of no avail.

It was also clear to Félicité de Genlis that as much as she had revelled in Dumouriez' feisty attentions at their frequent supper parties, his sudden arrest of the Comte de Beurnonville on the afternoon of April 2nd was unacceptable. She had heard the news at midnight and vowed to put a lid on her present playpen. The hurly-burly of army life had finally proved too *outré* for her refined tastes. She reasoned that her devoted charge, the fifteen-year-old Princesse Adélaïde, now also struck down with sores and fever, would be best contained at Boues de Saint Amand, and the dubious benefits of its thermal mud. In the cold grey April morning, the resolute de Genlis settled herself in a hired carriage. The postilions cracked their whips, when '*Alte-là!*' The convalescent Louis Philippe, guessing at her intent, had scooped his shivering sister from her bed and, with only a flimsy shawl and her watch (rescued from her pillow), thrust her into de Genlis' arms. A shrill, swift and decisive scene, which put paid to the Duc de Chartres' fond feeling for '*mon amie*'. The carriage headed for Switzerland; it was a risky journey, exposed to the conflicting and suspicious armies. Lanterns swung through the night over rough roads and narrow hill passes. Within the substantial old confines of Schaffhausen, on the Rhine, the two women were offered temporary safety.

De Genlis' acute sense of timing had served them both well. On April 4th the Convention ordered the arrest of 'La Citoyenne Femme Egalité' – Adélaïde's mother. There was now a death price on all heads of the extant Bourbons. The Duchesse d'Orléans broken-hearted after her father's death, had gone to pieces, groaning in her private oratory and refusing to eat. She was now considered a dangerous liability, with her pleasing domain of Bizy a nest of conspiracy. On this same morning Général Dumouriez, with Louis Philippe and the Comte de Valence left headquarters at Boues de Saint Amand, in haste for Condé, where the Austrian Générals still waited to discuss Armistice terms. As they passed a battalion of Republican volunteers, cries rang out: 'Down with Dumouriez! The traitor!' The little cavalcade galloped furiously on to the Austrian camp as they were showered with bullets. When Dumouriez' horse refused a ditch, Louis Philippe's valet, Baudoin, offered his own. Writhing by the roadside, feigning agonizing injury, the canny Baudoin redirected the angry volunteers the wrong way. Dumouriez had no option but to lead his young Lieutenant-Générals to safety – with the enemy; he reminded them authoritatively of how, in 1777, the nineteen-year-old Lafayette had absconded to the North American States to enlist in their War of Independence.

Louis Philippe lost no time in obtaining passports for Switzerland; 'strictly temporary ones', he was warned; no cantons of the country were safe for him. Word of Egalité, the regicide, the Duc d'Orléans, had spread across Europe. Louis Philippe noted in his diary: 'All I kept – one packhorse and my valet, Baudoin … I sold my horses and accoutrements at Basle.' His carriage, drawn by three horses, with three servants and his valet on the box, had attracted attention.

The Marquis de Montesquiou, an émigré friend of his father, with connections in Switzerland, stepped in to help the beleaguered itinerants. He had steered de Genlis and Adélaïde to a convent in Bremgarten. They had subsisted on the sale of one of Madame's 'Rousseau' manuscripts. Ensconced between the Swiss lakes and mountains, the resourceful de Genlis now produced her harp to ingratiate the pious community. For Louis Philippe, the Marquis had bleak advice: 'Your only hope is to roam about the mountains, and avoid being recognized.' With his inimitable flamboyance, Thomas Carlyle pictures the scene: 'Brave young Egalité reaches Switzerland … with a strong crabstick in his hand, a strong heart in his body:

his princedom is now reduced to that.' Louis Philippe's sole companion was his loyal Baudoin, who, being taken sick, was now mounted on their one horse. Peasants bowed their heads at this master of compassion trudging past. The two companions were reduced to thirty sous a day.

Louis Philippe had always thrived on leadership and responsibility. But his reserves of energy and discipline were momentarily toppled. As he stomped through the scenic Swiss Cantons from Basle, south to Neuchâtel, he assessed his priorities. He was a faithful patriot. He had no desire to join the émigrés. A military career was now tacitly barred him. He had always been 'a pacific prince'. He had good friends. Général Dumouriez believed in him; he had explicitly urged him to keep an account of his travels. '... it would be pleasant to read the diary of a Bourbon concerned with matters other than hunting, women and eating.' To the Marquis de Montesquiou, the Général had also written, '*Embrassez pour moi notre bon jeune homme.*' And, yes! The forlorn young Duc thought of Félicité de Genlis; despite her disgraceful behaviour in attempting to abandon poor feverish Adélaïde at Saint Amand. As the mountains loomed and the distant lakes glimmered blue, her voice came to mind.

> He was a Prince, I made him a man.
> He was dull, I made him clever.
> He was insipid, I brought him to life.
> He was a coward, I made him brave...

She had despised any soft treatment. Louis Philippe and his young brothers had slept on wooden beds, covered with hair matting. Daily, they took exercise to build the body. They would walk five or six leagues with leaden soles in their boots. She impressed on the Princes that their birth and fortune was of little merit in the face of their performance. Louis Philippe now chuckled at her hypocrisy. She had moulded them into honourable Republicans and yet her vanity desired them to remain Royal. Swimming, rowing, fencing and riding, carrying baskets of firewood; as a concession for good behaviour, they might visit a farm, a factory, a bindery or weavery. But never once did Madame de Genlis take her charges to a locksmith. A dirty trade, she assured them. Louis XVI's consuming interest in these appliances had given locks a bad name.

8

Philippe Egalité, Duc d'Orléans, and his two younger sons, were rounded up for imprisonment on April 8th, 1793. The Duc de Montpensier, serving in the Alpes-Maritimes as ADC to their good friend Général Biron, was astonished to see his revered leader on his knees before him, in an agony of despair. The Général had been ordered to arrest him; this seventeen-year-old son of his closest friend. 'Is that all? Let me go directly. I can amuse my dear father in our captivity.' Montpensier next assured Biron that he had not involved himself in Counter-Revolutionary, conspiracy, but now heartily despised the Jacobin ethic. The Général and his discreet Commandant followed Montpensier to his lodgings, where between them they destroyed and burnt all dangerous and potentially incriminating letters from Louis Philippe, the Duc de Chartres.

Général Biron arranged for Montpensier's return to Paris in a modest carriage, with his valet Gamache in the saddle and a single officer of the *gendarmes* in attendance. The provincial towns of Brignoles and Aix erupted in pockets of violence as Jacobins clamoured to obtain the soldiers' identity and to see their passports. The calm young police officer retaliated that he was delivering dispatches to the Convention, and urged on their postilion. The swelling crowds and disruption at Aix had frightened the Mayor and he quickly consigned Montpensier's small party to an apartment in the Town Hall. The valiant officer had already warned the young duc that if his identity was discovered, he was a lost man. 'They will hew you in pieces; but do not be alarmed, they shall take my life before they have yours.'

Montpensier slept in his clothes and bolted the Garde Room. The next day he was told that all proceedings in his case were instead to be administered at Marseilles, where an immense mob had already collected to glimpse the state prisoner in his carriage. Fears for his safety had mounted considerably. It was even mooted by the town officials that an empty cab be driven through the town centre while Montpensier and Gamache should walk the last lap along side streets. They complied, but the ruse was rumbled. The magistrates rushed out to receive them, as Montpensier sensed his immediate assassination. In the Palais de Justice, he and Gamache were imprisoned in a cell of nine feet square. The despairing valet was aghast at the filth. It had been left uncleaned after two thieves had contributed to its horrific state for six years.

Continually pestered by municipal authorities, hovered over, questioned, locked up and guarded, Montpensier was astounded one day to read that his brother Louis Philippe had exited France with Général Dumouriez. 'Your brother is a traitor,' announced the garde, pulling a newspaper from his pocket. Montpensier, momentarily dumbfounded, next learnt that the instant Louis Philippe had passed into Belgium, he had expedited him the news. Montpensier's courier, in a fast diligence, had not arrived until thirty hours after his brother's arrest in Nice. Montpensier was now interrogated even more closely by court administrators.

Why did his brother quit France?

What were his motives?

What were his libertine intentions?

To betray his country?

After twelve days of stinking confinement, Montpensier had unexpected news of his father and his thirteen-year-old brother, Beaujolais. They were to join him in Marseilles in the formidable fortress of Notre-Dame de la Garde. At midnight on April 23rd, he and Gamache were suddenly woken and marched under a strong garde through silent streets by the old port. They breathed deeply on the good pure air; and again Montpensier was assured that he would have been torn to pieces by a daytime crowd. At 4am, he was joined by his family; night hours had clearly been favoured for the movement of all the captives.

The jubilant embraces were soon ordered to stop; strict silence between prisoners was an imperative; a sentinel behind each door enforced the rule. But it was an altogether acceptable Orléans-Bourbon party; to the approval of both captives and gardes alike. Philippe Egalité, Duc d'Orléans, his sister, the Duchesse de Bourbon, her husband, the flamboyant Prince de Conti and the young Comte de Beaujolais. A prodigious spender, a dandy and bon viveur, Conti was the father of the ill-fated Duc d'Enghien, later murdered by Napoleon in 1804.

Their rough and eventful journey had started from Paris on April 11th.

The accompanying *Commissaires* – Laugier, Cailleux and Naigeon – had noted down their behaviour and idiosyncrasies. The Duchesse was fractious; could they start at eleven o'clock in the mornings? Could she attend *la Messe*? And the carriage would wait patiently through her confessions. They named her 'La Malheureuse'. Even so, her misery and indignant hauteur tore at their hearts. The Citoyen Conti was also hard to please. He felt his age and infirmities. He complained bitterly that Louis Philippe should have done well by himself and left his family as hostages. The Duc d'Orléans, Citoyen Egalité, a natural optimist, managed to dispel the boredom and sadness in the company of his youngest son, Beaujolais. A lack of horses had delayed them. At Vienne, the city magistrates had offered Rhône riverboat transport to Avignon, to include the carriages. It was a cheaper alternative; but when a strong north wind got up, becoming increasingly violent, the plaintive Prince had begged for rest; he had caught a fever. The boat was forced to dock soon after midnight, fifteen leagues from Vienne. The wind died at 3am on April 18th. The boat was buffeted through more rough wind and weather, when they finally moored in the early evening at Pont-Saint-Esprit. It was noted that the nearer the prisoners approached Marseilles, the more subdued and anxious they became.

The Duc d'Orléans had kept his own account.

Our sailors made lewd jokes about our necks being chopped at Marseilles. But we were still anxious to arrive at our sad depot alive. On 19th April, we departed Pont-Saint-Esprit '*par le plus beau temps du monde*'. It did not last – north wind and waves violent – twice the crew had to slacken the ropes. Arrived Avignon midnight. All appeared calm. There had been rumour of agitation. Due to the capricious weather we chose to leave the boat and secured more horses. We reached Orgon six o'clock in the evening. The Mayor contained us in a depot with ten guards for the night. All was quiet until drunken volunteers from the Italian army yelled menacing threats as they were shoved into the same quarters as ourselves. We all talked together and with reason and respect. But the wine and their raucous patriotism inspired them to even worse threats and loud-mouthed vilification; that we were émigrés – that it was necessary to chop off our heads –

'Bourbons to the guillotine!' They waved guns in the air and all hope left our little party.

The volunteers were to leave at dawn. Laugier had also left Orgon early; he was heading for Marseilles to check on the arrangements. The party spent the next night, April 21st, at Aix. A formidable crowd thronged the town's public places when the carriages arrived early evening. The prisoners were shacked up pell-mell with officers, *gendarmerie* and *commissaires*. The Duchesse was addressed as Citoyenne Bourbon – Madame Veto – with other expressions of hate and derision. Laugier, having reached Marseilles, sent word that they should delay their departure from Aix on April 22nd, until eleven o'clock at night.

The *commissaires'* final words on their illustrious charges read like an epitaph.

What was a tragedy for their stay in prison for them all, was the suspicion, fear and abject certainty that carrying the name of Bourbon they would be taken eventually to the scaffold. The energy of patriotism in Marseilles and their zealous hate of the *Ancien Régime* and the sentiments of individual worth were now inextricably stamped on the Republic.

Signé

LAUGIER, CAILLEUX, NAIGEON

Marseilles, *le 24 avril 1793, l'an 2 de la République.*

After the dank, dark dungeons of the Palais de Justice, the Fort Notre-Dame de la Garde was an improvement. The cells had more light, allowing Montpensier to sketch and write. He and Beaujolais were even permitted to play ball around the fort. This agreeable rhythm lasted for four days, until an order from the Convention, enforced by armed administrators beating on their doors, shattered all hope. No more talking or eating together! A few days into this crippling new regime, the officer garde stationed between their rooms shot himself.

By the end of May, they were transferred to the towering Fort St Jean at the entrance of the old port. As Montpensier observed, it took a battalion of

500 to escort an old woman, an ailing old man, a middle-aged father and the two young brothers to the satanic fort etched against the night sky. The Duchesse was mounted in a '*chaise à porteur*' and burst into tears at the sight of her room. 'It was barbarous to treat such nobility as herself, who had served her country well with every justice and reason.' Her shrieks echoing down the black tunnels and curling towers went unheeded.

Further up the narrow stairs, the darkness and fetid horror left Montpensier struck dumb in his allotted cell. The latrines pervaded the stench with a morbid infection. His door was being unlocked; an exercise that took six to seven minutes. He waited in terror. In the light of a lantern stood the resourceful Gamache with his trunk and with sugar to burn to dispel the foul smell. '*Dieu! Mon Bon Seigneur, Dieu!*' The two young men would throw themselves against the cell bars above the sea to breathe in any air possible. They read all day. Gamache was happy to start with the second volume; it was all the same to him. In the evening they played piquet until supper; each slice of bread cut in four, in case of a letter slipped inside; chicken cut about and inspected vigorously; fruit quartered. Montpensier and Beaujolais were destined to endure three and a half years of shock and torment at Fort St Jean.

Undaunted, Montpensier persevered with the observations which were later to colour his autobiography. His flair for description comes over well as his fastidious uncle surveys the execrable scene.

It would be impossible to give an adequate idea of the appearance of the Prince of Conti as he entered our dungeon; his head covered with curls in paper, a little three-cocked hat placed horizontally over them. Thrusting forward his cane, he called out to the gardes, 'I shall be smothered in this horrible place ... Lads, I will not conceal from you that it is all over with us; nay, I am bound to tell you that we have not four and twenty hours to live. I am only shut up here with you, as oxen are with the sheep, when the time is come for them to be slaughtered.'

9

Louis Philippe and Baudoin had been traipsing through Switzerland for four months. From Neuchâtel, through the mountains of Unterwalden, across Interlaken and to the soaring peaks of Grindelwald. A Damoclean fear of discovery hung over their rough and incognito roaming. Sleeping under hedges, their clothes in tatters, hungry and footsore, they had become veritable vagabonds. Louis Philippe took precarious comfort from his fertile mind, comparing his plight with Jean-Jacques Rousseau, whose maxim 'It is an important thing in life never to neglect the passing moment' gave him the impetus to put one foot after another. Aged sixteen, Rousseau had marched confidently into the world's wide spaces; he had spent nights on the street to keep his sous for bread rather than a bed. He praised the dawn and sunrise, the birth of a fine summer's day. Climbing through mountain forests, he would marvel at clumps of periwinkle and at the powerful song of nightingales.

With his facility to remember whole passages of text, Louis Philippe was especially moved by Rousseau's account in his *Lettres de la Montagne* of his pangs of hunger. Dying of thirst and fatigue, he had knocked on a peasant's door and begged a meal. He was given skimmed milk and coarse barley bread. The peasant, seeing his appetite and honest expression, returned with ham and wine and cooked an omelette.

A very different tale to Louis Philippe and Baudoins' hostile reception at the Hospitium on Mount St Gothard. Founded as an asylum for poor travellers, the Prince and his valet were given a signal refusal. It was dusk on August 29th, 1793, when they rang the bell of the humble wood lodge. A bearded Capuchin monk peered out from a first-floor casement window. What did they want? 'I request,' replied Louis Philippe, 'some nourishment for my companion and myself.' The reverend father assured them that he could not admit foot-passengers, and particularly not of their appearance. Closing his window, he waved them off to a ramshackle shed where muleteers were dipping into goats' cheese. In his future heyday of power and riches, Louis Philippe commissioned Horace Vernet, his favourite artist, to depict the scene; it was to hang in Palais Royal.

The summer was passing and the nights colder. On a particularly wet and foggy evening in Gordona, the two travellers were again refused a bed. After desperate pleas, they were finally given straw and shelter in the barn. Louis Philippe woke in the small hours to be confronted by a youth eyeing him at the end of a musket. He explained that his aunt who owned the land had ordered him to shoot if the wanderers attempted to thieve. Louis Philippe and Baudoin, with their overriding fear of being recognised, never stayed in any one place for more than two days.

Once again the valiant Général Montesquiou had devised a plan to relieve the young strays. His friend, Monsieur Jost, headmaster at the College of Reichenau, a boys' boarding institution, needed a geography master; a supplement of history teaching, mathematics and modern languages was desirable. A French émigré by name of Monsieur Chabaud-Latour had failed to take up the post. And so, the Duc de Chartres, aged twenty, whose distinction in serving his country was now ignored, became a schoolmaster. Another irresistible topic to stir the imagination at many future after-dinner conversations in the Tuileries; and Winterhalter was later commissioned to capture the scene. The young prince, tall, slim and handsome, his back to the window, with mountains behind, and his folios, maps and globe set out all before.

Louis Philippe moved to the Château de Reichenau near the village of Coire in October 1793. Its pretty gardens and views of the Upper Rhine and Lower Rhine, in confluence below, were a balm. He accepted gladly a salary of 1,400 francs a year and stayed for eight months, under the pseudonym of Monsieur Chabaud. His true identity was known only to Monsieur Jost, who referred to him fondly as 'Chabos'. The first few weeks passed well and peacefully. Chabos believed intrinsically in all education and had an authoritative air. His natural kindness and firm manner endeared him to his pupils. He found the library a disappointment, as was the food. And Monsieur Jost considered his mania for a clean shirt each day most extravagant. However, Chabos was judged an excellent teacher, although his benefactor was constrained to ask him to refrain from spicing his talk with all the important people he had met.

The news of his father's sudden death at the scaffold on November 6th, 1793 astounded Louis Philippe. He shuffled round the grounds of Reichenau, head down and inconsolable. He felt guilty; his ultimate complicity with Dumouriez was a key accusation in his father's trial. And now, his brothers were in prison; he had no news of his mother; his sister was still in the dubious care of Félicité de Genlis. Louis Philippe and his brothers had worshipped their father's gaiety, his wit and elegance, and even his *louche* behaviour, which they had judged as brave. But as many as had loved and admired the Duc d'Orléans there were those who loathed his genius deceits. Miss Elizabeth Wynne, writing her diary in Switzerland, recorded on November 15th, 'We heard today that the Duke of Orléans ... has been guillotined ... Hated by all mankind.' A typical and common reaction of the day.

Montpensier and Beaujolais, suffocating in their grim little cells through the long provençale summer, had been aware of their father's impending death. On the morning of October 22nd, Montpensier was woken by him and embraced. Surly attendants stood around. 'I come, my dear Montpensier to say Adieu ... it is always a painful moment but I had to see you again ... Goodbye my son...'

Montpensier was so seized he could say nothing. Tears flowing, he held his father to his heart. In his later account of their captivity in Fort St Jean, Montpensier included an idolizing tribute.

'Unfortunate and excellent father! You sacrificed yourself for the wrong projects ... Your enemies crushed your voice.' The first and last lines ring truer perhaps than the long and overwhelming eulogy of an adoring son.

The imprisoned brothers had agitated for some word. Their aunt, the Duchesse de Bourbon, was full of foreboding; was she preparing them? A letter came; it was from their mother. The Duchesse d'Orléans, in big disfigured writing spelt out, "*Vivez malheureux enfants, pour votre si malheureuse mère.*" What could this mean? What had become of their father? 'Condemned and executed,' said their aunt. Prince Conti read in a public paper that when the heads had been chopped off the remaining Royal Family, their Orléans cousins were next in the line of fire.

Général Montesquiou sent to the newly succeeded Louis Philippe an account of his father's death: his heroic last stand at the scaffold, unflinching, his hair fastidiously powdered, his dress elegant in yellow buckskin and a waistcoat of white piqué. He had helped the executioner untie his cravat and urged him on calmly – '*Dépêchez-moi vite!*'

Louis Philippe was now the Duc d'Orléans. The loyal Montesquiou also had solemn news of his mother. Cruelly labelled '*La femme de Philippe, le Guillotiné*', she had barely left her bed since the death of her father in early March. The Duchesse now felt fear and gloom all around her at Bizy, where Jacobin soldiers guarded the château. At dusk one evening a former forest warden of the great park had arrived exhausted and gasping for breath. He had walked from Paris with sinister news. The Convention had put out an order that the Duchesse be brought there for questioning.

The following day, November 5th, the Convention liquidated her 'service' allowance. Her five *femmes de chambre*, three *femmes de wardrobe*, six male *domestiques* and a chef were to be disbanded. The townspeople of Vernon were horrified at her frail demeanour as she descended the steps for her journey to Paris. A veritable ghost! Forty years old and near to death! She had consigned to her secretary, Monsieur de Chabrier, a casket of diamonds and mixed jewellery; he later handed it over, in fear, to the departmental authorities. She had urged Docteur Gueydan to escape while there was still time; he refused. It was her wish to obey the Convention, she told her troubled audience as she mounted the carriage for six days of inexorable pain and discomfort.

At St Germain-des-Prés, where the Duchesse had weakened considerably, she was allowed to sleep at the Auberge de la Chasse Royale, and had an ingenious exchange with her lawyer. She wept as she asked of him three things: to prevent the dilapidation of her cherished properties and lands; to save her inheritance; and to gain permission from the prison for her medical prescriptions. In the event, her prescriptions were taken to the tribunal's chief prosecutor – the hasty Antoine Fouquier-Tinville – for his didactic perusal. The Duchesse completed her journey to Luxembourg – that mercurial palace-cum parliament-cum-prison. The walls and façades closed around her. The rich changing colours of the chestnut trees, the lawns and ornamental pools and statuary could not allay her trepidations.

10

The newly titled Duc d'Orléans, went through the motions of his daily routines in a discombobulated daze. His family was crushed and scattered, each one of them born to breeding, and unimaginable fortune. In his twenty-first year, Louis Philippe now saw life as a deceptive ride, which needed a flexible hold on the reins. He had been devastated by his father's death; he felt lost and lonely and in dire need of comfort. The little Italian college cook, who had long been enamoured of the village carpenter, was now intrigued with this master of many subjects. She had watched him each evening pacing the gardens with Monsieur Jost, in a flow of animated talk. Louis Philippe, aware of her discreet admiration and her plump little body – reminiscent of Hendrickje Stoffels – fell on her with relief and gusto. By the summer of 1794, Louis Philippe's chaste record was violated by the charming Marianne Banzori. Monsieur Jost was incensed at the news that his cook was '*enceinte*' and wrote to Général Montesquiou: 'I am not angry with Monsieur Chabos for having fathered a child, but I am angry with him for fathering it on my cook.' The hapless Marianne was dispatched to Milan where she gave birth in December. The child was handed over to the '*Enfants trouvés*'. At this not surprising juncture, Louis Philippe had left Reichenau and wrote a series of sentimental letters in German to his Marianne:

> You see, my dearest treasure, that your Chabosli loses no time in writing to you. I can't talk of what I've been through since I had to leave you. *Ma petite, ma bonne petite*, you can only judge it by what you have been through yourself. After being dragged from your beloved arms I wanted to go back to you, my darling. I half turned round but you were already far off ... I got into the boat with death in my soul ... You were always present in my sight. I couldn't speak or think of anything else. *Adieu, ma chère petite* ... Your Chabosli kisses you and loves you with all his heart.

And later: 'I find your letters easier to read, my beloved treasure, and I see that you are trying to write more legibly ... You do well not to write very often, busy as you are with so much cooking. You are always before my eyes, and your Chabosli will never forget his treasure.'

The episode, tinged with his desire and remorse, was consigned to the rich tapestry of Louis Philippe's life. Monsieur Raymond Recouly in his *Louis Philippe, Roi des Français* revealed this incident through pertinent correspondence between Général Montesquiou and Monsieur Jost.

Louis Philippe was in stronger mode after his experiences at Reichenau. Monsieur Jost had afforded him a Certificate of Ability in Teaching; he had earned some money and he had become heir to the questionably proud House of Orléans. He was now intent on reaching England where a part of his father's dwindled fortune was still purportedly intact. And, should he and his brothers exile themselves to America, they could restart their lives well away from the cruel orgies and blood-letting of France. But when would his brothers be released from Fort St Jean? His mother from Luxembourg? And his sister? Princesse Adélaïde, now sixteen, had been extricated from Mme de Genlis' doubtful care to live in Fribourg with their great-aunt, the Princesse de Conti. They were soon compelled to move to Bavaria and then to Hungary.

Leaving Reichenau, Louis Philippe and Baudoin set off for Bremgarten to stay with kind Général Montesquiou in quiet seclusion. By January 1795, their retreat was discovered and bandied around by German newspapers: that the Duc d'Orléans was living ostentatiously in a specially built palace ... Meanwhile, the flirtatious Comtesse de Flahaut, who shared the attention of the Prince Talleyrand with his beautiful young niece, the Duchesse de Dino, had written appealingly to Governor Morris: 'I have seen the young Duc d'Orléans in Switzerland ... he is melancholy, but gentle and modest. His great ambition is to go to America and forget the greatness and suffering which have been part and parcel of his youth; but he has no money at all.'

Louis Philippe travelled to bustling Hamburg to meet his mother's old admirer from America. Governor Morris had initiated a speculative plan of mortgaging some Orléans estates to invest in thousands of acres on the right bank of the Saint Lawrence River. The young Duc, shrewd from hard experience of money matters, knocked the idea flat. Instead, Montesquiou arranged passports and limited credit with a banker in Copenhagen. Itching for space and exercise, Louis Philippe set off for the Scandinavian peninsula under the name of Müller. His friend Gustave, Comte de Montjoie, accompanied him; it was he who had successfully escorted Adélaïde and Mme de Genlis on their dangerous carriage journey to Schaffhausen. Louis Philippe's letters to Montesquiou, depicting the trials and triumphs of their wandering, concentrated his observation; his accounts were finally contained in *Mon Journal*, published in 1849, the year before his death.

From Copenhagen they crossed the Sound to Elsinore, where the castle defends its port and gardens of Hamlet, Prince of Denmark. Familiar with Shakespeare, Louis Philippe was always keen to indulge his literary appetite. Chugging up the west coast of Sweden through the Kattegat Sound he visited the prosperous town of Gothenburg, where he observed its industry and institutions. Was he prompted by Mme de Genlis' fervent enthusiasm for all industrial pursuits and their childhood outings to factories? His yen for history next carried Louis Philippe across the border into Norway to Fredrikstad in the Gulf of Skagerrak. Here fell the unpopular Swedish monarch Charles XII in 1718. He was thirty-six years old and his death was dignified in verse by Voltaire. But the Swedes had long despaired of his arrogance and his extravagant warmongering.

Listing to the Norwegian Sea, the Orléans party found a peaceful haven at Kristiana. The sweep of sky and space and the bracing air from the north served them well after the strains of travel. The villagers welcomed the three young Frenchmen unreservedly, never once suspecting Louis Philippe's true identity. He stayed several weeks, relishing his anonymity and the release from suspicion. They took picnics into the countryside and to the surrounding waterways and islands. A local youth, to become years later a lecturer at the Reformed Church in Paris, would be astonished to recognise in the Duc d'Orléans that clever, gentle young man from Kristiana.

Considerably refreshed and leaving an impression of exceptional good behaviour, the travelling trio set off in launches up the west coast of Norway to Lapland. Passing through Trondheim, they continued through the Lofoten Islands and the surround of spectacular fjords; they were regaled in lurid detail with tales of the treacherous evils of that great whirlpool: the Maelstrom in the Gulf of Salten. A notorious phenomenon that could suddenly swallow up the largest ships, their wrecks never to be recovered. Their voyage headed lastly for Hammersfeldt on the North Cape; the most northern town in Europe. Louis Philippe had engaged a wig-maker from Iceland to guide and interpret. A wise precaution; the mountains, the precipices, storms and haphazard temperatures could prove fatal. They reached Hammersfeldt on August 24th, 1795; the last part of their journey had been achieved by reindeer sledge and three weeks of camping out in the wilds.

Louis Philippe revelled in his experiences of this striking land: the inhabitants, their customs and their stories of survival in that arctic cape. Written off by Ovid as a glacial region of Scythia – 'sad, lonely, barren, no trees, no fruits, and dark'; but for Louis Philippe it proved a time of rejuvenation and happy readjustment to the human race. Wearing the local thermal tunic, he visited the humble tents of the Laplanders and gave vent to his perennial thirst for knowledge. The tents with their conical roofs were wrapped around with skins and rugs. He was intrigued with the Lapland stone houses where the winter stocks of food were stored in wooden hutches, similar to dovecots and raised on poles to a height that guarded against raids from wildlife or burial in snow. Louis Philippe could not resist climbing up to see a store hutch; he was warned that a ravenous bear was known to break the poles and drag away entire supplies – including the proprietor.

Crossing the Lapland–Sweden border with a following of admiring Laplanders and their reindeer, Louis Philippe wended his way down the Torne Valley to a remote town called Muonio. He stayed with a priest in his rectory and, as always, under the name Müller. He there met the sister of the priest's wife. She was the housekeeper and was called Beata.

Resolving to conclude his adventurous explorations of Scandinavia, Louis Philippe crossed the Gulf of Finland to the Aland Islands and finally embarked at Stockholm. A few months after he had left Scandinavia, Beata Caisa Wahbom gave birth to a son, whom she named Erik.

Resident in Stockholm was the distinguished ex-minister of Louis XVI's disbanded household, the Comte de Saint-Priest. He had heard talk of a young traveller, one Monsieur Müller, arriving in the capital of Sweden. He was further astounded to learn that the Duc d'Orléans had 'fallen from the skies on Stockholm'. They met and Louis Philippe talked at length of his existence. The comte was impressed with Louis Philippe's survival tactics through the tortuous twists of the Revolution: his army service and his resource in dealing with so many hurdles. The young Duc poured out his sadness and frustration to the trusted aristocrat; all his youthful aspirations of liberty had been plunged into useless excesses of blood and turmoil. The Comte de Saint-Priest sat silent and sighing; what a litany of regrets from one so young. He then told Louis Philippe that the ten-year-old Louis XVII had died in the Temple prison on June 8th, 1795.

11

That smiling little boy, with his head of long chestnut curls; the proud little Prince in his uniform of the Garde Nationale, prancing atop the banqueting table to the delight of the Swiss officers.*

The Comte de Saint-Priest was talking again: of the arrest and pitiful bullying of Louis Charles, the second Dauphin, in his closing days. With their father and mother decapitated, the Convention had ruled that the two Capet children should languish in the Temple. Simon, the old cobbler from the Tuileries, had clipped the boy's curls. The joints of his wasting body were swollen with scrofulous infection; he could hardly walk. Simon, now assigned keeper, delighted in yelling to him at night: 'Capet! Capet!' With his aching knees and the soles of his feet burning, the boy would stumble through the dark at his brutal master's bidding. 'I am here, Citizen'. 'Come nearer, wolf cub.' Louis Charles would brace his frail body for the kicks and blows to come. Collapsing and faint with pain, he would be taunted further. 'Suppose you were King, Capet – what would you do to me?' Replied the Dauphin: 'I would forgive you.'

His father's dying words at the scaffold were ever in his mind. His mother and his aunt had soon followed. Calm and upright in an open cart, the Queen of France, his own beloved mother, had been rattled to the scaffold; her hair shorn, her hands tied behind her. She regretted nothing, it was not a shameful death. She thought of her Petit Trianon (nicknamed "Little Vienna" by her detractors) and her favourite grotto; that last sight of the little stream, uncleared and choked with autumn leaves ... Above all, she anguished over her adored children. 'I am distraught to be leaving my poor children,' she had last written to Madame Elisabeth, who was next to be taken to her death six months later.

Louis Charles was subsisting on a contemptible diet of broth, lentils and burnt chestnuts, with a glass of sugar and water when his throat was on fire.

---

* Louis Philippe remembered accompanying the heart of the first Dauphin in 1789 to the Val-de-Grâce, with its overwhelming dome, set in the fields of Port Royal.

A doctor was called in on account of his worsening condition. Fresh air was prescribed and Louis Charles was moved up to a breezy room with a window open to the sun and skies. He was given a new doctor and new keeper, a kind and gentle man called Gomin, who tended the Royal orphan with devotion.

Gomin would carry him up to the battlemented platform by the left turret. It had been a wet spring in 1795; with the frequent storms and through the rains of ages, a shallow basin had formed and was kept constantly supplied. The boy would gaze intently at the sparrows, dipping their beaks to drink, wetting their breasts and wings and shaking their feathers dry. With his back wedged against the wall he would stand enthralled, hanging on Gomin's arm. 'My birds,' he called them, and would walk a little closer and closer still; at first they would fly away, but as he became more familiar they waited until he could almost touch them before they spread their wings and thrilled him with their swoops and chirping.

His fifteen-year-old sister, Madame Royale, implored repeatedly that she might see her brother. She had been told his bed had been infested with bugs. She wanted to nurse him and show him her love. Always the protective sister who, on the terraces of Versailles, had walked beside her toddling brother, holding his little hand firmly. She had also been informed that her mother and aunt had 'gone to take the air ... We advise you to take patience and to trust in the justness and goodness of the French'. Madame Royale's memoirs: *Filia Dolorosa: Memoirs of the Duchesse d'Angoulême*, recount the excruciating fear and loneliness of her imprisonment; the dread of the unknown and the ultimate despair at the siblings' separation.

Gomin was happy to see his 'little Capet' so calm and smiling on that June afternoon. He lay exceptionally still. Was he even now in pain? 'Oh yes,' said the boy, 'but the music is so beautiful.' There was no music. 'From above!' And he raised his fluttering fingers. He was in ecstasies, his eyes sparkling. He cried, 'From amongst all the voices, I have distinguished that of my mother!' Gomin knelt beside him. Again he was exultant as his large eyes wandered to the window. 'I have something to tell you!' But as the keeper rested a hand on the heart of the young Louis XVII, it could beat no more.

It was Louis Philippe's turn to sigh. Saint-Priest leaned towards him confidingly. 'Your cousin, the Comte de Provence, exiled in Verona, has already declared his succession. He styles himself Louis XVIII. It is clear that he wants a restoration of the Ancien Régime.' The Comte lowered his voice; and Général Dumouriez was again promoting him, the young Duc d'Orléans, as the only possible means of bringing together the Republic and the Monarchy. The Comte advised Louis Philippe not to linger in Stockholm. Although he had been welcomed and treated most graciously by the Swedish court, the modest Müller had been recognised at a state ball for which he had rashly taken a ticket out of curiosity. The officious French envoy had uncovered his alias and informed His Majesty; whereupon the Royal Family had extended even more invitations and kindnesses.

Absorbed in his travels and undaunted, Louis Philippe left Stockholm at the start of 1796. Up through Uppsala, he followed a trail in deference to the brave young Prince Gustavus who, 270 years before, was destined to be king like himself; he also had fled persecution. Further inland they were shown the copper mines of Falun and the fascinating subterranean towns. Next they reached Mora, the lakeside where his hero Gustavus had stood on the famous rock, goading his troops to beat off Northern tyrants. Finally the Duc was eager to see around the renowned docks at Karlskrona, set on a headland of the South Baltic Sea. Hewn out of the rock, a vast arsenal of the finest ships was stored within and repaired. Louis Philippe was first refused entry. Strangers were not admitted. The commissary was adamant. Inured to disappointment, Louis Philippe turned away, when suddenly a message was relayed from the Regent to give every permission. Making a leisurely return through Copenhagen to Hamburg, Louis Philippe took stock of his parlous circumstances.

He was virtually destitute and, fearing anew for his identity, changed his lodgings constantly. The Directory, which had replaced the Convention in November 1795, was anxious to find this wandering Prince of the Blood; ostensibly to ensure that he was not courting dissent across Europe. Headed by a five-man consortium rather than a President, the Directory was now determined on Louis Philippe's voluntary exile; but in America, well separated by the Atlantic Ocean. He was finally tracked down in Friedrichstadt, a calm little town set inland from the North Sea and the distant red rock cliffs of Helgoland. The tree-lined canals, crossed with narrow streets and quaint houses with their gabled roofs and pediments had proved a welcome haven for Louis Philippe and his modest party. The local sweet and sour soup of eels and prunes had served them well.

The French *chargé*, handing a letter to Louis Philippe from his mother, explained that she had been released from prison earlier in the summer and had persuaded the Directory to free her two younger sons from the Fort St Jean. She had also managed, through her obliging lawyer, to send them a heap of books, two waistcoats, two dozen table napkins and, at her special request, 'please give my poor boys some good wine'. The Duchesse reiterated in her letter to Louis Philippe, the demand of the Directory that she and his siblings cross the Atlantic for asylum in America. It was their ardent desire, she promised him, that 'we put the seas between us and restore tranquillity to our country'. Montpensier and Beaujolais were to be released in November.

Louis Philippe was delighted beyond belief to set off for America and to avoid tensions between Palais Royal and the Tuileries. He had also refused adamantly to join the émigré army under Louis XVIII, now under Austrian command. He next learnt from his mother's letter that Governor Morris had offered substantial credit for her sons' voyaging in America.

Louis Philippe wrote tenderly to his mother, before he embarked on *The America*.

September 24th, 1796, from Hamburg to Philadelphia.

When my loving mother receives this letter, her arrangements will be exonerated and I will have parted for America ... I do not believe that happiness is irretrievably lost for me since I still have the means to soften the blows to a mother so dear, whose fate and sufferings have torn my heart for so long.

I like to dream and think that soon I will embrace my brothers and that we will be reunited. I do not complain of my destiny. I do not feel it could ever be so miserable again. I hear that our dear mother is as well as she can be and, if I still have a chance to serve my country, to contribute to its tranquillity and happiness, there is no sacrifice I would not make for it; as long as I live I shall be ready to serve.

Louis Philippe and Baudoin boarded ship in thick fog over the Elbe. They had chosen Danish passports for their identity. Their Captain Ewing, an acerbic and suspicious man, had looked askance at the accompanying Baudoin. He suggested the young dependent would be of no use to Mr Müller on board and would desert him on landing. Another passenger was curtly dismissed for complaining about the tough American biscuits. 'There is my beef, there is my bread – if you do not like them, leave the ship.' The planter from San Domingo was snubbed and had to resign himself to the hard fare. He had no teeth and the cook no will to bake fresh bread. He instead fell on Müller, using him relentlessly as an interpreter, which well secured his identity.

The generous Governor Morris had also written to Louis Philippe with news of his mother and her final imprisonment. Her close friends, Madame de Chastellux and Madame de la Charce, had joined her at Belhomme prison, euphemistically named a 'health house'. The Duchesse's dogged pleas to the Convention for fresh air and better care had been heeded. Belhomme, in the rue de Charonne, with its cultivated garden and vineyard, was a 'paradise' compared with the horrors of Luxembourg. The kind old retainer from her father's estate at Lesigny-en-Brie brought her fruit and cheese and flour and sent two cows.

Milk was the only sustenance the Duchesse had allowed herself. Her fellow confined friends were alarmed by her greenish pallor, her flabby flesh, her puffy breath. The small cluster of the *'ancien régime'* at Belhomme cheered the Duchesse. They took pleasure in greeting each other – Madame la Comtesse, La Princesse, Monsieur le Maréchal, le Comte. And, in heroic defiance, they revived their spirits with games and singing in their rooms. An intrepid lady would mount on a chair and, singing with her skirt lifted, would proffer an opera hat. To much mawkish laughter, another would align two facing chairs, to concoct an execution block and kneel in waiting. But the painfully hobbling Duchesse would remain on the ragged mattress with the wilting bolster, her bed drawn up between an old monk and a prostitute.

She was lowered each day, inert on a stretcher, to the garden. Shuddering gently in the sun, she would re-live her brush with the guillotine. Four gardes had halted by her bed. She was to be consigned to the *conciergerie*, the last remove to the scaffold; the ultimate death knell! But the Commission of

General Security, confronted with the effigy of a dying woman and the Doctor's report of a clogged liver, a feeble pulse and strange spasms, waved the Duchesse aside as so many unwanted goods. The elegant façade of Madame de Pompadour's former hunting lodge frowned anew on the frail lady resting in the garden.

Mystery, fear and tragedy lurked behind every wall in Paris. And it was a considerable shock to the inmates when Mr Belhomme himself was condemned to prison. In his zeal for hand-plucking rich prisoners from whom he could exact ready payment, he had also increased his fees to an extortionate sum of 300 francs a month. This pie-in-the sky behaviour was hardly commensurate with the eight apples between thirty mouths for supper. But had he not served La Citoyenne, La Duchesse, each day her cream of chicken soup? As a palliative to his prison sentence, Mme Belhomme was allowed to run the 'home' and presumably the accounts.

In the lugubrious confines of Belhomme, the Duchesse d'Orléans in her forty-fourth year was introduced to Monsieur Rouzet; a fellow prisoner, he had been a respectable Deputy at the Toulouse Convention. The Duc de Nivernais had recommended him to her for advice and counsel. Rouzet was to become a lifelong soul mate and an acutely divisive element within her family.

The Duchesse was offered her tentative release in the early summer of 1796, but she preferred to languish in uninterrupted reveries and boredom at Belhomme, where she felt safe from the uncertain outside world. Lunching and supping with Rouzet and other legally inclined prisoners (to include Jean-Lambert Tallien, an angry young man), appealed to her. Tallien's radical tirades against the King and the Royalists had become more and more vituperative, largely contributing to the Monarchy's demise on August 10th, 1792. The Duchesse's newly assembled friends were a surprise to her. The ferocious Tallien was certainly astonished to be placed beside this last Princesse of the Bourbon blood.

Rouzet himself was essentially '*peuple*'. France had now attained changed social strata; if the Duchesse felt *déclassée* by the Revolution, she was too shrewd to show it. Rouzet, approaching sixty, with his rough manner and dress and deportment, his literary talk and his many cerebral attributes, all propounded in his country accent, pleased her. She saw in him an able mind, devoted to her interests. Others were to suspect him of genius designs on her fortune. But had he not courageously defended Louis XVI and his cause? He had openly judged the Convention wrong for not saving the King in the interest of crown and country. He had fled Paris in 1793, where 1,000 heads had fallen between June 15th and July 27th. Arrested in Toulouse, he had been proclaimed '*hors la loi*' and returned post-haste to Paris. Rouzet was clearly complex and set to run.

12

After a pleasant voyage of twenty-seven days, Louis Philippe and Baudoin arrived in Philadelphia on October 21st; it was a prosperous city with a genial and prestigious society. They stayed in the Reverend Marshall's basement, in Walnut Street, adjacent to the church. Louis Philippe had been separated from his brothers for three years and now speculated anxiously on their arrival. Montpensier, twenty-one years old and Beaujolais, seventeen, had embarked early November on a Swedish boat. On leaving Fort St Jean, Montpensier later recounted in his autobiography: 'It is impossible to describe the sensation experienced in crossing the drawbridge ... the gratifying reflection that I now trod on it for the last time, could with difficulty impress itself on my mind, and I could not avoid fancying that the whole was a sleeping vision...'

Battered and buffeted by refractory winds in the Mediterranean, they put in at Gibraltar. The Princes, travelling incognito, were astonished at the friendliness of the English, after the contrast of bullying from their own people. Completing a journey of ninety-three days during which time Louis Philippe had fretted endlessly over their delay – thoughts of piracy, abduction, and uprisings in France to repudiate the Directory's bill of freedom, their vessel even sunk to the seabed – Montpensier and Beaujolais walked joyfully back into his life on February 8th, 1797. They were never to part again. But death already lurked unseen. After three years spent cooped up in stench and infested humidity, both brothers had contracted tuberculosis.

Louis Philippe opted that they should spend the remaining winter amongst the kind and charming Philadelphians and rented a house from the Spanish consul. Unaware of their hidden disease, the younger brothers relaxed and luxuriated in the peace and comforts of daily living. With the horrors of Fort St Jean still torturing his mind, Montpensier evoked his memoirs. The shouts and shots and screams of pain; slit throats and cannon fire; the stink of seared and burning flesh. The *Massacreurs* and gardes, with bloodied sabres banging on their doors, thrusting into their cells with their venomous shrieking '*Misérables — vous nous faites horreur! Nous n'avons fais que venger nos péres, nos fréres, nos amis, et c'est vous-même qui nous y avez excités.*'

On November 18, 1795 at half past five in the afternoon, Montpensier and Beaujolais had attempted an escape. Wrapped in a cloak, Beaujolais was at first to cross the drawbridge; he was to then walk nonchalantly across the beach to their rendezvous with the captain of a Tuscan boat. Montpensier stood motionless by his *grille*. 'I had death in my heart. Not one minute to lose; to jump from the window; I had locked the door. I tied the cord round a bolt that fastened the window and stepped out.' Way down his dizzy descent, the rope cord snapped. He lost consciousness and came to, after fifteen minutes, waist high in the sea, his eyes dazed by moonlight.

Montpensier had landed on sand but his leg and ankle were broken and swelling alarmingly. He hoisted himself on a harbour chain. Where was Beaujolais? The Captain? The boat? But Beaujolais had been apprehended by the fierce Commandant of the fortress the moment he stepped off the drawbridge; he had been marched back to his cell and guarded by a sentinel and a fusilier.

In the two hours that Montpensier lolled in the glacial sea, seven boats had passed. Who was he? They had no time to stop! 'I am dying – I have money!' He must be a bad lot out at this time of night – a pirate – a corsair! The eighth boat had no time but promised they would pick him up on their return. They came and helped him board most painfully; his mounting fever and inflamed joints had staved off his numbness and shock. He was taken to his friend Maugin, a wig-maker, where he spent the night. In the morning, after assiduous application of warm bricks to his friend's limbs, Maugin called in a surgeon. Montpensier was bled extensively and his broken bones and joints were set. He was given the choice of recuperation in hospital or a return to the fort. He chose to be at the fort with his brother.

The Commandant next interrogated him: 'Why did you escape? What were you doing? Where is your brother?' Replied Montpensier indignantly: 'We wanted to escape the atrocious tyranny which we have suffered for nearly three years and to recover our liberty of which you have no right to deprive us.'

Montpensier was confined to his bed for forty days, when he was able to walk a few steps with crutches. It took fifteen months for the swelling to subside and for the complete recovery of his leg; but he would always sense a phantom limp.

The spring of 1797 found the three Orléans Princes, invigorated from their stay in Philadelphia, setting off on horseback to Baltimore. Passing views of Chesapeake Bay, they reached Washington. Continuing on past the Shenandoah mountains, they rode 200 kilometres to Mount Vernon, the country home of the retired President George Washington. Their host, aged sixty-five, was to die just two and a half years later. A distinguished General of the War of Independence, and President of his constitutional government (1787–1797), he was delighted to entertain the Duc d'Orléans; he even looked upon him as an equally fine General.

Washington's portrait had just been painted by the acclaimed Gilbert Stuart. Magnanimous he stands, his hand held out in appeal, from a froth of lace at the wrist; his highly coloured cheeks reflect the leader of the hunt and successful surveyor of his own estates.

Louis Philippe was impressed by the great man's modesty, his common sense and methodical approach to men and management. Washington inwardly applauded the Princes' heroic spirit and charm. He gave them letters of introduction and marked their map to the far west, with places and objects of special interest. The two liberal protagonists parted on a wave of respect and admiration

George Washington was never considered a great orator, nor even an author of books; but his *Rules of Civility and Decent Behaviour in Company and Conversation* is a gem. It was compiled at that most observant age of fourteen years. The concise rule number 35: 'Let your discourse with men of business be short and comprehensive' would have appealed to Louis Philippe and would have given him more leeway to talk of himself. Rule number 100 might have pre-empted Beaujolais' future behaviour: 'Cleanse not your teeth with the table cloth, napkin, fork or knife; but if others do it, let it be done with a pick tooth.'

Strapping saddlebags, knapsacks, firearms and moneys on their horses, the three brothers wended their way through West Virginia into the lush and fertile Shenandoah Valley. They were heading for the old town of Winchester, an important frontier post in the War of Independence. More particularly, they were anxious to reach 'The Golden Buck' a small and comfortable tavern on South Cameron Street. It had been earnestly recommended by their previous host, who had often stopped at the inn. The landlord – a Mr Bush – was a stocky, florid old man; he especially liked to reminisce on the War, sitting beside the brook, in his wide-brimmed hat, under the willow tree. And it was true that Washington had presented a bill 'to prevent hogs running at large within the town of Winchester ...' (1761).

On arrival, their horses were led off to the stable block; inside Louis Philippe and Mr Bush shared an exchange on their respective travels. It transpired they had both been to Mannheim, the cultural city on the Rhine, with its pleasant river port. As they chatted happily in their halting German the guests were kept waiting for their supper. The long journey on hilly, rough roads had taken a toll on Beaujolais. Louis Philippe, always concerned for his siblings' stamina, felt it prudent to have a quiet meal in their own rooms. 'Old Sam', the servant, was quick to attend to their orders, but was waylaid as he scurried around by his dreaded landlord. Mr Bush was furious; his pride and honour were at stake; 'meals in the rooms' were unheard of. That initial conversation with Louis Philippe – so full of sympathetic interest – was flung to the winds.

'Since then you are too good to eat at the same table with my guests, you are too good to eat in my house; I desire, therefore, that you leave it instantly!' No assurances from Louis Philippe that he had intended no insult could avail the old man's scorn. Stipulated on the sign of his renowned tavern was the landlord's obligation: 'to feed all comers who could pay and were decent'. When the Prince had the audacity to point to this golden rule emblazoned on his Golden Buck, Mr Bush turned on his heel. Seizing his axe from the woodpile behind the tavern, he rushed towards them and his eyes were reported to look 'unwholesome'. The Princes were momentarily alarmed, but it was the tavern's sign that was in danger. 'Come on Buck!' shouted Mr Bush as he made to strike it to the ground. Seeing no chance of food or rest at the widely considered 'fashionable hotel of the place', the Orléans party left. They were already inured to wood cabins and huts; and on one occasion were happy to see a little inn with its board offering 'Enter-tainment for man and horse'. After a hard day's riding through the barren tracts of Kentucky, and an ample supper, they had fallen sound asleep on the soft side of the planks on the cabin floor. Louis Philippe had woken in the early hours to see that their host and his wife had joined them. They were cogitating quietly on why such intelligent youths were running wild across the face of the earth instead of settling down and purchasing a piece of land.

But it was ever the Princes' aim to explore their adopted country, to observe humanity and to assimilate some practical skills for their own survival. Indeed, the Indian settlers and tribes who came into their orbit even benefited from Louis Philippe's own first-aid attentions. When continuing their arduous approach to the Niagara Falls, he fell and cut his leg. As a precaution, he whipped out his lancet to bleed himself (another useful attribute imparted by the resourceful Madame de Genlis). A crowd of Chippewa Indians emerged from the forest and gathered round. When he had stemmed the blood and closed the vein, he gestured to his audience that he was cured. He was led off purposefully to a sick old man. He gave him a gentle bleeding, and it was soon noticed that the patient looked better. Promptly assuming the status of a god in their midst, Louis Philippe was offered the highest accolade: a straw mat for the night between the chief's grandmother and his great-aunt.

Hugging the deserted shores of Lake Erie, they heard the distant thundering of the Niagara cataracts, as the green waters beat down on the ledged rocks. Closing in on the mist and froth, the Princes were mesmerised by the sheer volume of water swirling and racing down the turbulent channels. It was effectively the entire St Lawrence Seaway with any overflow from the Great Lakes massing in cascades of nearly 200 feet.

Leaving Buffalo through more swamp and stifling dark forests, which Louis Philippe reckoned was their hardest and roughest ordeal yet, they had a surprise encounter; namely with Alexander Baring, whom they had met in Philadelphia. Baring, to become the Lord Ashburton, was a financier in the tradition of his forebears. His new wife, Anne Louisa, was the daughter of Senator William Bingham. The little party halted in the dismal swamp and compared notes. Baring warned the brothers of the savage and intolerable terrain that lay ahead of them by Canandaigua Lake. Louis Philippe assured him in return that he had an equally appalling passage to Niagara.

By July 1797, they had regained the remembered comforts and sophistication of Philadelphia, but to their horror and dismay a virulent bout of yellow fever had swept the city. Their erstwhile friends had fled. The Orléans, who were born to privilege and priceless domains, had no means of escape. They could only watch for the deadly symptoms of black vomit and headaches. Montpensier took the opportunity to write a long and descriptive letter to their sister Adélaïde; it was dated 14th August, 1797. They had been travelling for four months and Montpensier shuddered as he recalled their struggles through the mosquito-ridden forests.

We journeyed, during that time, a thousand leagues, and always upon the same horses, except the last hundred leagues, which we performed partly by water, partly on foot, partly on hired horses, and partly by the 'stage', or public conveyance. We have seen many Indians, and we even remained several days in their country. They are in general the best people in the world, except when they are intoxicated, or inflamed with passion. They received us with great kindness; and our being Frenchmen contributed not a little to this reception, for they are very fond of our nation. The most interesting object we visited after the Indian villages was certainly the Cataract of Niagara ... I have made a sketch of it, from which I intend making a watercolour drawing, which, my dear little sister shall certainly see at our beloved mother's home; but it is not yet commenced, and will occupy me for some time, for it is not, I can assure you, a trifling undertaking.

To give you an idea of the agreeable manner in which they travel in this country, I must tell you, dear sister, that we passed fourteen nights in the woods, devoured by all kinds of insects, often wet to the bone, without being able to dry ourselves, and our only food being pork, a little salt beef, and maize bread; independently of this adventure, we were 40 or 50 nights in miserable huts where we were obliged to lie upon a floor made of rough timber, and to endure all the taunts and murmurings of the inhabitants; who often turned us out of doors, often refused us admission altogether, and whose hospitality was always defective. I declare I should never recommend a similar journey to any friend of mine; yet we are far from repenting what we have done, since we have all three brought back with us excellent health and more experience.

Adieu, beloved and cherished sister, so tenderly loved; receive the embraces of three brothers, whose thoughts are constantly with you.

Adélaïde, now twenty years old, was acutely clever and marked to become a formidable adjunct to Louis Philippe's future life – to his throne, his directives, his marriage and his children. But, whilst languishing in Switzerland with her questionable mentor Félicité de Genlis, the frustrated teenager had written four years previously to her maternal uncle, the Duke of Modena, in a torrent of despair. Dated 22nd August, 1793, she had chronicled a 'cruel situation'. She had no money. She wished passionately to come to Italy and be with him, her dear uncle. What should she do? Would he receive her? She would confide in him her pain and fears, knowing of the tenderness he had for her mother. Should she enter an Italian convent? She next stipulated a fanciful sum of money she would need for such a journey to include a maid and two '*domestiques*' and the means to purchase a '*trousseau*'.

She signed herself – honoured to be his unhappy niece, Adèle Bourbon d'Orléans. A tenacious letter from a sixteen-year-old, with undertones of the grip hold that she would bring to play in her majority. The Duke of Modena never replied. (In 1802 Adélaïde was to join her widowed mother, the Duchesse d'Orléans, at Figueras. In this quaint, sleepy village, nestling at the foot of the Catalan Pyrenees, Adélaïde fretted once more – there was peace and comfort but unmitigated boredom.)

In September 1797, the brothers received a surprise windfall from their mother, the Directory had reinstated her fortune, with the proviso that she exiled herself to Spain. With a war breaking out in the Mediterranean between Spain and England, Louis Philippe knew that it could be a hazardous passage to visit her. But with more money and their health intact, they planned to leave Philadelphia for New Orleans in December. First established in 1718, from the Mississippi boom, on the rubble of Tchoutchouma, a deserted Indian settlement, it was named after their great, great-grandfather Philippe d'Orléans, the Regent to Louis XV, who had promoted the project. At the time of the Princes' long journey, New Orleans was still under Spanish dominion with ongoing communications with Cuba, and ships sailing from Havana to Europe. The Princes were confident of finding their mother.

Meanwhile the Duchesse had suffered an epic journey from the jaws of Belhomme prison to Barcelona. Together with her sister-in-law, the Duchesse de Bourbon, the Prince de Conti, and her close aficionados, Madame de la Charce, Madame de la Chastellux, L'Abbé Kayser and the undaunted Docteur Gueydan, the story began. The two cumbersome berlines from the *Ancien Regime* swayed on their grinding wheels and groaning springs; the old horses stumbled in their mouldy, worn harness. Whenever they passed through a village, Conti would lean out of their carriage window. Raising his faded tricorne from his powdered head, he announced to any passers-by – 'We are being dragged out of France against the wishes of the law.' The observant and naturally curious Duchesse de Bourbon guessed their *gardien* to be around twenty years old; a blond youth, with tender blue eyes, he was squashed up against the three women – the Duchesse Douairière, her maid Victorine, and herself. He tried to contain his swaying limbs; but the sensual Duchesse found her knees hopelessly knocking against his. She assured him she was no prickly porcupine and the relieved young man felt free to throw out an arm and leg to ease his constrictions. In the third week, the road became intolerable, with dangerous ditches and mud. The berlines swerved and staggered and the alarmed Duchesse de Bourbon called on Saint Michel. When their *gardien* revealed his name as 'Michel' she called him '*mon bon ange*'. She was to evoke the adventurous journey in her account: *Voyage Tragique et Tendrement Burlesque*. The Duchesse Douairière had taken a more reserved view of their debonair *gardien*. She had been frightened for her life at the hazardous going, but had enjoyed the robust companionship.

The amicable party had survived rough meals and rougher bedding; leftover scraps and straw. By mid-October, the berlines approached the Spanish frontier. A fortress loomed ahead as they rambled through narrow ways to their leave of France. Municipal agents searched the two berlines, when suddenly there were cries of astonishment. At the bottom of the Bourbons' carriage, secreted beneath a pile of coats and papers, a man had been found. Was he a thief? Much embarrassed by his discovery, he stammered out his name and profession. 'Jacques-Marie Rouzet, *membre du*

Conseil des Cinq-cents. He fell with a swoon and the Duchesse, overwhelmed with her emotions and amazement, fainted also. It was established that Rouzet had no valid passport and no express authority to leave France. In fact, he was to be considered a criminal. The officer of the garde and his agent smelt a plot. The Duchesse, recovering her senses, announced that she refused to pass the frontier if Rouzet was detained. Rouzet finally persuaded the varying authorities that he was essential to the Duchesse's well-being; her financial and her legal affairs. The gardes and agents sensed a romantic attachment. Rouzet was permitted to rejoin his Duchesse for their continuing journey, through the Pyrenees to Spain. He vowed never to be parted from her again. They had become curiously indispensable to each other.

In the glacial cold of mid-December 1797, the Princes boated down the Ohio valley into the Mississippi, through ominous ice slabs, swells and racing waters. The four boatmen became exhausted and the Princes helped to row. They checked the river level day and night and scanned the seemingly deserted swampland for savages. They arrived in New Orleans in February 1798 after a harsh forty days' journey. They were immediately welcomed, seized upon and fêted as the legitimate Princes of the Blood. After waiting five weeks for a Spanish corvette, they finally settled for an American boat. So anxious were they to see again their fond and cherished mother, they risked the enemy. When an English frigate, flying the tricolore discharged its guns in the Gulf of Mexico and dispatched captors on board, the Princes quaked in their cabin below; any vestige of the Republican flag aroused their fear and alarm. Louis Philippe with his inborn authority and calm, strode up to the Lieutenant of the frigate and urged him to convey to his Captain the correct identity of himself and his two brothers. Whereupon Captain Cochrane (to become Admiral Sir Thomas Cochrane, Earl of Dundonald) assured them they should have no apprehensions on board his ship. The deck of the frigate was considerably higher than their American boat; a rope was lowered for the Princes to clamber up her side. Louis Philippe, mishandling his grip, fell into the Gulf. Recovering himself, he swam coolly round to the stern where a boat was lowered to hoist him up. Confidence established all around, the Princes disembarked in Havana on March 31st. Louis Philippe made notes on their continuing travel.

We had been the first Princes of the House of Bourbon to appear in America – let alone Havana. The *San Pedro*, 64 guns, conveyed letters to our mother in Spain, telling her of our arrival in Cuba. She said she would approach the King of Spain to obtain this permission for us to join her. She had no reply. For eighteen months, we pleasured in Havana, living in a fine old house with carriages and horses. It had been lent to us by a rich lady – Doña Leonora de Contreras.

But in May 1799 a thunderbolt struck from the Madrid government. The Secretary of State, Señor Urquijo, sent an order to the Captain General of Cuba that the Orléans Princes were to leave immediately.

The long-envisaged visit to our mother in Barcelona was forbidden us. A demand from the French Government had instigated our departure. And a cabal of suspicious and despotic Spanish Ministers had tired of the French Prince who had once pitched into battles for Liberty. We were offered no means to quit except for passage on a war schooner: the *Santa Elisabeth*, 16 guns and a crew of 80. We had nowhere to go. We chose Nassau; it was to be our first port to England. Our Captain was warned to keep his cannons in firing position when we were on board. Corsairs and pirates infested the seas. From Nassau, we made a 20-day crossing to Halifax, where the Duke of Kent, a young Commander-in-Chief, received us most amicably. A son of the King of England, George III, he was to become the father of Queen Victoria. We next boarded a ship leaving for New York, where we would find the regular packet to Falmouth. Two wearisome crossings ensued; 23 days from Halifax to New York and 27 days from New York to Falmouth, where we landed on January 1st 1800. Four months' travel from Havana – and so to England, where renowned and generous hospitality had been afforded to so many French – whether émigrés or 'refugees', as ourselves.

13

The arrival of the D'Orléans Princes in England, their father's bright, adopted playground, was to bear them winds of change and dire portents. Neither Montpensier nor Beaujolais would see their country again; Louis Philippe would not return to France until 1814, at the age of forty. Their immediate situation was precarious, financially and socially. Louis Philippe was not averse to *de haut en bas* leadership from the elite and educated; he was no society rebel. But the name Orléans still stank and sent shudders down the spine; he and his brothers, the unwitting sons of a Regicide, would be despised by the émigrés now in and around London. In the unpretentious purlieus of Baker Street, the Comte d'Artois, younger brother of Louis XVIII, had already corralled a veritable Court of Versailles made up of admiring aristocrats and parasites. A charming lightweight, the debonair 'Monsieur' was causing considerable worry to his elder brother. Eking out his exile in the Russian Federation, under the questionable aegis of Tsar Paul I, Louis XVIII was becoming nervous of Monsieur's mounting popularity. The root rationale of the émigrés was to hold together against Bonaparte, the victorious little Corsican usurper; Louis Philippe knew it was essential he hang in with his legitimist cousins. Général Dumouriez, also established in England, urged him to submit to Monsieur in reconciliation and a renewed oath of loyalty. Louis Philippe could not afford to be ostracized from the Bourbon body. He needed funds, a restored name and every social position and acceptance.

Frantically busy settling himself and his brothers into a rented Victorian villa by the Thames, in peaceful, wooded Twickenham recouping any discernible moneys from their father's lavish escapades: a rented house in Belgravia (at 3 Chapel Street); another at 35 Portland Place; his racing world at Newmarket and the hunting with the Quorn, his stray pleasures with the Prince of Wales, in that young man's hedonistic heyday.... Putting all such pressing matters aside, Orléans wrote to his cousin, the Comte d'Artois, for an audience. Monsieur gave an instant acceptance to his younger cousin; he hoped to finally persuade him to wear the white cockade, the time-honoured symbol of the senior Princes' émigré army; the Prince of Condé's vengeance in war for the devastations to the Bourbon family.

The *Annual Register* gave a slanderous report of their meeting. The suggestion that the Duc d'Orléans had approached Monsieur with humble apologies and persuasive flattery, was repudiated by Louis Philippe as 'fairy tales on the subject'. There had been no hint of grovelling humility from Louis Philippe; no pleading of 'the folly of youth', or excuses for his former Jacobin loyalties. And he had not conceded to 'errors'. 'Errors?' he had retorted to Monsieur. 'I have committed a few … like yourself. We should talk instead of *our* errors.' The interview had been frank and dignified; it left Monsieur in no doubt of Louis Philippe's sharp mind, his love of fair liberties and his grasp of events. He compared the young Duc with his own two sons, the Ducs d'Angoulême and de Berri; their lack of such manners, culture and command made Louis Philippe a demonstrably superior specimen. A formal and modest letter to the Comte de Provence ensued; Louis Philippe, swearing allegiance on his sword, asked for reconciliation with the reviving Bourbons. The self-styled Louis XVIII was gratified and promptly granted full recognition of rights and privilege to the three Princes d'Orléans and their sister, Princesse Adélaïde.

Still shunned by supercilious French émigrés, with their show of sanctimonious court manners, the Orléans made themselves scarce at Monsieur's recreation rooms at 46 Baker Street. However, the doors of the highest echelons of English Society were flung open wide. George III, a reputed benefactor, received them kindly, introducing his Prime Minister, William Pitt the Younger and his sons and daughters. The Duke of Kent, his third son, was already a friend; and the Prince of Wales asked them frequently to dine at Carlton House. The Marchioness of Salisbury, the incomparable châtelaine of Hatfield, invited 400 of impeccable rank and distinction to meet the Princes. State banquets, embassies and private parties were not complete without the crowning élan of the charming and well-disposed Orléans brothers. But it was at Donnington House, the Leicestershire home of the Irish peer, Lord Moira, that they felt most at ease.

Donnington was a huge conglomerate of Georgian stone, nestling in a Repton-landscaped park, with rooms vast and comfortable. The drawing-room had a coffered ceiling and handsome fireplaces and led off to a long library, hung with engravings. There Louis Philippe would sit at a long table, engrossed in tomes by the Earl of Clarendon, on his code, his politics and the Civil War in England. Thomas Moore, a regular guest, would sit composing poetry and songs; Montpensier, looking pensively through the array of tall sash windows, would sigh over his gnawing feelings for Elizabeth Forbes, their neighbour in Twickenham, who was musical and artistic. The peace and solid comforts at Donnington were not to everyone's taste. Elisabeth Vigée-le-Brun recorded in her memoirs: 'I remember feeling very comfortable there ... but what a shame it was so dull!' The rigours of the English dinner party, when the ladies rose from the table, leaving the men to drink and talk politics, did not amuse her. Neither did she care for the segregated line-up of women embroidering or stitching tapestry, and the men returned opposite, curiously silent and reading. When she had asked Lady Charlotte, Moira's sister, if they might walk together in the moonlit park, she was told that the shutters were closed and could not be reopened.

Our petulant guest was clearly not invited for the diverting weekend, as described by the exuberant Thomas Moore in his poetical works, Vol. VII. The Orléans brothers, together with Monsieur and his suite had been dining with a carefully selected party of French émigrés. Beaujolais, now initiated in the fashionable modes of English Society, had powdered his dark hair and, with a deft touch, had added an artificial *queue*. On the departure of the ladies, Monsieur, turning in his chair, noticed that Beaujolais' *queue* had come adrift. With a screech of delight, he pulled at the limp tail and, to the hilarity of the dinner guests, popped it into poor Beaujolais' mouth. On other jolly occasions, Louis Philippe would attempt to teach Thomas Moore French lays.

Hostesses jockeyed for the Princes' acceptances to their homes and parties. A magnificent dinner at Stowe incurred a caustic report by Elizabeth Wynne, despite elaborate staging and no expense spared, to include the hiring of four French cooks, 'the dinner was neither good nor *bien choisi*'. The Comtesse de Boigne, the daughter of the Marquis d'Osmond, also known for her curt aperçus, was more lenient in her appraisal of the Orléans Princes. At the impressionable age of sixteen, she was taken to their newly rented villa in East Twickenham, High Shot House; substantial and white-stuccoed; 'High' to indicate its position above the river, 'Shot' referring to an open area of land.

Beaujolais, she portrayed as 'young, a bit unkempt, light, frivolous, unoccupied – fallen into all the pitfalls of a young man about town. Good figure, distinguished bearing – but no manners in *soigné* company. Coming out of the opera one would avoid him, fearing he might be drunk'. Montpensier, she considered 'plain – but his manners so noble and gracious that his face was not noticed. He loved art and music. Louis Philippe, she accorded 'a quite good figure – no distinction – neither in bearing or manners. He never seemed to be really at ease. His conversation always extremely interesting but a little pedantic.' But the general 'on-dit' held that Louis Philippe was fairly good-looking, clever, his conversation reflecting a great depth and knowledge.

The Orléans brothers were now set to live happily and modestly together in 'dear quiet Twick'. The Crown Inn, once a 'Home for Inebriates', set opposite High Shot House, played a chivalrous role in the Princes' lives. The comfortable benches and coloured glass windows made for pleasant retreats. The landlord kept an eye on their adjoining land and made time to run the local postal service. Their entourage consisted of their childhood tutor, Chevalier de Broval; later joined by Gustave, Comte de Montjoie, four menservants, a cook and maidservant. A flow of Royalty, both French and English – aristocrats, Ambassadors and émigrés, now settled in Richmond and Twickenham (including the youngest and richest diplomat, Prince Esterhazy, at York House) – would come to dine. Concerts, whist drives and French amateur dramatics were staged regularly at York House, the handsome seventeenth-century brick riverside house, purported to be once owned by the Earl of Clarendon.

Louis Philippe, Montpensier and Beaujolais were exceptionally fond of each other and soon became absorbed in their own interests. Louis Philippe took up gardening and asked that manure from the Richmond road should be spread on his flowerbeds. Montpensier, having fast acquired the reputation of a romantic *'grand seigneur'* would call regularly on Elisabeth Vigée-Le Brun, staying nearby with the Comte and Comtesse de Vaudreuil. He would stroll with her through Petersham Fields alongside the Thames, where cattle grazed; and then above to the Terrace of Richmond Hill. There they sketched that renowned panorama of the curved sweep of the Thames below. Beaujolais, despite regular rowing and walking had plenty of time to exert himself with all the carelessness of youth. Louis Philippe hated any inactivity and lack of mental exercise; he studied the political economy and government laws in England. Le Brun remembers seeing him 'seated at a long table covered with books, one of which lay open before him'. He loved to visit England's industrial plants – of engineering, agriculture and every manufacture.

King George III would invite the three Princes to the London military reviews. They wore morning dress and no white cockade. Louis Philippe's persistence in not donning this ultimate badge of the toppled *Ancien Régime* infuriated Monsieur. 'All this must stop,' he growled. 'It is the white cockade that you don't want to wear.' Replied Louis Philippe: 'Very well. Yes, Monsieur, I think that is exactly it; it is the white cockade that I don't want to wear; and *I shall not wear it.*' Another sore in Louis Philippe's life in this year of 1804 was the tragic death of his cousin, the Duc d'Enghien; they had been devoted childhood playfellows. Writing to the distinguished Bishop of Llandaff on July 28th, Louis Philippe refers to the 'Corsican usurper' and his determination to wipe out all the Bourbons. The murder of the Duc d'Enghien, together with his dog at the Château de Vincennes, by Napoleon's firing squad, was premeditated; the grave had been dug ready.

Despite all his diverting and improving occupations, Louis Philippe was chronically aware of his ineffectual presence on the European canvas of events. Napoleon, his own contemporary, was slashing through the Mediterranean with victory after victory. His megalomaniac attacks for the sea ports were achieved. Louis Philippe wrote to the London Foreign Office. Could he not put his unusual position into some account? As a French Prince but also an Englishman in principle, could he not be useful in their mutual links with the Continent? Keeping up his modest appearances, driving from Twickenham to London and back in a curricle was beginning to pall.

He was next surprised and gratified to hear from his cousin, Louis XVIII, writing from his exile in Russia. In effect, could Louis Philippe arrange refuge for him in England? To his chagrin, his good friend the Tsar was now considering reconciliation with Napoleon! Louis Philippe's approach to the

English Government was irrefutably refused. He replied to his cousin: 'I feel assured that should Your Majesty arrive unannounced, alone and without a suite, nobody would dare to oppose Your Majesty's entry into England; it is certain, Sire, that, immediately, the King's Ministers would receive you and arrange an abode for Your Majesty.' The putative King shortly disembarked at Yarmouth. He was received with little enthusiasm and taken to Hartwell House, near Aylesbury. In grand Jacobean comfort, with secluded gardens of gravel paths and high trimmed hedges, he lived until May 1814, when with the ignominious fall of Napoleon after his defeated campaigns, Louis XVIII was restored to the Bourbon throne. He was a lonely man and now in his fifties; his wife, Josephine de Savoie, was to die childless in 1810. He had a distinguished head, but was obese and plagued with chronic gout. Highly intelligent and with a shrewd mind, he managed a plausible reign of ten years, after all the revolutionary upheavals.

One Sunday morning, Louis Philippe paid a dutiful visit to Hartwell House. He arrived early and found himself alone in the hall with Marie-Thérèse, the daughter of Louis XVI and Marie Antoinette. She cried out in horror, collapsing on the floor, to see before her the son of Egalité, her father's deadly betrayer. Louis Philippe stepped forward to help her, but was waved vehemently aside. Marie-Thérèse (now the Duchesse d'Angoulême) was married to her cousin, the eldest son of Monsieur; he was a good soldier with limited intelligence, later to verge on insanity. Her troubled life was never destined to be easy. Her childless marriage was compensated by the admiration of close friends. She even won special approval from Napoleon who confided to one of his Ministers: 'She is the only man of the family.' Acclaimed for her gallantry and spirit, her sudden swoon was all the more astonishing. Louis Philippe, aghast and embarrassed at his effect on his long lost cousin, suggested to their host that he should leave. But the King assured him it was a passing malaise; that the Duchesse would join them for lunch; that, more importantly, he had wanted to show Louis Philippe his huge gratitude for securing his fine new refuge. But future visits to Hartwell became as rare as those to Baker Street.

In May 1807, Montpensier developed consumption, the legacy of his foul imprisonment in Marseilles. His cold, with incessant coughing and spitting blood, was treated by the doctor with asses' milk, apple water and honey, and judicious doses of laudanum. His devoted brothers were in constant attendance. A recommended stay at a country inn near Windsor was taken; convalescence in peace and quiet with clean air made sense. But the wretched Montpensier died on May 18th, his first day away. His funeral took place at the French Chapel, Portman Square. A few days later, his body was given an honoured tomb in Westminster Abbey. Standing with Beaujolais at the ceremony, Louis Philippe was suddenly aware of the haggard lines streaking his youngest brother's features. Consumptive coughing soon set in. A warm climate was advised on to save him. In the early spring, Louis Philippe sailed with his second dying brother to the warmth and sun of Malta. On leaving England, Beaujolais had protested to him: 'I feel my life ending in the same way as Montpensier. What is the good of going so far to seek a tomb?' The close air of Valetta proved unbreathable for young Beaujolais. Aged 28, he died on May 29th, 1808, soon after their arrival. He lies buried in the magnificent Church of St John.

14

The Duchesse d'Orléans had heard of Montpensier's death, the previous May. Her helpless grief went untended as war between France and Spain plunged into even more violent action. How often she had taken her barouche to the hill from where she would gaze on the frontier of her beautiful France! She had prayed and asked God for peace, for the restoration of the Bourbons, for the chance to see her country again. And now her own land was intent on bombing her adopted fief. And now, it was of Beaujolais' death that she heard. Her little Beaujolais! So much beloved!

Just days before setting off with Beaujolais for Malta, Louis Philippe had written to King Ferdinand IV of the two Sicilies, on the possibility of hiring a villa near Mount Etna. The King, always sensitive to the wretchedness of others, had managed to assign Louis Philippe and his dying brother a retreat at Catania, by the base of Etna. But Beaujolais had died too soon.

There had been another reason for Louis Philippe's approach to King Ferdinand – an oblique introduction to his daughter, the Princesse of Naples, Marie-Amélie. Louis Philippe was on a mission: to find a bride; to make an advantageous marriage to a Princesse of serious provenance, distinguished, intelligent and raffinée. He had Marie-Amélie firmly in mind, but fully appreciated that he was hardly the most eligible prospect: the son of the regicide Egalité, who had effectively murdered Marie Antoinette, the sister of Queen Maria-Carolina, who was the mother of this envisaged bride. He was 35 and now variously described as of manly appearance, tall and well proportioned; dignified, calm and resolute. Marie-Amélie was an eminently suitable Princesse with several suitors to her name, to include Eugène de Beauharnais, the stepson of Napoleon; but he had been roundly repudiated by Marie-Amélie's family as a 'parvenu'. Now, at a mature 26 years, Marie-Amélie could not presume on many more offers. On a scorching hot day in the early summer of 1808, Louis Philippe arrived at Palermo. He was still in mourning for Beaujolais and made his way rather diffidently to the Palazzo Reale. Marie-Amélie recorded her first impressions in her diary: 'Mamma sent for Isabel and me, and presented the Duc d'Orléans to us. He is of middle height, inclined to be stout; he is neither handsome nor ugly. He has the features of the House of Bourbon, is polite and well educated.' She herself had been consigned to a remarkably intelligent governess – Donna Vicenza Rizzi (née Signorita Ambrozio), widow of a renowned Neapolitan lawyer. Appearing so delicate at birth, Marie-Amélie had been first wrapped in cotton wool, but at the age of two and a half had delighted her grandfather, King Charles III of Spain, by reading to him. Riding with her brothers and sisters in the exquisite grounds of Caserta (widely considered the most vast and beautiful palace in Europe, and set in the fertile plains around Naples), Marie-Amélie had an exceptionally happy childhood. Philip Hackert, the admired landscape painter, lived in lodgings on the estate and gave the children drawing lessons.

Facing her unexpected future, Marie-Amélie gives herself an even more dispassionate portrait: she is tall, her face is long, her eyes blue, not particularly large, but lively. Her hair is not thick, but it is gold. her nose is aquiline. She has a round chin with a pretty dimple. Her teeth are not beautiful. She has a long neck, good shoulders and a small bosom. Long feet, a good leg but hands and arms rather ugly. '*Dans l'ensemble,* I have an air of modest but imposing nobility which makes people realize who I am.'

Marie-Amélie's exceptional bearing and dignity once even impelled the crafty diplomat, Talleyrand, to label her 'the last great lady in Europe'. Her formidable mother admitted that Marie-Amélie was the prettiest of their daughters and had infinite tact and an excellent heart. The Comtesse de Boigne, on a first official sighting in Paris, pitched in with 'plain, tall, thin, a high colour, little eyes, uneven teeth, well-held head, a long neck and *distingué* air and deportment'. She found her expression encouraging; 'pure, noble and vivacious'.

Did Louis Philippe feel that he had found the last port in a storm? Although not struck by her looks, he recognized in Marie-Amélie a happy *mélange* of good character, vivacity and moral strength. And might he have guessed that her strong, upright body was to bear him ten children? His comment to his family and friends – '*Elle me plaît*' – became her implicit hold on him and his own lifelong attachment. Marie-Amélie's father, to whom she was acutely devoted, was affected by the genetic insanity, chronic in the Spanish Bourbons. His tutors had been urged not to tax his brain. Ferdinand evolved as a sixteen-year-old with virtually no knowledge or interests except for hunting and fishing. He was also reputed to have a ferocious temper. However, Marie-Amélie's mother, daughter of the Austrian Empress, Maria Theresa, could compete with that trait; described by many as a witch and mistress of intrigue, she soon took charge of the whole island, while her 'Ferdinando' contented himself selling fish in the market place, adorned in a white cap and apron, holding high his head and his proud yield. He was also prone to sing out of tune. The ravishing Lady Hamilton would sing duets with him. 'He sings like a King,' she would assure all with commendable tact. Meanwhile, the Queen of Sicily saw to the dwindling resources of the military, the schools, museums and libraries, the newly proposed *Rights of Man* and the protection of the coasts from the corsairs of Barbary.

When Queen Maria-Carolina had first taken Louis Philippe's head between her hands and stared at him intently on that hot summer afternoon, she had murmured, 'I ought to detest you – and yet, I feel I like you.' But she intended trouble and persuaded Ferdinand to delay any marriage. Napoleon had just placed his favourite Général, Joachim Murat, on the throne of Naples. He was a fierce fighter and married to Napoleon's sister, Caroline Bonaparte. It occurred to Maria-Carolina that if this family became linked to the exiled Duc d'Orléans, Murat could stir up jealousies and agitate Napoleon. However, with Napoleon busy thrashing through the Mediterranean, seizing ports and denying all entry to the English fleet, Maria-Carolina alerted Ferdinand to the plan of sending their son, the Prince of Salerno, as Regent, to guard the ransacked Spanish throne. This idea grabbed Louis Philippe's immediate attention. The eighteen-year-old Salerno, obese and jejune, clearly needed accompanying. The Queen was triumphant and compliant; she had delayed this young Duc's intrusion into the family.

With England and Spain now joining forces against the Napoleonic invasions, Louis Philippe saw his chance to gain prestige from his own lynchpin position; his wholehearted repugnance for the usurper fired him. He wrote courteously to Louis XVIII of his intent to join the British expeditionary forces and help rout the enemy. His dream of Command, to befit his military rank, was mounting.

'Ah! If you only knew how dear you are to me! Do not forget me!' pleaded Louis Philippe to his Marie-Amélie as he set sail with her youngest brother from Palermo to the key Atlantic port of Cadiz. She called back to him: 'I never change. My affection once given is given forever.' The British army in Palermo, approving the measure, had obtained them a passage on a British warship, *The Thunderer*. Arriving on Sunday 13th August, 1808 at Gibraltar, the British governor and Admiral Lord Collingwood, lying off the Rock, made it clear to the French and Spanish Princes that their endeavour was misconceived and a disaster. Any such meddling with the balance of diplomacy between France, Spain and England was a gift to Napoleon's peninsula strategy. Louis Philippe was persuaded by Collingwood to continue his journey on *The Thunderer* to Portsmouth. And he well needed to arrange affairs in England for his marriage; he also had to look to his mother, whose house in Figueras had been bombed, and there was also his sister, Adélaïde to attend to. A request that his mother and sister be added to the pension list was given grudging consent; it had needed a letter to the English government, written at Kensington Palace, under the kind concern of the Duke of Kent.

Re-embarking at Portsmouth for his return to Sicily, Louis Philippe was surprised and delighted to be joined by his sister Adélaïde. They had been parted for 15 years; ever since that hectic moment when he had thrust her into the escaping carriage, with Madame de Genlis. Adélaïde now stood before him, seemingly bereft of looks, with a gawky figure. But Marie-Amélie was later to describe her sister-in-law as tall with fine eyes, beautiful fair hair and a wide mouth. (She would later make liberal use of this last attribute, as her brother's favourite mentor.) With the shared voyage ahead, Adélaïde relished her chance of telling her adored brother of her past years. Her scorn for their mother's '*chancelier*' knew no bounds. In their mother's infatuation for the odious Rouzet, he was now upgraded to le Comte de Folmont. The King of Spain had granted her this fatuous request. Naturally indolent, the Duchesse had given de Folmont the full rein of her money and the running of the house at Figueras. This included some twenty persons – her suite and servants had lived quietly behind the Moorish façade from 1801 to 1808. Adélaïde would stomp behind her mother, visiting the modest villages, hospitals and schools. Monotonous strolls in the shaded gardens off the main square were always a chance for the Duchesse to ingratiate herself as the kind Princesse with the gentle face.

Several friends visited and stayed including Madame de Chastellux and Madame de la Charce. According to Madame de Lage, 'the hours passed pleasantly'. Painting, drawing, talking, and especially listening to long readings by de Folmont. Adélaïde shuddered at the memory. Their mother had found his high-pitched voice a ravishment as he touched on novels about Cléopatre and conversations with Cicero: 'How to grow old' and 'Friendships'. This *diminué* life had suited the Duchesse's slender spirit.

On 12th June, 1808, the Catalan people had torn up the proclamation of the French government. The French immediately bombed Figueras. The Duchesse's house was the first to be hit. She and her household assembled their effects but escape was barred to them. On the evening of June 14th the firing halted. At nine o'clock the Duchesse and her daughter took their chance. Adélaïde lowered her voice: 'Monsieur de Folmont now lives on at the house, and with his wife!' Through all her miseries, the Duchesse was magnanimous. 'My faithful friend,' she later wrote to Madame de Folmont, sending her thanks and blessings for the lady's tolerance and kindnesses.

The Duchesse, her daughter and their suite were first confronted with a crossing through the Manolda River. The night was already dark and the current flowing fast. Their mother was passed from arm to arm. She lost a shoe, became totally dishevelled and transfixed with fear. She finally collapsed on a convent mattress halfway up a mountain. The nuns nursed her through her prayers and sorrows; but three weeks later there was no hope of descending to Figueras. The French had spewed forth and lit up the whole area. After months of uncomfortable peregrinations along the Mediterranean shores, the Duchesse had found a pleasant new exile on Minorca, in the village of Mahon. Here she settled with her loyal suite of twelve, with her hairdresser entailed.

15

Reunited with Marie-Amélie, Louis Philippe was satisfied that he had allayed any ill-conceived suspicions and rumours that he had been entangled with the French and the British mission against the throne of Naples. The British Foreign Office, such loyal friends in his exile, were now assured that pitching his zeal into the Mediterranean madness was of no significant account. Louis Philippe now sank back with relief and expectations of his happy marriage. He had written to friends in buoyant vein: 'What an advantage this means to me! What a blow to the prejudice against me; what a benefit is the close union of the House of Austria with mine! It will be a great boon to marry a Bourbon, and probably, at least I hope so, to have children. I hope that the British Government will realize that I can be of service to them in Sicily; in England, I am quite useless. This uselessness puts a kind of extinguisher on the top of my head, which is no help to them or to me.'

But Maria-Carolina! The words of Admiral Collingwood seeped back into Louis Philippe's mind. 'God protect you from Queen Carolina. She is the wickedest woman he ever created.' Not only had she scattered seeds of slander in his absence, warning that émigrés circles in London were hinting at Louis Philippe being an English agent, with orders to mount a constitutional revolution, she finally ruled that there would be no marriage without the presence of the Douairière, Duchesse d'Orléans. Precipitate word from the Duchesse announced her refusal to give her consent to the marriage, fuelling speculation that the odious Rouzet de Folmont was determined on intercepting any reconciliation with her children. In spite of these prevarications, permission was finally granted from the Duchesse and from a delighted Louis XVIII for the marriage between this first Prince of the Blood and a Bourbon Princesse. The Duchesse arrived at Palermo on the English frigate *Opposition*. Keenly anticipating events, she disembarked on October 15th. It is interesting to note that both Louis Philippe, Duc d'Orléans and Marie-Amélie de Bourbon-Sicile were descended from Louis XIII,

King of France. The bride from the elder son, Louis XIV, and the groom from the younger son, Philippe Duc d'Orléans.

The disciplines of Marie-Amélie and her Catholic devotions were to be a mainstay of her long life. She was to approach tragedy and vexing circumstances with every acceptance. Days before her wedding on the evening of 15th November, 1809, it was again postponed. Her father had fallen down the Palace stairs and broken his leg. However, the marriage contract was signed and the ceremony finally enacted in King Ferdinand's bedroom on 25th November. An altar was erected. Marie-Amélie stepped into the room, in cloth of silver, a diamond tiara and white feathers slipped into her golden ringlets. The bride stood radiant with her love and happiness, as the winter sun streamed into the room, highlighting the flowers and candles encircling her. Marie-Amélie later confessed to such great emotion that her legs 'tottered under her'. But Louis Philippe's 'yes' in his firm and resolute voice gave her courage. In the Palatinate Chapel on the first floor of the palace, where the Byzantine mosaics dazzled and the dome soared, they later knelt at the altar. The Cardinal presided with prayer and blessings. A bas-relief displayed in a recess still portrays the ceremony and the principal figureheads; Louis Philippe's mother, the Duchesse Douairière, is distinctly recognizable.

Louis Philippe's esteemed marriage gave lustre and gravitas to his standing. The European courts were impressed. And, in a letter from the Duke of Wellington to Général Dumouriez, His Grace confesses: 'I have often lamented the lot of the Duke of Orléans. He is a Prince of the most estimable character, great talents and deserved reputation; he will one day prove a great benefactor to his unhappy country.' Queen Maria-Carolina expressed her feelings more candidly: 'Naughty Amélie has married the Duc d'Orléans, dreadful name; they have nothing to live on, are poor but happy and love each other infinitely.' Finally, the Duchesse Douairière wrote happily to Louis XVIII, the Comte de Provence, of her charming daughter-in-law and her pleasure at the Palermo Court.

Louis Philippe and Marie-Amélie settled into the Palazzo Santa Theresa – to become the Palazzo Orléans. The building was much in need of repair, and the young couple became absorbed in its renovation. Louis Philippe, waving a plaster-smeared trowel, surveyed the building work; a precursor to his considerable future restorations of his own family Palaces. Marie-Amélie made a good friend of her sister-in-law, Adélaïde, who in turn gave her lessons in French. Marie-Amélie was too wise to grudge the exceptionally close sibling connection, but doubly relished the brief moments when she and Louis Philippe were left alone. Reflecting on her blissful marriage, she realised how blessed she was and how lucky; she had been allowed to choose her husband rather than be harnessed to some political candidate.

The newly married couple attracted a stream of the intelligentsia and sophisticates passing through Sicily. But there were rumblings of trouble. The Orléans were running short of money; mother, son and daughter found their pension allowance from the English government arriving less and less punctually; this necessitated more help from the Duke of Kent. Political differences between Queen Maria-Carolina and her son-in-law soon caused more friction and embarrassment; Louis Philippe's liberated outlook and his acceptance of the French government reforms was an anathema to her. Marie-Amélie was devastated by such fraught family scenes. Her mother-in-law had also exacerbated matters with petty complaints that her Rouzet felt neglected and demoted in this regal ensemble. And nobody quite knew why he had presented himself anyway. Louis Philippe himself began to weary of their Sicilian idyll, referring to Palermo as 'this *dortoire*', and 'this sleepy hollow'. In March 1810, the mounting clouds parted for him, with an option for change. The Spanish Council wrote to King Ferdinand, inviting a Prince of his Household to undermine the Imperial *Régime* in France; to command the Spanish army and to excite rebellion with the French, and effectively defeat the oppressor. Louis Philippe, flattered to have been called upon, set sail on *La Venganza*, with his valet, de Broval, on May 2nd.

They landed at Tarragona, where they found the Spanish in retreat and a group of mere French deserters to command. Louis Philippe refused such a puerile commitment and sailed on to Cadiz, on the south-west coast. He was treated with respect, but given no troops to command. Downing Street had already censured the whole venture as folly. Spirited letters were sent off from Louis Philippe to the London Foreign Office. On board *La Venganza*, in the Bay of Cadiz, on 20th June, 1810, he wrote first to Comte d'Antraigues; stipulating his disregard for English diplomats who rarely understood the language or characteristics of the countries in which they are posted. To Général Dumouriez, his loyal protagonist, and now established in England, he suggested that the old veteran was badly needed to modernise the Spanish army. Lastly, to his factor in Twickenham, de Guilherny, he wrote: 'my wife will soon make me a father, ALLELUIA!'

He was mollified with the letters from his adoring wife. Despite her pregnancy, Marie-Amélie had encouraged this Spanish adventure.

> Everybody believes your son will be the heir presumptive to a French throne and that with the grace of God and his parents, he will not be an idiot and will achieve something – my dear friend, I swear to you that I wish, wickedly, to have a daughter, because then you will be more in haste to unite me with you and because I always remember, tearfully, that terrible phrase that you have said to me many times: 'If I have a son, I die happy.'
>
> *Ton* Amélie

Their son and heir, the Duc de Chartres, Ferdinand Louis-Charles, was born September 3rd, 1810. His father, back from Cadiz in October, was jubilant. He reported proudly on Ferdinand's large Orléanic head. Two daughters were to be born in Sicily: Louise, the future Queen of Belgium, in 1812, and Marie, to become the Duchess of Würtemberg, in 1813.

Despite the happy birth, the rumbling bickering prevailed between the two grandmothers. The Duchesse Douairière, who was happy enough to give and attend dinners at her assigned Palazzo de Santa Cruz, was nevertheless piqued by the self-persecution of her dearest Rouzet. Louis Philippe was constrained to write to Queen Maria-Carolina, to thank her for all her tender consideration given to his poor dear mother, effecting a happy reunion with her children. She would understand that the incompatibility of the '*susdit personnage*', the Comte de Folmont, with the family, had made victims of them all. On January 12th, 1811, the Duchesse and the Comte, taking no personal leave of the court and her newly acquired family, embarked in a huff for Minorca. Recovering from the terrible storms, she soon regained her quiet and charitable disposition in her exile home at Mahon. Starting her day with two eggs '*à la coque*', and drinking tea from a cup of finest porcelain, she would next visit churches and appear at all civic audiences and festivals. She was considered a veritable '*personne de haute marque*'. Folmont by her side proved a total impediment to any accord with her family. On September 24th, 1811, Louis Philippe wrote curtly to his mother: 'I am persuaded that Folmont is a wrecker. My sister tells me that if he died, she would come to Mahon; I suggest that you do not hinder him...'

Early in 1812, it became clear to the Sicilians that Queen Maria-Carolina was a dangerous liability. They felt threatened by her cruel caprice and her idiosyncratic taxing system. Crowds clamoured beneath her Palace windows for a constitution. Lord William Bentinck – the British Ambassador at Palermo, was swiftly upgraded to Captain General of Sicily. He simultaneously commanded the Queen to return to her treasured Vienna. Her banishment greatly relieved Louis Philippe; he had always suspected her secret scheming, and with military foresight, had even kept a horse saddled up for flight. King Ferdinand was next persuaded to retire to his country estate. Louis Philippe also took the precaution of removing himself, his wife and little son to the countryside, a few miles from Palermo. He had maintained a circumspect friendship with Bentinck, who had previously spoken highly of him, regretting that the Sicilian government had not gained by his excellent presence. Indeed, Louis Philippe was now admired throughout Europe for his balance of loyalty with the Sicilian Royal Family and the demands of their country. In a final clampdown on any insurrection, Bentinck ordered an embargo on all English support, arms and money. Wrote Louis Philippe to his friend the Vicomte de Rohan Chabot, an officer in the English army: 'Our position here is precarious ... we can't tell what's going to happen; I simply don't know from one day to another ...' Wrote Marie-Amélie in her journal, separated for the first time from her mother: 'My heart was torn by conflicting emotions – love of my country, compassion, justice, honour. I seemed to float in a sea of anguish.' Her mother, Maria-Carolina, Queen of the Two Sicilies, Archduchess of Austria, was to be struck dead by apoplexy in 1814.

Louis Philippe's own Shakespearian cry of 'a sea of troubles' was mollified in the summer of 1812. Napoleon's reckless advance on Russia left his army desecrated; the freezing winter spelt his tottering defeat by April 20th, 1814. He had abdicated and was exiled to Elba to the relief of all the European powers. On April 23rd, an English frigate – The *Aboukir* – brought to Palermo the sensational news of Napoleon's defeat and of Louis XVIII's return to the throne. Louis Philippe hurried into Palermo to verify these reports. At the Marine Hotel, the Ambassador's residence, Bentinck greeted him. 'I congratulate you upon the downfall of Napoleon, and on the Restoration of the illustrious race, of which you are yourself a member, to the throne of their fathers.' He handed the stunned Louis Philippe *Le Moniteur* and its detailed account of events. The *Aboukir* was immediately put at his disposal. On May 1st, with loving farewells to his wife and sister and his little Ferdinand, he embarked for France. With the modest complement of Captain Gordon and his English valet, George White, the Duc d'Orléans was on course to end his challenging exile of twenty-one years.

16

In a show of summary command, Louis Philippe reviewed the troops at Marseille and then at Lyons. Wearing a Général's borrowed uniform, he was anxious to assert his position as a Prince of the Blood and clearly expected deference and honour. Arriving in Paris on May 18th, 1814, he sent Captain Gordon ahead to book rooms at a hotel in the Rue Grange-Batelière; he had been warned that his family home, Palais Royal, had been seriously degraded during the Republican and Napoleonic governments. The stately rooms had been turned into dishevelled repositories for unwanted furniture. Cobwebs swung in the broken windows and the damp walls revealed huge blank spaces, where Royal portraits and gilded mirrors had once hung. Every passage and corner was blocked by destitute families, let in to lodge, at Napoleon's behest. Louis XVIII had especially asked that Palais Royal be made ready for the Orléans family, but the crowd of builders and beggars had only increased the chaos.

On the evening of his arrival, Louis Philippe made an incognito visit. Stepping tentatively through the rubble-strewn gardens and arcaded galleries, he crossed the front court and entered. An Officer of the garde, still in Napoleonic livery, came up swiftly behind. Where was he going? Louis Philippe, in response, knelt sobbing and kissed the lowest step of the white marble Grand Staircase. The officer and assembled attendants again demanded his business. Louis Philippe recovered himself. 'I am the Duc d'Orléans,' he replied dismissively, and added the well-documented retort: *'Je suis ici, chez moi!'* He stood tall and took his carriage on to the Tuileries. How would he be received? With that old Bourbon reserve and calculated suspicion? Louis XVIII greeted his cousin, sitting in his wheelchair. Despite his throbbing feet, firmly bandaged, his mood was affable. He assured Louis Philippe that he had pleasure in conferring on him his old rank of Lieutenant Général. The following day, the King issued a decree that the vast Orléans estate and *appanage* be released to the family. On June 7th, the *Journal des Débats* stated that the Duc d'Orléans was once again in residence at Palais-

Royal. He had been much moved by the applause of a large crowd as he drove out in his carriage. Re-established with a considerable fortune, he next called on the best workforce to restore the family home.* He immediately engaged Monsieur de Fontaine, the former architect to Napoleon. Louis Philippe secretly admired the Emperor's restorative sweep through Paris; a progression of bold new bridges and façades. When he saw the old familiar Palais Royal grandeur taking shape, Louis Philippe embarked on a French ship, *La Ville de Marseille*, to retrieve his young family from Palermo. Baron Athalin, a former Général and topographer in Napoleon's army, sailed with him. He was to become his longest serving and best-liked Aide-de-Camp, despite his opportunistic switches to the Imperial Front.

On the evening of July 26th, the grand and gilded *La Ville de Marseille* approached Palermo, under full sail, and dropped anchor. The Duchesse d'Orléans, Madame Adélaïde, the young Duc de Chartres and the Princesses Louise and Marie boarded without ceremony. A large suite was in attendance, to include the children's nurses, ladies-in-waiting, footmen and valets, doctors, governesses, secretaries, a court usher, priests, cooks and two aides-de-camp. Three Commandants, together with the Admiral from Toulon were to manoeuvre the ship and stand on strict guard of the three children. The islanders had turned out to see this momentous embarkation. Church bells and the thunder of cannons rang out. There were frenzied calls for their cherished '*Donna Amalia*.' She breathed in the deep scent of roses and jasmine, swept to her across the warm swirl of water. She gazed on the flowers and wooded hills of Sicily; she would see them no more. But for Louis Philippe it was his epiphany; a break for freedom, for activity and new adventure. He had fretted in fallow exile long enough. The anchor was lifted at two o'clock in the morning and the ubiquitous thumping on deck had kept Marie-Amélie awake.

She lay overwhelmed with unknown fears and melancholy; of the separation from family and country to a life in France, which only four months earlier had been their enemy. She thought of her father, King Ferdinand, dubbed 'the Nose' by his fond people with his profile of a bird of

---

* Palais Royal was built by Prime Minister, Cardinal Richelieu in 1624. It was first known as Palais Cardinal. It was inherited by Louis XIV and given to his brother Philippe d'Orléans, whose Palace dinner parties were notorious.

prey and his keen blue eyes and strong jutting jaw. Ever his favourite daughter, he wanted to hold her once more in a last tender moment. At six o'clock on that restless dawn, King Ferdinand boarded *La Ville de Marseille*. He breakfasted with the cherished family. A much-loved father and grandfather. They would none of them meet again.

Their ship set sail through a calm Tyrrhenian Sea, past the Aeolian Islands, named after Aeolus, the God of winds. But the long days and nights passed languidly with the heat suffocating. In the evening, the three children were allowed on the bridge to catch the breeze. They would watch the green flying fish, darting around the ship, and were fascinated by the tiny sea horses. A sailor held up a turtle with its feet and flippers wriggling wildly as it tried to escape his strong grip. Three-year-old Ferdinand was curious about everything he saw and needed a firm hold; he had the crew in his pocket with all his questions. Through the clear visibility, they sailed up the length of the Italian coast, past Porto Ercole, and the islands of Monte Cristo and Elba; they did not know that the warmonger was already plotting a further foray into France. After two days becalmed in torrid heat, the Admiral sent out to Bastia, on the near peak of Corsica, for water and fruit. *La Ville de Marseille* was saluted with twenty-one cannon shots. Even in these waterways, once so proud of their son Napoleon's celebrated warring, they now received the French with open arms.

Louis Philippe continually gave orders to keep clear of heavy rough swells. He had specifically made arrangements for their long journey from Palermo to Paris to be made by sea rather than jolting carriage drives. He was anxious for his wife; she was in the last two months of her fourth pregnancy and suffered from seasickness. The strong westerly August winds, blowing the sea to big swells, gradually calmed. The party felt refreshed with the breezes at the stern as they sailed jubilantly past the Alpes-Maritimes. At the foot of the mountains, the arresting Corniche with Monaco, Nice, Juan-les-Pins and Cannes now spread before them. The children were excited to see snow on the distant Alps and Marie-Amélie was captivated by her first glimpses of France.

Passing the Côte d'Azur, the wind dropped. Coasting towards Hyères, the current pulled the ship close to the 'Golden Isles'. The crew tightened the sails and tacked with dinghies – Porquerolles, Port-Cros and Le Levant –

each smothered with rocks, heather, pine woods, eucalyptus and vineyards. The ship dropped anchor and the party clustered by the bridge to admire the Maures mountains. At nightfall the chain of peaks was sharply etched against the purple sky. The Mayor of Hyères descended with a flurry of greetings and flowers. He apologised for not entertaining them on shore.

On August 13th, after eighteen days at sea, they arrived at Marseille, and disembarked for a week of punishing ceremonial and accolade – '*Vive le Roi! Vivent les Bourbons!*' Louis Philippe's favourite horses from Sicily were also unloaded; the whole party was accommodated on the Quai du Lazaret in spacious rooms overlooking the sea. Town authorities called; Admirals from fifty British war boats, Commandants, beautiful women in white with lilies in their hair and everywhere children, with frenzied screams of '*Vivent le Duc et la Duchesse d'Orléans!*' Faces were crammed into windows and banners and white flags fluttered from houses. Générals accompanied the Orléans' open carriages to civilian receptions and military reviews, with Louis Philippe himself mounted on parade. Grand corporate dinners were followed by magnificent fireworks and pretty girls bearing flowers and reciting verses; swinging flashlights, they danced in the moonlight. Marie-Amélie stepped gingerly over cobbled streets and rough paving stones, fearful of stumbling with her unborn baby. She was admired for her gentle smile and charming manner; this blonde Neapolitan with her blue eyes; a young mother with a handsome son and two daughters. She had seized their sympathy. And Marie-Amélie was impressed by these vivacious Provençales; their sharp perception and their excitability. In one bound, she had become a joyful patriot of the French. At the ancient Byzantine-style cathedral, the Orléans knelt by the altar and sang the 'Te Deum' with a large choir. Suddenly, they were confronted with collection bags. The Royal party was unprepared and embarrassed. The resourceful Athalin came to the rescue.

A smaller boat, constructed in Toulon for Napoleon's younger Austrian bride, the Empress Marie-Louise, had been arranged for the Orléans' passage to the mouth of the Rhône. But a wind blew up with an ominous sea. Marie-Amélie was sick and the sailors, tired from their exertions, put in at the fishing village of Sausset-les-Pins. They were greeted by two fishermen who gave them all refreshments in their hut. Marie-Amélie, Adélaïde and the children retired to sleep on board. But Louis Philippe, Athalin and entourage preferred the grass bank under the stars. This amused everybody. Just before midnight, the Mayor passed by and was astonished by this adventure from the Royal voyagers. In a worried state, he woke the sleeping men with a start. As the storm had quietened, the Orléans party re-embarked to set sail at midnight. The Mayor and fishermen were thanked profoundly for their hospitality. At the mouth of the Rhône, as their boat passed sedately through the marshes and plains of the Camargue, the children were ecstatic to see big black bulls and white horses. Docking at Arles, Marie-Amélie flagged at the sight of more merry bunting and the promise of more flowers, thanks, grand dinners, speeches and fireworks... Louis Philippe took little Ferdinand with him to attend the military reviews, leaving Marie-Amélie to rest. On August 24th, they left Arles on a large, comfortable boat. The even flow of the Rhône was appreciated by all until a violent storm whipped up the water and conditions became as rough as the Mediterranean. The boat listed badly – to everybody's terror. Through a pounding deluge of rain and hail, the crew and stewards managed to right it, and again the wind calmed.

Louis Philippe was so happy at Marie-Amélie's genuine delight in his beautiful France. Through the fertile Rhône valley he was proud to point out the old fortified river ports at Tarascon and Beaucaire; the castles and the châteaux. The swift water thoroughfare swept them along, past vineyards and sweeping plains. At Avignon there were more public promenades, ceremonial banquets and Royal toasts, and little Ferdinand was blessed by the Cathedral priest. The party next stepped into the vineyards of Châteauneuf-du-Pape, reputed to be the most intoxicating wine of the Rhône. The villagers, headed by the Mayor, kept pace with the boat from the bank side; girls danced along behind with tambourines. At the Roman city of Orange, there was more delirious shaking of white handkerchiefs; the townsfolk crammed the banks in frenzied excitement for their resurrected Monarchy. Rowing against a rapid current, it took an hour to pass under the bridge of St Bénézet. The famous structure with twenty-two arches was originally conceived in 1177 by a shepherd boy, Bénézet. He had been persuaded by voices from heaven to build this first span of the Rhône. Considered mad until he was seen to lift a massive boulder when approbation and the wherewithal poured in. The legend might recall Sainte Bernadette of Lourdes, the *voyante* shepherdess who, despite the disdain and disbelief of her elders, established her shrine to the Virgin Mary. The endless journey continued with little halts into September; Port d'Annonay, Saint-Pierre-le-Boeuf and Sablon, and each time the Orléans disembarked they were applauded by huge crowds. With his natural charm and cordial *badinage*, Louis Philippe won the hearts and esteem of those rustic audiences. It was the basis of his enduring popularity, this ability to relate on every level. His subtle rapport with the people caused incessant jealousy and suspicion amongst the restored Bourbons.

Towards Lyons, they crossed three boats full of returning soldiers. A caustic cry: '*Vive l'Empereur*' winged shrilly over the water. At Vienne, Marie-Amélie had raved over the Gothic basilica, the tombs and painted windows; but in Lyons she was blinded by the Northern winds and dust. The austere grey façades and the obsession with industry did not appeal. 'A city of two thousand souls with a fine river,' she noted. Seeing her suffering from the cold, as never experienced in her warm climate, Louis Philippe urged her to walk ashore with him for half an hour; to stir her circulation.

As they neared Dijon, word came from Monsieur le Comte d'Artois: he would like to meet them. Two miles before the town, their six carriages were halted by two Générals. They were to escort Louis Philippe, mounted on a horse, to meet Monsieur. The ladies and children were led off to the local *préfecture* to clean themselves after the journey. Monsieur made an excellent impression on the family. Marie-Amélie described him as of middle height, slim, a fine aquiline nose, beautiful brown eyes, silver hair, elegant, charming, and with a broad smile to show good teeth. He took her by the hand to his private study at the *Préfecture*, where the three children met him and all played together. There was six o'clock supper with military and civil authorities; Marie-Amélie sat between Monsieur and the *Préfet*. After the meal, Monsieur, with every courtesy, returned mother and children to their carriage and took his cousin Louis Philippe out to the theatre.

On September 15th, the road from Dijon through rocky country was rough. Again Louis Philippe feared for their unborn baby. A premature birth would seem inevitable with such merciless shaking and jerking. They arrived, thankfully, at Avalon, in the middle of artillery practice to blasts of military music and 'Bravos!' Through Sens, Montereau and on to Fontainebleau, where the precipitate retreat of Napoleon that very spring, and the convulsions of war, had left their scars: broken bridges across the Seine; bullet-ridden façades and city walls torn down. Louis Philippe's valets went on ahead to the Château. In the magnificent grandeur of the apartments of Princesse Pauline Borghese, Napoleon's favourite sister, their rooms had been made ready. The sculptor, Canova's striking attitude of her, as Venus, in a dress so revealing that she would laugh off her nudity, was much admired by the Orléans. They were told how she would airily say, 'Oh, but the studio was heated!'

The Seine et Oise was seized with torrential rain on their last lap. The horses were forced to a walking pace. After five hours, the carriages reached the outskirts of Paris where the bawdy market women pressed flowers on them. Picking up speed, the cavalcade trotted past the Hôtel des Invalides, the Tuileries, the vast colonnade of the Louvre Palace, over the ancient Pont Neuf and into the rue Saint Honoré, and to Palais Royal. Marie-Amélie was startled to see the line-up of shopping arcades flanking the court to the Palace, but was immediately reassured by the Grand Staircase, exquisitely curved in a double flight. The journey from Palermo to Paris had lasted forty days. She sent up a silent prayer of thanks for their safe arrival on that day, September 22nd, 1814.

17

The travel-worn family was received by Comte de Montmorency. Archbishop de la Fare and Abbé Saint-Albin; the two sons from Philippe le Gros' 'left-handed' marriage to Madame de Montpesson, stood by. The Duchesse de Bourbon waited at the top of the magnificent stairs, smiling down at her nephew, Louis Philippe, his Duchesse and their beautiful children. She showed Marie-Amélie her room. It was charming but noisy with the unaccustomed sounds of Paris below. In the morning, she was visited by the King's doctor; a priest and a gynaecologist followed. Her advanced pregnancy was thoroughly checked. The Orléans now took immediate rank after the Royal Bourbons and were integral potential heirs to the throne.

On that first afternoon, the Duc and Duchesse were invited by Louis XVIII to the Tuileries. They found him small and plump in his invalid's chair. He was taking snuff. Any carelessness in his appearance was redressed by a powdered wig and *queue*, a handsome head, sparkling eyes and an extreme courtesy and intelligence. Louis later made notes on this first family encounter; an incisive report of Louis Philippe ran as follows: 'He has been Prince, Republican, soldier, an emigrant professor of maths and geography, a citizen of America, an English gentleman, a Sicilian noble – but now returns as a Prince of the Royal House of Bourbon ... He has been marked by his years of experience; his character is complex.' But the good qualities he sensed in 'Amélie' 'have quietened my apprehension over the Duc d'Orléans'. He did not like Adélaïde. He looked on Louis Philippe and his sister coldly, whereas Marie-Amélie was greeted with exceptional warmth. She was a Royal Bourbon after all. He granted her the title of 'Royal Highness' with Louis Philippe and Adélaïde pointedly downgraded to 'Serene Highness'. Thereafter, when they entered the State Rooms of the Tuileries, the double doors were thrown wide for Marie-Amélie and immediately shut, to be half-opened for Louis Philippe and Adélaïde. At Notre Dame, the kneeling cushions put out for the Orléans were ordered to be removed; they knelt instead on the marble floor. The Royal box at gala Palace performances was denied them. The Opposition noticed the King's petulant jibes. Was he appeasing the Ultra-Royalists who were seasoned detractors of the Orléans? Louis XVIII's bigoted Court etiquette deepened his cousin's anger and humiliation.

In their first evenings together, the Orléans walked incognito round the lit-up crystal glass boutiques of Palais Royal. The whole of Paris exuded joy and confidence, to reflect those early days of a restored Monarchy and Government. The people of France were on honeymoon, reborn, exultant; of their own will, they had beckoned their King back to the throne. The return of the Bourbons had been decreed and signed by the Republican party as well as the Legitimists. The reinstalled King was enjoying this unaccustomed applause. A daily drive in his carriage with his horses at the gallop soothed him in his invalid discomfort. He was also attended by the pretty Comtesse du Cayla; she would call at the Tuileries three days a week for three-hour sessions of tête-à-tête. Despite admitting to the 'old King's caresses', Zoé du Cayla assured all interested parties that 'He knew her not'.

Louis XVIII had been surprised by the renewed deference and esteem of the French people. But social and political distinctions already simmered and soured; the Bourbon fabric was fraying. Squabbles broke out between the new nobility – 'Les valets de Bonaparte' – and the enriched Bourgeoisie, and the traditional tiered system. The King's chance credibility was in doubt. His inability to please both the émigrés with the return of their estates, and any loyal Republicans who refused to relinquish their gains, spread resentment across the board. It was Napoleon who had destroyed the Revolutionary party; it had now resurrected itself in form of new Constitutional liberties. Aware of the King's boredom with bickering, the Orléans aficionados stirred up interest in the younger Lieutenant Général with his figure brilliantly decked in uniform, his clever talk and repartee, his charisma. This former fighter at Valmy and Jemappes carried weight with the Republicans. He was soon considered streaks ahead of the Bourbons. Louis Philippe was aware of these risqué exchanges; with his usual caution, he took every care not to involve himself. There had been quite enough upheavals; the end of the Napoleonic wars had brought peace and relief to the people, who were now content to get on with their lives. Louis Philippe likewise stood back to a quiet existence at home, tending his growing family. Instead, it was a côterie of Orléanist enthusiasts who cautiously drew in the Republican party. These included the Marquis de Lafayette, the heroic Général of both the American and the French Revolutions; Jacques Laffitte, the rich banker, and Benjamin Constant, a revolutionary author and intimate friend of Madame de Staël.

Ferdinand, the young Duc de Chartres, now four years, took pride in donning his uniform of the Hussars. Driving in his mother's carriage to the border towns of Vincennes, Vichy and Neuilly, he watched the military manoeuvres. Marie-Amélie found the horses below standard. At Palais Royal, Louis Philippe had put the stables in good order with superb horses bought from England.

On October 25th, 1814, after hours of hard labour Marie-Amélie gave birth to a second much desired son. Doctor Errard gave the news in a shrill, excited voice to the family and the court, who had waited in nearby salons. The Senior Prince de Condé had been the actual witness. The baby was swept up on to a cushion and paraded through the Palace. Louis XVIII later congratulated the happy mother; at the start of her life in France, she had given him the best of presents. As a further mark of approval, the King saw fit to send her twelve dozen boxes of sugared almonds, to be shared with the family, friends and household. At the christening of the newly born Duc de Nemours, his grandmother, the Duchesse Douairière d'Orléans, was piqued and petulant when not invited to give the first signature on the civil record. But it was decided, in the name of the King, that this privilege, even dis-counting the Duchesse's *froideur*, be given to Marie-Amélie.

Louis Philippe was soon presiding over a full programme of audiences, receptions and dinners in the revived grandeur of Palais Royal. Ambassadors, Ministers, Maréchals, artists and eminent literati flocked to the Orléans magnificent table. The noble Chateaubriand was a popular guest; his com-bative oratory and weather-beaten face suggested an open invitation to a fight. Having dumped Napoleon over the Enghien murder in 1804, he had since become a Minister of the Restoration. Fouché, Duc d'Otranto, was another contentious heavyweight, circling Palais Royal parties. Chief of Police from 1799, he had been instrumental in bringing Napoleon to power. Unprin-cipled and feared, he nevertheless impressed upon Wellington the valour and virtues of the Duc d'Orléans: 'Nothing can be done with a Bourbon,' he warned, and indeed Wellington had always been Orléans' champion.

The rigid Tuileries' etiquette and the inherent boredom had no place at Palais Royal. Madame Adélaïde, who balked at any humdrum convention, was a popular catalyst at the parties. She became jolly and voluble and enjoyed her wine. Her friend, Prince de Talleyrand, was inveigled along to air his intrigues and flattery. It was Talleyrand who could gauge the mood of the people: their need for social change and liberal ethics; their growing identification with the Duc d'Orléans, whose blood was Royal but whose gut instincts were Republican. With his surprise demotion from Minister of Foreign Affairs to Grand Chamberlain, Talleyrand now begrudged the Bourbons whom he had served so long.

On December 8th, 1814 the Orléans received the Duke of Wellington and his Duchess at Palais Royal. He came with a letter from the Prince Regent, congratulating them on the happy birth of the Duc de Nemours. The Orléans waited on the staircase balcony with their court, to include the Duchesse Douairière. Wellington, later to earn the sobriquet 'The Iron Duke', found parties and pretty women irresistible. Handsome and compelling, he relished a grand dinner followed by quadrilles in the cooler ballrooms. Wellington's visit to Paris was exuberantly fêted with a succession of dinners, theatre parties, court balls, and the élan of his military genius.

After a year of settling into life at Palais Royal – the sightseeing of fine old churches, gardens, museums, the preoccupation with her four children, her charitable concerns and social receiving – Marie-Amélie felt tired. She was also plagued by her mother-in-law who, after thirty years, was still bitter over de Genlis' influence on her precious children. Louis Philippe and Marie-Amélie were receiving endless recriminating letters with whining requests for more money and more respect. These missives, prompted by Folmont, were politely replied to by Louis Philippe. But it had been a golden autumn; the young Chartres and his father had ridden regularly together in the Bois de Boulogne and through the ravishing great park of Saint-Cloud, the King's residence. With his loathing of intrigue, Louis Philippe had absorbed himself with his military duties at Vincennes, commanding and receiving the Regiment of the King's Hussars. Meanwhile, disaffection for Louis XVIII seethed and suppurated among his ministers and courtiers. On February 7th, 1815, in a bid to keep the people of Paris amused, a Mardi Gras carnival was staged. The hefty butcher ferried his fat bull around the town. It entered

Palais Royal courtyard, preceded by a rumbustious crowd, with a thrilled little boy perched in the saddle. And Talleyrand, stomping on his lame leg through influential salons, was again promising that Napoleon was 'finished'; his back to the wall, his rumble over. His description of the romanticised hero held his audiences in thrall; 'a pale exhausted face with fine eyes; a charming face'. Alas! On March 1st, Napoleon had landed at Cannes with a thousand men. He had escaped from Elba! The French were thunderstruck. Talleyrand had blundered. Louis Philippe was sent for by the King, who had greeted the astounding news with his habitual nonchalance. He saw no particular danger and outlined his plan for stationing the small complement of Bourbon Princes to key Southern outposts. He, Louis Philippe, was to serve under Monsieur at Lyons. Was it prudent to send out the Princes without troops? The King waved aside any alternatives; the Princes would amply convey their reinstalled Bourbon dynasty against that rascal Bonaparte. Louis Philippe, shocked by the King's cavalier assessment of such critical events, felt further humiliation at serving under Monsieur; that dandy, the Comte d'Artois. The King stared at him fixedly, with his bulging black pupils that filled the whites of his eyes. Louis Philippe was ordered to grease his boots and left the next day for Lyons; he himself did not underestimate Napoleon's allure. The ex-Emperor was a magnet to the scattered French troops; an irresistible force to follow. On 7th March, Napoleon entered Grenoble; on the 8th, he and his Hussars entered the Faubourg de la Guillotière on the outskirts of Lyons. At his lodging in the Archbishop's Palace, Monsieur had proved a useless guard; his Maréchals and aides, his horses and his suite had been geared for his escape alone. Any resistance had been proved an anachronism. Louis Philippe returned to Paris on 12th March, offering the King his help in any other direction. Meanwhile, he saw to the safety of his family, with a crossing to England; by 2.30am on 13th March, Marie-Amélie and the children, with the Comte de Grave in overall command, were bowling along in an anonymous travelling coach to Calais. Louis Philippe had feared that a carriage with his coat of arms could have incited hostage taking.

Marie-Amélie would often recall to her family and friends the cruel experience of their sudden departure from Paris. The separation from Louis Philippe, the dark cold night, the sinister speed and secrecy, the fear of the unknown. The children had been woken from deep sleep. Louise had a fever; Marie was silent and frightened, clinging to her mother; Nemours, at five months, sobbed, uncomprehending in the arms of his wet nurse. Only Chartres, a natural daredevil, could promise his mother, with bravado, that he truly found the whole adventure amusing. They had reached Calais at midday and, after the proverbially rough crossing, arrived exhausted in Dover early evening. Marie-Amélie settled her brave little brood at the Ship Inn, and anguished for news of her husband. Word was trickling in from France; the country was staggered by this volte-face in their fortunes. The King of France with his armies, fleets and fortresses was being vanquished yet again by a brigand-chief: Maréchal Ney had defected to Napoleon. He who had toadied to his King with the boast and promise to deliver Napoleon in an iron cage. Expostulated Louis XVIII: 'Eight days ago everyone was ready to die for me.' Was it conceivable that he was to drop the sceptre after holding it for only a year?

18

On 16th March, Louis Philippe was ordered to command the Army of the North. He set off for Lille with his trusted Maréchal Mortier, the Duc de Trévise, as his Adjutant. Instructions were sent out to the troops: to avoid civil war; to rally round the King and the Constitutional Charter; and on no account to admit foreign troops. Louis Philippe went on to Valenciennes to check the armed forces. He found them lagged with lethargy. He returned to Lille on the 19th to meet up with the King. It was already demonstrably clear that the nation held the Charter more dear than their tottering Sovereign and that the troops were fast declaring for Napoleon. On the evening of March 20th, a colossal boil was lanced. The Emperor entered Paris. A collective shriek rang out. 'Down with the nobles! Down with the priests! The Bourbons to the scaffold!' Louis XVIII fled from the Tuileries with the Duc de Decazes, one of his favourite and more unreliable Ministers. The Duc left an authoritative order: 'If Napoleon asks for a woman, give him one with a disease.' In a dither and flurry of inept posturing, the King arrived in Lille on March 22nd, whereupon Maréchal Mortier urged him to leave for immediate exile in Ghent. The wavering King's parting words to Louis Philippe were: 'Do what you think best.' On March 23rd, an apology was sent by Louis Philippe to his Maréchal.

> My dear Maréchal, I have just resigned to you the whole command in the Department of the North. I go to bury myself in retirement and oblivion. The King no longer being in France, I cannot transmit you any further orders in his name ... your pure patriotism will suggest to you everything most beneficial to the interests of France ... Farewell my dear Maréchal ... I admire your loyalty and your noble disposition...
>
> L.P. d'Orléans

Louis XVIII had deserted his men with no bidding. Jubilant soldiers in tricolore cockades had lined his relief route with roars of '*Vive l'Empereur!*'

Louis Philippe, sensing the country's state of collapse, left for England. A month later, Talleyrand wrote provocatively to Louis XVIII, respecting the Congress of Vienna; he reported a comment heard between Tsar Alexander I and the Irish diplomat, Lord Clancarty, in which the Tsar had mooted: 'I see no one so fitted to conciliate all parties as the Duc d'Orléans; he is a Frenchman, a Bourbon and he has sons. He also, when young, served the Constitutional cause. He has worn the tricolore cockade, which I often maintained, when in Paris, should never have been discarded. In him all parties would be united.' Talleyrand softened this recorded blow by adding that, naturally, the Tsar had no idea of European Sovereign legitimacy. But despite Napoleon being declared an outlaw at the Congress, the brief Restoration of the Bourbon throne had proved a catastrophe.

Throughout these dramatic entries and exits, a tormented mother tended her fractious children at a seaport on the south coast of England. Marie-Amélie had been joined by her close friend, the Comtesse de Vérac, and her faithful Italian maid Saveria. But the Duchesse's anxiety was relentless. There had been no news of Louis Philippe. Relief came on March 25th when a berline and post-chaise bounded the Duchesse d'Orléans and her children and entourage from Dover to London. Freed from days of raging wind and the thudding waves, the party was fascinated to set eyes on England for the first time. One continuous garden seemed spread before them. Horses were changed at Canterbury, Sittingbourne and Rochester, a pretty town on the Medway, where they dismounted at a warm, clean inn. The distant skyline of London gave way to Westminster Bridge. The French visitors were amazed at the opulence of the shops, the luxurious carriages and the large population. Marie-Amélie found the residential 'squares' particularly enchanting with the oval centres of grass and trees, enclosed in iron banisters and privacy. Circling Hyde Park and its brilliant rows and promenades, they arrived at No. 13 Great Cumberland Street, Oxford 'Road'. There, the Orléans' old Sicilian friends, the Prince and Princess de Castelcicala, gave them all dinner. As the exiled Ambassador to Louis XVIII, the Prince and Marie-Amélie had much to talk of. At ten o'clock, they were escorted to the Hotel Grillon (to translate as 'Cricket') at No. 20, the north end of Albemarle Street.

Marie-Amélie slept with the feverish Louise in her arms. The young family's new refuge was a Georgian brick front with five tall, narrow windows contained behind a fine iron balcony. Rooms had been set aside for the Orléans on the piano nobile, to include a lofty long room with pillars and fine chimney pieces. Attentive service was aided by a dumb waiter, used on cords and pulleys. The following day was Easter Sunday, and Marie-Amélie joined her Sicilian friends for Grand Mass at the nearby Chapel Royal for French émigrés; a modest, stuccoed front with a galleried interior. It was built in 1799 in the name of St Louis of France. She remembered how often Louis Philippe had talked to her of this Chapel; bitterly alone, she opened her heart to her Dieu. That same evening, Lord Castlereagh, Minister of Foreign Affairs, presented himself. A cold, correct and serious man, his sombre visit was totally eclipsed the next day by the Duke of Kent, the youngest brother of the Prince Regent; he was described by his hostess as a lovely, big, fat man with a kind, open face. Slow and tentative in talk, he was warm and friendly. The English Royal Family was sympathetic to the Neapolitan Duchesse d'Orléans who had become French. The upper floor reception room fast became a focus of *entente cordiale*. Rumours of Napoleon swirled through London. On March 28th, news came that the Duc d'Orléans was in Belgium. In the evening, the Prince Regent came to meet her. There was now a flurry of excitement at the 'Grillon'. The Duchesse adorned herself nervously in brocade and emeralds; she had heard that the Prince could become easily bored. Saveria had decked the dull drawing-room with flowers. The stately visitor stayed three hours and talked of France; and the restabilising of the Monarchy; a French Monarchy was essential to the peace of Europe, he said. He praised his friend, the Duc d'Orléans: 'A big man, an extremely polite manner – a little affected perhaps – loves to talk – a real raconteur. When one listens to him one sees him as a strong, lovely man.' Marie-Amélie noted that this description of Louis Philippe echoed her own observations of her husband. It was also apparent to her that the Regent's looks and figure were on the wane.

More and more distinguished émigrés were pouring into London. Many had met difficulty securing horses to leave Paris and had been forced to wait on the Imperial Government for consent. The Minister of Police, Joseph

Fouché, an acknowledged renegade, was in charge of passports. At six o'clock on the morning of April 3rd, a faint knocking stirred Marie-Amélie. Saveria opened their hotel door and in walked Louis Philippe with outstretched arms. He looked well and deeply moved to find her. Marie-Amélie's indescribable joy and relief were patent. 'I forgot all my worries and jumped out of bed and threw myself at his neck.' Two days later, the Orléans were invited by the Prince Regent to a soirée at Carlton House. It soared in Georgian grandeur, overlooking St James's Park. The dazzling staircase curved up through a circular wall to twin domes and a skylight far above. The party was led into a small room swathed in Chinese lacquer. Their host arrived thirty minutes later and led them on to a room with walls of black velvet. There they found his mother, the German Queen Charlotte; small, stout and affable, she circled the guests and led them down another staircase to several more galleries with low ceilings. Peers of the realm, diplomats and their wives were grouped in talk and card games until eleven o'clock. There was no mention of dinner or wines in Marie-Amélie's diary; she professed they were happy enough to sit and drink coffee and were immensely touched by the warmth of the Royal Family.

Lord Castlereagh next asked Louis Philippe to Westminster to 'talk Napoleon'. Should England prepare for war against the incorrigible Emperor? Had he usurped all power and capability in France since his return? And after her recent peace so arduously gained? Louis Philippe had been following the situation closely, fearful that Napoleon would kill and exhaust the French people. He recognised the necessity of the return of the Bourbons and the security and sympathies of Europe. All countries had become drained and impoverished by Napoleon's incessant warfare. The Orléans were again invited to Carlton House, by Princess Charlotte of Wales, the nineteen-year-old daughter of the Regent and his estranged wife, Caroline of Brunswick. Living in an annexe close to her father, she rarely saw him and found his cruel indifference to her mother abominable. Sad and lonely, Princess Charlotte was an awkward girl, but the Orléans and their enchanting children clearly delighted her. A friendship developed fast with this blue-eyed frolicking prospective Queen of England; Louis Philippe, always the circumspect observer, took care that it did not offend her father. Towards the end of their stay at the 'Grillon', Général Dumouriez called. He was greeted affectionately. The Duchesse well knew how her youthful husband had been given the chance to fight well under him; and how the Général had enabled him to reach exile and escape the Bourbon regicides.

On May 2nd, the Orléans family left London for the Star and Garter Hotel in Richmond. It was to become a favourite haunt in turn for the future Emperor, Napoleon III, King Victor Emmanuel and Maréchal Soult, the Special Envoy to the 'Last King of the French'. The late Georgian mansion with its fine display of bow windows towered above the grass hill sloping to the Thames. It was from the terrace adjoining that Montpensier had so often painted the renowned river view below. The Orléans found the location 'delicious' and relished the country air; the children were walked in Richmond Park, just across the road. They loved to see the deer, but their mother found this wide expanse with sad old oaks depressing. She and Adélaïde, on the last day of May, took the little ones down the hill to Ham Common to join the summer fair. They were all amazed to see specially staged shows of ballet and gymnastics, and sheds with animals. The party stayed two hours, enchanted by such novelties in this grassy seclusion, bordered by fine eighteenth-century homes. Louis Philippe had himself embraced the leafy suburbs and was held in fond regard after his earlier seven-year stay at Twickenham. He and his young brothers had always been warmly welcomed at Hampton Court.

The old Queen Charlotte and her son, the Duke of Kent, next invited the Duc and Duchesse to spend an evening at Frogmore. During the excellent dinner, Louis Philippe was suddenly taken ill and made a rapid retreat from the dining-room. The Queen sent for the King's doctor, who was at nearby Windsor; she suggested that Marie-Amélie should leave the table and be with her husband. Louis Philippe recovered himself quickly but was queasy for some days. Marie-Amélie was terrified; she had never seen him ill before and tended him obsessively; he had always been so exceptionally strong and active. But the new war in France had plagued Louis Philippe's sleep and appetite. The forecast from the Congress of Vienna that Napoleon, the 'outlaw' and 'villain' would ultimately fall did not cheer him; it had all been said before. The allied Sovereigns and political presses in England were even hounding their wily quarry as a 'notorious criminal' with 'a special charge of murder'. Any letters and documents variously signed by Napoleon as 'N-NP-NAP or

NAPOLE' were eagerly sought. Louis Philippe had always found the liberal English with their largesse and logic a tonic. He now chose to lie doggo in their peaceful country, anonymous and in waiting; his chance would come. It was now the turn of the fractured Bourbons to shake France into sense and action. When the heroics of Napoleon had wrung the country dry, the Bourbons would again jump on the wagon – and Waterloo was nigh...

On 12th June, Louis Philippe installed his family in Twickenham, his favourite Thameside haunt; and a cheaper and more congenial alternative to London. He had leased a plain Georgian mansion from Mr George Pocock for £270 a year. A handsome pilastered octagon, rising thirty feet with high-arched windows and *lunettes*, was contiguous with the façade. It was designed by James Gibbs as a ravishing garden room but was swiftly relegated to a reception and dining-room by the Orléans. The house, set on a bend of the river, was surrounded by woodland and spacious lawns rolling to the water's edge. Birdsong and an ever-changing view of passing boats spelt peace and retreat. Wrote Louis Philippe to his friend Chabot: 'Here I am back in *Old England*. Unhappy France! ... what a mess they're in there! I bless heaven, *morning, noon and night* that I'm in my peaceful house in *old Twick*, on the *banks of the Thames*.' This glade of green, with its rustling chestnut trees and sycamore wrapped around the growing family.

News of England's victory at Waterloo came to Twickenham three days after the battle. Louis Philippe was profoundly upset. As the English screamed their triumph and relief, the Duc and Duchesse stayed at home. Despite their own liberation, they felt sickened with this National rejoicing and received only French visitors. The battle had engaged around noon on Sunday June 18th. The fighting ground was only three and a half miles wide; edged with woods and villages, it was congested. Wellington described the scene of combat as 'a close run thing'; he was seen running everywhere between his men, encouraging and giving advice. By seven o'clock, Napoleon was ruined; his men and horses depleted or dead. His opportunistic 'Hundred Days' had run their course. He surrendered to the British with an ingratiating appeal to the Prince of Wales: might he install himself 'at the hearth of the British people?' He was instead rapidly dispatched to the South Atlantic isle of St Helena.

After the battle, Wellington had returned to the inn at Waterloo. He slept on a pallet, allowing Alexander Gordon, his favourite aide-de-camp, to lie dying on his bed. The next day, he wrote to an unidentified correspondent:

What do you think of the total defeat of Buonaparte by the British Army? ... It was really the battle of the Giants ... My heart is broken by the terrible loss I have sustained; of my old friends and companions and my poor soldiers...

Three young Générals, all good friends of the Orléans, had survived the blood bath of Waterloo: Comte Etienne-Maurice Gérard, Comte Théodore de Rumigny and Baron Athalin. They had all chosen to form up with the Imperial forces; and they were all to become Louis Philippe's closest aides-de-camp. Napoleon's 'Hundred Days' had now culminated in the 'White Terror'. The ultra-Royalists were demanding redress and malicious reprisal from those who had defected to the Emperor's army. The formidable minister, Joseph Fouché, was busy compiling a long list of the said deserters. Louis Philippe watched closely the restless and vengeful mood in Paris from his secluded Twickenham home. The Prince Regent and the Duke of Kent, together with their mother Queen Charlotte and her daughters, Elizabeth and Mary, visited the family often. They would talk for hours; the Prince Regent especially, on the state of France. The ladies strolled by the river and frisked on the lawn with the children. One afternoon, the Duke of Kent brought along a small military orchestra to play through tea and an early supper.

It was a time for travelling round the ancestral homes of England; both Louis Philippe and Marie-Amélie were avid for historical knowledge. With his earlier stay in exile from 1800 to 1807, his accomplished military career and his grace and poise, Louis Philippe was afforded the aristocracy's every friendship and sympathy. At Blenheim, the Duke of Marlborough ferried them around the magnificent park. After spending the night at the 'Cobham Arms' in Buckinghamshire, they continued on to Stowe. Marie-Amélie noted assiduously the styles of architecture and the statuary. They approved some oak trees, recently planted by Louis XVIII and all the Royal Princes. An inscription beside declared that they had been overwhelmed by the warm attention of the Marquis of Buckingham, in this delicious venue. Impressed by their interest, the Marquis opened up two cabinets of historical curiosities. From the documents of Royal English History, a collection of letters from the Bourbons was revealed, to include wisps of golden hair cut from the renowned waist-long locks of Mary of York, who on 9th October, 1514 was married to Louis XII; the sacrifice of 'perhaps the loveliest Princess in English history' to a weak and worn old King. The Duc and Duchesse next visited Woburn Abbey, where they were given permission to drive their carriages round the park. They found it not as *soigné* as the others, due to the wide acreage for deer herds and cultivated fields. They later saw the inside; it was described by Marie-Amélie as a large and grand house, in which she could easily sense the origins of a Cistercian abbey, founded in 1145. They stayed at the nearby St George Hotel.

On September 3rd little Chartres' fifth birthday, the Orléans ended their four-day tour. Sustained by a '*solide breakfast Britannique*', as noted by Marie-Amélie, they made a morning visit to 'Penganger' (sic) – (Panshanger) in Hertfordshire; the house was romantic and Gothic and lay in a valley, with the river Mimram spilling over into adjacent lakes. At 'Heathfield' (sic) (Hatfield House) they were shown round by Lady Georgina Cecil, daughter of Lord and Lady Salisbury. Emerging from the Gothic interior, they were led to a dark and narrow courtyard at the end of the garden. Here Queen Mary had kept her younger sister, Elizabeth, prisoner. The visitors were shown a little iron cage; to taunt Bloody Mary, Elizabeth would threaten to fasten her oppressed little head inside. At three o'clock, the sightseeing party set off for Twickenham. They arrived at eight o'clock, delighted to see their darlings, who in turn showed great joy at seeing their parents again.

At the end of the month, the second Restoration had begun. The King summoned Louis Philippe back to Paris for the opening of the Chamber of Peers. He crossed the Channel the next day, leaving his family happily employed in their mother's disciplined routine. Never waste a precious moment of God's given time, she would urge as she sat stitching and painting in the comfortable drawing-room beside the Thames. When the autumn mists obscured the view, she would call to the children: 'Have sunshine in your soul' and cheer them with her lovely, gentle smile. She was ever the best of mothers.

Mounting the Tribune at the Chamber on October 13th, a look of indignation crossed Louis Philippe's face; and resolution. The assembly was visibly hostile; baying for the blood and mass assassination of all those who had gone over to Napoleon. But now they were impressed to see this Prince of the Blood, the Duc d'Orléans, standing so powerfully before them in all his nobility. Solemn and dignified, he stoutly repudiated the majority Royalist will to murder all defectors from the King's army: 'I propose the total suppression of the obnoxious clause.' He added that public order was patently more in demand than further malevolence and disruption. Any such evil, he warned, could 'convert into weapons for disturbing the repose of the nation'. There were cries of 'Support! Support!' from the nobility. The people cheered his sense and generosity; the King and his côterie condemned it. Louis Philippe's hard-hitting speech was an electrifying performance; the English papers reported the debate at length and praised him; he who was 'entitled to the respect and admiration of foreign countries'. Louis Philippe was again made aware of Louis XVIII's tottering tenure to the throne and the disenchantment of his people. The King and his entourage had been transfixed by Louis Philippe's cool reserve; his audience, from every per-suasion, was jubilant. His Majesty, in a petulant protest, put out an ordinance that in future no Princes of the Blood were to appear in the Chamber unless by special authority. The King's contempt fuelled the Duc's popularity. Always sensitive to the distrust of his Bourbon cousins, Louis Philippe was careful to keep his distance; to perform only if called upon. He returned to Twickenham and his preferred anonymity. The furious Bourbon ultras chased him across the Channel to drum up their hackneyed calumny and defamation.

The French Ambassador to London, the Marquis d'Osmond, was warned by the Paris diplomatic of slanderous publications being printed at Orléans House. The Ambassador, who had the highest regard for Louis Philippe, called on him and his family; his diarist daughter, the Comtesse de Boigne, accompanied him. They found the family clustered round a toy press, engrossed in printing a poem, written by the children's heroic uncle Montpensier. The rumour that malicious reportage was being sent post-haste to France from the Orléans stronghold had been a myth. The disdainful Duchesse d'Angoulême was also given a wide berth by Louis

Philippe; she had been sent to London to keep a cursory watch. But the Comtesse de Boigne, whose pen was prone to sarcasm, paints a mellow family scene:

> The Duc d'Orléans led a retired life in the society of his family. He was perhaps never at anytime so brilliant in his conversation as he was in these days. He had passed the age when his knowledge, as extensive as it was varied, appeared a little tarnished by pedantry. The impartiality of his mind enabled him to grasp all situations and to discuss them with generous moderation. The happiness of his home life soothed the occasional vexations caused by his political position and altogether I have never seen him to such advantage or in such a state of contentment as in the little drawing-room at Twickenham.

Louis Philippe adored his children, his wife, his home and the companionship of his happy marriage. Their son Chartres, so bright and full of charm, the blonde and gentle Louise, the dark-haired and vivacious Marie, and their bemused little Duc de Nemours. Their admirer, Princess Charlotte, visited often to race with them through the trees, across the lawn, romping, laughing and singing.

Marie-Amélie, in pain for some days, gave birth prematurely to a daughter on March 28th, 1816. She was christened Françoise by the priest of Twickenham. Her mother's bedroom made a pretty chapel and the tally of twenty inches and seven pounds seemed more than adequate for a newborn. News of Françoise's arrival was sent to the Queen and Prince Regent by the Comte de Montmorency. On May 2nd, there was great rejoicing over the marriage between Princess Charlotte, the heir to the English throne, and Prince Leopold de Saxe-Cobourg and Gotha (later to become Leopold I of Belgium). Marie-Amélie stayed at home, still tired from giving birth. It was a magnificent ceremony, in the precincts of Carlton House; the couple purported to be passionately in love. Both young and handsome, they seemed the future resplendent. But their union was to be cut cruelly short ... The crowd was ecstatic as the radiant bride, the symbol of cherished Monarchy in perpetuity, drove off to Weybridge, where her uncle, the Duke of York, had lent them his home.

Charlotte and Leopold soon visited at Orléans House. The two men established an immediate rapport. Although Leopold himself was a traditional legitimist, he appreciated Louis Philippe's liberal arguments and his formidable intelligence. Three weeks later, on October 10th, the Orléans visited Charlotte and Leopold at Claremont, the gift to the Royal couple from the nation. The vast Palladian-styled country house, with its imposing portico of four Corinthian columns, is set high on a rise over parkland and the small town of Esher. From the Belvedere, across the undulating Surrey landscape, both Windsor Castle and the dome of St Paul's were then clearly seen. Little could the Orléans have imagined that thirty years ahead, Claremont was to be their last exile from France; when Marie-Amélie's golden curls would be swept white with shock and sadness.

The New Year of 1817 beamed bright and calm, but by January 5th it had disintegrated into hard rain and floods. The Thames rose alarmingly, leaving Orléans House marooned. The men of the household amused themselves walking on stilts. '*La Tamise est effrayante!*' shrieked Marie-Amélie as the downpour quickened. She was carried in a makeshift sedan to behind the house, away from the ominous swell of water. Lower Twickenham was flooded; Kingston and Hampton Wick were under water as the Orléans went off again to Claremont to celebrate Charlotte's twenty-first birthday. She was beautiful and vibrant in her adoration of her handsome husband. But the most arresting man of all, her father, the Prince Regent ... had taken himself off to Brighton with the Austrian Ambassador, Prince Esterhazy. Louis Philippe was well aware of the Regent's *louche* excesses; he was widely described as the greatest reveller and boozer in England. His 'aventures', the neglect of his daughter and his scandalous behaviour towards his wife, the German Caroline of Brunswick, was a *cause célèbre*. But with his remarkable wit and intelligence, his irresistible charm and personality, he remained popular, keeping the affection and loyalty of friends, wives, paramours and any stray offspring. He had a marked esteem for Louis Philippe and for all the French aristocrats exiled in England. A real affinity had sprung up between the English Royal Family and the Orléans. This mutual kindliness and deference was never lost.

Impressed with the English politicians, Louis Philippe had also become a good friend of Wellington, who in turn looked favourably on France and her finally restored liberty. The newly established regime under the Minister, the Duc de Richelieu, appeared set on a correct recovery. But there were still rumbling reports on both sides of the Channel, of disorder in the French Parlement. The abysmal harvests of 1815 and 1816 were regurgitating in bouts of tumult and repression. France was still crushed and confused after the wars. Meanwhile, Louis XVIII was confiding to his memoirs his fears of his cousin Orléans' emerging credibility. 'I do him justice in saying that he will not conspire to obtain my throne, but he will not refuse it should it one day be offered to him...' Yes, the Orléans factor was becoming more prominent. And, despite his cousin's facility for making good friends with the distinguished and esteemed English galère, Louis XVIII was now loath to recall this distrusted Duc and his family back home to France. Finally, his mother, the Duchesse Douairière, stepped in and entreated the King for their return. The po-faced Duchesse d'Angoulême, in her love and sympathy for Marie-Amélie, also pleaded for their recall. The King had always felt a special fondness for the Douairière, whom he would call 'Justine' (inspired by the Marquis de Sade's novel *Justine*, published 1797). His time-honoured respect for her won the day.

The end of March 1817 saw the remaining days of the Orléans' two-year stay in Twickenham. It was a considerable wrench to leave their many friends. Both the English and the French felt sickened at their approaching departure. Condolences, good wishes and invitations winged their way from Lord Bristol and Lord North of North House, Putney; from Lady Pembroke of Richmond Park; from the genial Duke of Devonshire of Chiswick; and from Lady Caroline Waldegrave of Twickenham.

On March 29th the Prince Regent gave a dinner at Carlton House, which included the entire Royal Family, politicians and a complement of Ambassadors. The table had never been more elegantly arrayed, with its dinner service of silver gilt. At nine o'clock, the ladies strolled through the enfilade of galleries, well lit and magnificently furnished. The men joined them for coffee and the Regent offered the Orléans the King's yacht to take them to France, under the command of Captain Owen.

A thick crowd of well-wishers had massed around Orléans House and the riverbanks on their departure day, April 8th. The family mounted into seven carriages. Aunt Adélaïde, sustaining a high fever, had to be lifted in carefully and the whole cavalcade was anguished to leave this peaceful, happy home; for two years they had been distanced from a world of perpetual intrigues. After a night in Rochester, their escorted rumbling carriages arrived at Dover in total fog. The following day was swept with snow and storms, and Captain Owen judged the wind too violent for any crossing attempt. Chartres, agog and restive, persuaded his mother to walk him along the white cliffs, a reckless venture in the high winds, which they found hugely exhilarating; the breaking waves and the little bathing cabins had enchanted them. At five o'clock on April 11th, the Royal launch took the party through a rough sea to the Royal yacht. As the vessel rolled and shook in the wind and surging swell, Louis Philippe pointed out to his faint-hearted women that the interior was fortified with mahogany panelling, gilded, and with padded red damask wall covering. At dawn, Captain Owen hoisted the sail and entered Calais at eight o'clock. The Garde Nationale met the party and Captain Owen and the Mayor of Calais were offered a meal by the Duc d'Orléans. Arriving at Boulogne at 12 noon, the family was given an ecstatic welcome. As the carriages passed through the thronged crowds in Normandy with their enthusiastic cries, Louis Philippe saw with relief and gratitude that his popularity had not been dimmed by absence.

19

The Orléans settled once again in Palais Royal with renewed vigour. The three elder children were bemused with their grand new living. They were given spacious bedrooms and were taken regularly to the Théâtre-Français, later to become the Comédie-Française. Built by their grandfather, the opportunist Philippe Egalité, in 1790, it was linked by a private passage to Palais Royal. Louis Philippe would lead his fledglings to the family box and leave them to assess the performance on their own, retrieving them at the finish. He was keen they should be familiarised with drama.

For the past two years, Louis Philippe had been painstakingly re-establishing rights to his property, the Château de Neuilly. Close to Paris, in a sheltered arm of the Seine, it would prove the jewel of the family's reclaimed seats. On their first visit, April 17th, 1817, they had found the park and gardens scuffed and desecrated by allied troops, from the 1815 manoeuvres. But the situation was exquisite and the air wonderfully fresh after the comparatively cramped and humid precinct of their urban Palais Royal. The estate was set in acres of calm, screened with trees and the glint of the Seine beyond. The prospect of galloping in the park, tree climbing, hay making, swimming and boating, captivated the children. Neuilly always evoked the most cherished childhood memories. The château itself was an unpretentious stone façade; a long, one-storey conglomerate of high-arched French windows, to resemble an orangery. The Orléans were to divide their life between Palais Royal in the winter and this beguiling new home with its open style, for the spring and summer.

The doors were soon opened to a wide consortium of diplomats, politicians, liberals and rising young members of the Chamber of Deputies; notably Pierre Casimir-Périer, François-Pierre Guizot and André-Marie Dupin; all of whom were forming up with their liberal views for the eventual 'Orléans solution'. Despite the open *froideur* of the King for his younger cousin, the public esteem and interest for Louis Philippe was steadily rising.

Louis Philippe had an avid appetite for parties; he relished informed talk, the stimulant of mixed views amongst an eclectic source of guests. His old friend, Thomas Moore, invited to a dinner at Neuilly, was amused to find Louis Philippe's English a bit 'rusty'; he was greeted by his host with 'I wish you a very good night, Mr Moore.' Striding through his newly embellished salons, Louis Philippe was all charm and smiles to both friend and servant. On one future occasion, when hosting a ball at the Tuileries, extra help had to be brought in. The head chef, Lapointe by name, had included a good-looking dairyman who was particularly eager to see a great party at the Palace. At the end of the ball, the good man, on clearing the table, was tempted by the look of a young leftover partridge, cold and intact on a plate; he quickly put it in his coat pocket. But he had been seen by Louis Philippe, who came up to him and murmured: 'Hands off!' The dairyman stood terrified. 'Come,' said Louis Philippe in a genial tone. 'Cheer up and run for it. If Lapointe sees you, he will give chase!'

Up the Grand Staircase of Palais Royal, the flow of guests was also unabated. Ambassadors, Ministers, Généraux, Governors, fellow Royals and the aristocracy were grouped as always in lively exchange on the politics and zeitgeist of the day. The Comtesse de Boigne, observing the arrival of guests at these gatherings, commented in an aside that many of them were of the Opposition. A member of the household answered, 'Monsieur le Duc has made no distinction; he has sent the invitations indiscriminately.' Marie-Amélie felt rather removed from these rigorous receptions. She preferred to listen and ponder. She kept her observations to herself and her diary, and made a rule never to repeat or question an argument. Settling in a corner, she would lower her eyes to her Dieu and her tapestry. It was for Adélaïde to sparkle with her clever repartee; her cheeks flushed from the wine or indeed from the discreet attentions of Général Athalin. ('La Princesse Athalie' had become her sobriquet in the press). Her admirer, Talleyrand, with his sensational girth and overbearing wit and cunning, would lend her his ear. His Excellency, the Russian Ambassador, Pozzo di Borgo, was a wild favourite with the children; big and bulky, he was always jolly, full of jokes and stories.

In the midst of these revived festivities, the Orléans' sixth child was born: a daughter named Clémentine. She arrived so rapidly, the family was caught unawares; a robust baby, she was handed immediately to the time-honoured wet nurse, Henriette Marten. Clémentine was destined to live ninety years from 1817 to 1907. Her father later described her as ambitious; she was certainly a beauty. She married the Prince Auguste Louis de Saxe-Cobourg and Gotha, called 'Gusti' by his young cousin, Princess Victoria. Their son, Ferdinand, became the King of Bulgaria.

In this same year, 1817, on a cold damp November evening, Sir Charles Stuart, the English Ambassador, hastened round to Palais-Royal with tentative news of Princess Charlotte; she was in labour, at Claremont. The following day, on November 8th, the family read shocking news in the English *New Times*. After a gruelling confinement, Princess Charlotte had finally lost her stillborn son during the night of Thursday November 6th. Between the spasms following her delivery, she hardly moved her eyes from her husband's face, until her own death in the early hours of November 7th. Marie-Amélie and Louis Philippe despaired over such an unexpected fate; they imagined the destitution and misery of Prince Leopold. Excusing themselves from their expected dinner guests, they passed the day in quiet and sadness.

Charlotte Augusta of Great Britain and Ireland, their vivacious and joyous friend. She had suffered from her father's temper and his jealousy of her growing popularity. He had hidden her from her rightful world, when suddenly her luck had changed. Prince Leopold of Saxe-Cobourg, the most handsome consort in Europe, had stepped in to share her love and infatuation. Just days before her death, *The Observer* of November 2nd had commented expansively on the huge National excitement over the imminent birth. The Princess had been keeping fit and well, riding and walking. She was seeing no visitors; those who called were asked to leave their cards in the hall. A Mrs Harrison of Dover Street had assembled and already delivered to Claremont 'a princely and costly wardrobe for the illustrious stranger'. It was now the turn of Mrs Bell of 52 St James's Street to advertise her services for specially made mourning dress. She could offer a wide choice of velvets, bombazine, georgette and crêpe – and at a low price.

Grave concern next flooded establishment speculation on the succession to the English throne. Although it was acknowledged that fourteen Princes and Princesses were all in the line of succession, none seemed to fit the calling. Finally, the Duke of Kent, the Prince Regent's youngest brother, agreed to relinquish his mistress in Canada. For the sake of the Monarchy, he was prompted to marry the widowed Victoria Maria Louisa, sister of Prince Leopold. Princess (Alexandria) Victoria was born in 1819, the phenomenal fruit of her father's sacrifice. The Duke of Kent wrote to his good friend Louis Philippe: '*La petite* is rather a pocket Hercules than a pocket Venus.' A year later, he died.

It was little Françoise, born in Twickenham and barely two years old, who was now causing anguish. For several weeks, Marie-Amélie had sat beside her consumptive child, knowing there was no hope for '*ma petite ange*'. The doctor had advised a move to Neuilly. Her bed was placed on an upper floor where she could breathe the fresh air from the grass and trees. On sunny days, mother and daughter would ride in the landau; but Françoise, Mademoiselle de Montpensier, always gentle and serene, was fast losing her hold. On May 20th, 1818, Marie-Amélie entered in her diary the resigned and sorrowful words: 'I saw her change for the worse ... her limbs became stiff and blue ... the appearance of near death. I kissed her and had to leave.' The child slept peacefully through the night, watched by nurses and the devoted doctor. In the morning the little girl asked for a drink of water and died painlessly. Added Marie-Amélie: 'However prepared we all were for this cruel event, the blow was no less grievous. I am her mother and it is the first time I have lost a child.'

The Orléans' third son, François, Prince de Joinville, was born at Neuilly on August 14th. He was a strong, substantial baby greeted with general joy. 'My Orléans cousin has worked hard!' cried out Louis XVIII, happy with this increase of Princes. Marie-Amélie, exhausted from her tending and mourning of Françoise and the new birth, was urged by Louis Philippe to rest herself.

The following year, Princesse Adélaïde came up with a provocative idea. With her chronic awareness of the people's low threshold of boredom, she knew that they had to be kept amused; if not astounded. She suggested to Louis Philippe that he have his sons educated in an ordinary school with ordinary pupils. Such an idea would never have occurred to him. What a slap in the face of established Royal tutorship! But what a boost for democracy! What a chance for class divisions to forge links; to revalue and revamp the bourgeoisie. Louis Philippe, with his ear to the ground, knew that such a step would make him popular. He also knew that Marie-Amélie would loathe the idea; to pander to the people was not in her remit. She would wish her sons educated in all the inherent dignity of their Royal breeding. Adélaïde persisted with her plan. She urged Louis Philippe to consult the Palace tutors; they were unanimously persuaded. Louis Philippe, now convinced by the whole concept, faced up to Louis XVIII who was appalled. They talked at length, both firmly entrenched in their own priorities. The King considered the plan a gross indignity. Louis Philippe insisted that his sons should mix with the populace; to be men as well as Princes. A compromise was arduously reached. The Princes should be sent to the Collège Henri IV as mere day boys, with no meals or games in common and as little access to the other pupils as possible.

And what was Marie-Amélie's opinion of this wondered the surly Monarch. He had more confidence in her values than in those of Louis Philippe. She wrote him a pacifying letter, assuring him of her absolute agreement with her husband. On 15th October, 1819, a press announcement appeared: 'The young Duc de Chartres, eldest son of the Duc d'Orléans, will enter this year the lowest secondary form of the Collège Henri IV.'

'I was a fellow pupil with M. de Chartres,' noted Baron Haussmann, the creator of Paris's broad boulevards, after he had demolished the labyrinth of its quaint old streets. 'We were on friendly terms and he was a good student.' He described how the Princes were accompanied everywhere by their tutors and had their meals served on silver plates. Their food was always different to that of the other boys. The original notion of democratic equality was somewhat swept aside by these exclusive niceties. Louis Philippe was criticised as much as he was applauded for this liberal line in the education of his sons. The Royalist Court detected Louis Philippe's motive for advancing his popularity. The National majority expressed approval that their sons would have the chance to meet their Princes and be known to them. The perennial Madame de Genlis, who had kept in gentle touch with the Orléans, praised them as a unified and exemplary family reared in the highest principles. She even reported that the Prince de Joinville, at two years, could speak as clearly as a child of seven. (This he refuted in his memoirs.) 'I knew nothing. At six years, I was backward despite my mother and assorted tutors teaching me to read.' He later joined his elder brothers at Collège Henri IV.

The days began early with the Princes and tutors walking to the Collège with its daunting high walls. Louis Philippe followed their reports closely. They were commendably free of flattery. But the Princes' involvement at receptions and social duties met with disapproval. Louis Philippe was swift to repudiate this attitude; he argued that his sons had to be equipped for all facets of their future. Meantime, he commended the criticism that Chartres' banter and *badinage* disrupted class and that Nemours should curb his indolence and impertinence. By the time the younger Joinville, equipped with Latin conjugation and rudimentary arithmetic, entered the Collège, their father had become adept at agreeing and disagreeing with the reports. However, the complaint of Joinville's misconduct on his promenades pro-voked imaginative correspondence. The boy would pick the flowers in the park, despite being reprimanded. Louis Philippe added his own judicious opinion to this latest diversion. 'If Joinville continues to amuse himself with this devastation, I will be forced to take severe corrective measures. He must pick nothing without having first asked permission. He behaves himself on the boat, and in consideration of this, I forgive him the rest for this time; I hope that he will not give me grounds for regretting this indulgence.' Louis Philippe's third son, François, Prince de Joinville, was indeed destined for a naval career, sporting a thick black beard.

A seesaw of birth and death had creaked through 1820. On New Year's Day, Marie-Amélie was seized by a premature birth. Despite the advanced pregnancy of her eighth child, she had spent the morning on her feet at the Tuileries, attending to official duties; notably receiving homage and pre-sentations from Générals of the Garde Royale. She returned to Palais Royal for a family lunch. In the evening, she was unexpectedly overcome. Her son, born three weeks before time, appeared weak; but he was given the habitual numerous forenames, to precede the Duc de Penthièvre, in memory of his great-grandfather. Any imperfection in the brain of the child could not have been perceived, until his mind failed to develop. Marie-Amélie adored him in his vulnerability; his affectionate gurgling, his falling down and rolling around her feet. On his early death in June 1828, Adélaïde had checked his mother's tears. It was the best thing that could have happened to him, she commented curtly. The ill-fated child had fallen into a languor and sensed that his death was near. He murmured pitiably *'Moi mourir – moi mourir.'* The family fell on their knees beside him, amazed that any such realization had entered his mind. His small figure is captured in marble at the Royal Chapel of Saint-Louis of Dreux. It was sculpted in 1845 by Jean-Jacques Pradier, renowned for his sympathetic work, its grace and elegance. The fingertips of the prone little Duc are joined and lifted in prayer above his crowned head. His two-year-old sister, Françoise, lies close by, veiled in a shroud, delicately construed in marble.

On 13th February, 1820, Monsieur's younger son, the Duc de Berri, was assassinated on leaving the Paris Opera. As he and the Duchesse were settled into their carriage, a man in a black cloak was seen running in from Rue de Richelieu. He lunged at the Duc, stabbing him in the chest. Berri was helped back to the house, to the mocking strains of a carnival ballet set in Venice. Still able to walk, he mounted the main stairs to the small private salon behind the Royal Box. Marie-Amélie was there to recall the morbid scene. Doctors, surgeons, bejewelled and *décolleté* ladies peered at their reclining and bloodied hero. The salon was suffocating, the music and applause unabated. Dr Dupuytren had probed the wound and advised another bleeding to cool the blood. 'Leave me in peace – do not torment me – you do me a fearful wrong,' cried Berri. 'The King! I must see the King.' Louis arrived around five o'clock, in the grey light of day, in time for his ravaged nephew to cry out to him, 'Sire! Sire! Spare the man's life.' The dying Duc had one final request of his revered uncle: would he consent to be guardian to his two illegitimate daughters, Charlotte and Louise? The girls were conceived in England by one Amy Brown. (Berri's wife Marie-Caroline, a Bourbon Princess from Naples, had always declaimed against them.) With admirable quick thinking, one of Louis XVIII's more respected attributes, he conferred rank on the two girls: the Comtesse de Vierzon and the Comtesse d'Issoudon. Their provenance would be rectified by these two pretty towns in the Province of Berry in the Loire district. The King did not spare the assassin's life. Louvel, a thirty-six-year-old saddler from Versailles was tried and executed. His crime had been propelled by a morbid hate for the Bourbons.

Six months later, on September 29th, the widowed Duchesse de Berri gave birth suddenly at Pavilion Marsan, in the Tuileries. It was two o'clock in the morning and there were no witnesses. '*Vite! Vite!*' cried the Duchesse, as her waters broke. There was no time to lose. Mme Gontaut, the family nurse, fled to her bedside, but the baby was well out. Three blushing Officers of the Garde Nationale, accompanied by Maréchal Suchet, stamped and shuffled up to the birth scene as witnesses. They were able to confirm his male sex before the umbilical cord was cut. The Orléans arrived on the scene as the King was being wheeled in to Pavilion Marsan. 'You are late,' he growled to Louis Philippe 'You failed me.' Mme de Gontaut, still in her nightgown, held the precipitate baby fast on her knees, and bound firm in his wrappings, which she would gently part to reveal his manhood.

The country was overjoyed at the sudden posthumous Royal birth of the Duc de Bordeaux. The sovereigns of Europe had hailed him as the future King, to preserve the peace. For the Orléans, it was a huge disappointment. They had hoped for their own son to finally succeed to the throne. The birth of a male Royal child had always been prone to ugly rumours and calumnious speculation. Louis XVIII, Duchesse d'Angoulême and the Orléans now deplored this rapid delivery with no suitable witnesses. Indeed, an old supposition still lurked that the Duc d'Orléans himself had been an exchange. As the expected male baby of an Italian gaoler from Modigliana it had been pre-arranged that he should replace the feared female Orléans baby. This mischievous slander ran its course for 200 years, to be soundly demolished in 1950 by the painstaking biographer, André de Castelot. Finding letters, reports and dossiers pertaining to the birth and '*ondoiement*' of the Orléans baby son, the Duc de Valois, he next discovered that these pertinent papers had been wrongly filed. They had been concealed in grievous error in the cabinet of his grandfather, Louis XV. It evolved that the rightful baby's birth, in his mother's bedroom at Palais-Royal, had a considerable attendance: Louis Philippe's father, the Duc d'Orléans, his maternal grandfather, the Duc de Penthièvre, the full complement of Bourbons, the Household Chamberlains and Gentlemen of the Bedchamber. Mindful of the sleights of circumstance and not a little piqued at being pipped at the post, Louis Philippe questioned Maréchal Suchet aggressively over the Duchesse de Berri's accouchement. Was she really the mother of a Prince? As sure as the Duc was the father of the Duc de Chartres was the timely rebuff. There was always a hint of the haphazard with the Duchesse de Berri.

Château Neuilly was a cherished retreat from the exigent demands and constraints of Paris. Superb in autumn with the woods ablaze in red and gold; in spring and summer flowers carpeted whole fields and everywhere the scent of roses. It was a relief to step outside informally dressed, and Marie-Amélie enjoyed calling on the schools and hospitals and orphanages. She would take her children and encourage them to hand out little gifts. They competed with each other to give away the most. But her eldest daughter, the eight-year-old Louise, always remembered a chilling incident that flawed the peace of Neuilly. One afternoon, Marie-Amélie was returning through the park from a charitable outing with Louise, Marie, Nemours and little Clémentine. Lolling by the boundary wall, some distance from the entrance gate, she saw two *louche* men. They strode towards her. She gripped Clémentine in her arms, telling the other three children, who were clinging to her, not to be afraid. The men faced her menacingly. 'Who are you?' they challenged. They barred her way. 'A mother – let us pass.' With perfect composure, she fixed them with her piercing blue eyes. Crushed by this creature who showed no alarm, they ordered her to 'Pass on – with the little ones.' Marie-Amélie later admitted she had been full of fear for the children. The family lived thirty happy summers at Neuilly, through their successive joys and tragedies.

It was the Comte de Folmont who next took the Orléans by surprise. His death on November 22nd was announced in *Le Moniteur*. A pompous eulogy described him as 'Faithful to his King and country.... he died calmly beneath the eyes of the august Princesse, who ministered to him with all respectable care.' Such sycophantic applause was undeserved. A vain and irritable man, he had proved a divisive force in the Orléans family. The Comtesse de Boigne sharpened her comments. 'He regarded the real estate of Mme la Duchesse as his own and made no attempt to protect it. He was master of the house, like a husband.' She next described him as an excessive gourmand. 'La Duchesse would trouble herself to procure for him the tongue of a carp or the tail of a pike and would see that he never sat in a draught – "This is M. de Folmont's place" – and she would remove anybody from the appointed chair.'

The Duchesse had insisted ad nauseam that her *chancelier* had delivered her from all perils in attending to her affairs and her money. She had no idea of the price of anything. Talking with the newly appointed Ambassador to Constantinople, the Marquis de Rivière, the Duchesse asked him if he could secure for her the best, most exclusive, moka coffee produced in the East. She explained that M. de Folmont drank coffee round the clock. The Marquis made a note of her request. 'How much coffee would Madame want?' 'I don't know. Lots of it. It keeps, does it not?' 'Yes, Madame, it improves even.' 'Good! I would like a large supply – a good twelve pounds.' Her friends laughed; she could just as well have asked for twelve hundred pounds.

Although Boigne did not believe that Folmont had robbed the Duchesse, she noted with her customary disdain that he had no idea of how to run grand estates after his own bourgeois provenance. Since the Restoration, he had lived with the Duchesse at Château Ivry, close to Paris. A modest pavilion of brick and stone, with flowered parterres and lawns sloping to the Seine. Occasionally, she enjoyed visiting the family at Palais Royal, showering her grandchildren with gifts. She had become frail, with her little face framed in a mass of layered curls, caught in a lace bonnet. The Duchesse commanded that M. de Folmont be buried at the newly built family Chapel at Dreux; well aware of her children's disgust for her *chancelier*, she instructed that his ashes be respected. Twenty-three years on, when Orléans renovated the chapel, he removed Folmont's tomb from beside his mother, to a crypt below.

Exhausted by the shock of her mentor's death, the Duchesse Douairière went into a decline. Her health was further exacerbated by a strange mishap in her boudoir; a footman had knocked into her left breast with the sharp corner of a book. She would describe the blow as a stinging pain, as though a sharp knife had passed through her. Weeks later, her breast smarted and swelled. A tumour was diagnosed. She refused all surgery. By May, she knew she was dying and gave serious thought to her final legacies. On Friday June 15th, 1821, the whole family visited her at Ivry. Despite the contrary upsets their mother had caused them, Louis Philippe and Adélaïde were both reconciled towards her. Although the Duchesse found Adélaïde too liberal, she had strongly repudiated her son and her daughter's court rebuffs from the King. As she reclined on a chaise longue in her pretty salon, with her hair newly curled and dressed, she assured the family visitors she felt better. She had eaten a little semolina, a few cherries with two small glasses of wine. Louis Philippe, Chartres and Nemours arranged to visit her every day; on June 20th, they moved into Château d'Ivry.

In great pain, and with a final show of determination, she had sat up in bed. Pointing to her hair, always admired and still abundant, 'Cut it! Cut it!' she gasped 'I should like it given to all who have loved me.' The following day, the Royal Court came to her side. These '*Visites d'Etiquettes*' were a clear signal of the end. The Duchesse was now silenced with creeping paralysis. She gazed intently at each face, with an implicit 'I recognise you.' Tended by Archbishop de la Fare and Abbé Saint-Albin, her passing was soothed with prayer and sprinkled water. She died in the afternoon of June 23rd. Her body was embalmed and placed for viewing in the main salon of Château d'Ivry. Louis XVIII, perhaps in a gesture of redress for his bigotry towards her children, accorded her the posthumous accolade of 'Princesse Royale'. The death of Louise-Marie Adélaïde de Bourbon-Penthièvre, Duchesse d'Orléans, prompted the *Journal des Débats* to similar praise. '... her face recalled a likeness to her great-grandfather Louis XIV's but her features were softened with the most touching kindliness.' Her devoted Archbishop later commended her grace and candour and her almost mediaeval fortitude in struggling with the many torments of her existence. Louis Philippe finally transported his mother's mortal remains to the Royal Chapel at Dreux. The hearse, harnessed to six fine horses, set off through the hills and woodland of Lower Normandy. Several lancers of the garde escorted the journey.

Returned to Neuilly, Madame Adélaïde lay on her bed in a state of operatic despair, refusing to eat or drink. Why? She had never cared for her mother. Chartres succumbed to measles and Nemours followed suit. Marie-Amélie ran from one bed to the next and remembered, with a certain satisfaction, Louis Philippe's concern when she suffered the rigours of childbirth. 'There are no more Amélies,' he had cried repeatedly, while the household crept through the rooms in silence. And she had murmured, 'I thank God for having allowed me to see how much my husband loves me.'

Left: Marie-Adélaide, Duchesse de Chartres, born 1753 and to become Duchesse d'Orléans. Painted in 1778, when her son, Louis Philippe, was five years old. *Elisabeth Vigée le Brun, private collection.*

Below: Queen Victoria arriving at Château d'Eu, September 2nd 1843. *From L–R:* Prince Albert, Queen Victoria, Louis Philippe, his daughter, Louise, the Queen of the Belgians, Queen Marie-Amélie and King Leopold. *Aquatint by Nicolas Eustache Maurin. Collection Louis Philippe at Château de Balleroy.*

Left: Marie-Amélie, Queen of the French, b.1782. A niece of Marie Antoinette, Talleyrand described her as 'the last great lady of Europe'. *Painted by Louis Hersent. Exhibited at the Salon, 1831. Collection Musée Louis Philippe, Château d'Eu Normandie.*

Left: Adelaide, Princesse d'Orléans, the revered sister of Louis Philippe. She proved a keystone to her brother. *Collection Musée Louis Philippe, Château D'Eu Normandie.*

Left: Louis Philippe, as tutor, in exile at Reichenau College, by the Alpine village of Coire, Switzerland. He stayed for eight months from October 1793. *Portrait by Winterhalter.*

Bottom left: Louis Philippe's hedonistic father – Louis Philippe Joseph, Duc de Chartres, to become D'Orléans. In September 1791, France was proclaimed as the First Republic, and Orléans was promptly accorded the name of 'Philippe-Egalité'. He was guillotined in November 1793. *Painting by Reynolds.*

Bottom right: The charismatic and scheming Félicité de Genlis, daughter of the Marquis de St. Aubin. She seduced the Duc d'Orléans (Louis Philippe Joseph) and was rewarded with the tutelage of his three sons. *Portrait by Antoine Vestier.*

Top left: Adolphe Thiers: a loyal, if quixotic, Prime Minister for the worst of times. He aimed to steer Louis Philippe towards an 'administrative monarchy'.

Top right: Casimir-Pierre, referred to as Casimir-Périer, the second Prime Minister to Louis Philippe in 1831. 'Hard-line' and effective, he was widely described as 'the energetic maniac'. His sudden death from cholera in 1832 was a calamity.

Above left: Molé; a lithograph from the picture by Ingres.

Above right: Lamartine; by Cattier.

Left: Ferdinand, Duc d'Orléans. Heir to the King of the French. *Portrait after Winterhalter, Chapelle Royale Dreux.*

Bottom left: The grocery store in Neuilly, into which Orléans was carried, to finally die after his carriage accident. *Watercolour, 19th Century French School.*

Bottom right: Ferdinand, Duc d'Orléans, Prince Royal 1810–1842, painted five years before his sudden death. *Oval portrait on ivory by the miniaturiste Amélie d'Aubigny. Exhibited at the Salon, 1837.*

Above: Louis Philippe signing the visitors book at the Eton College Library, October 12th 1844. *Lithograph by Edouard Pingret.*

Left: Louis Philippe in 1835, five years into his reign. *By the royal portrait painter Ary Scheffer.*

Left: The Octagon Tower, contiguous with Orleans House, was built by James Gibbs, 1721. It became a conservatory cum dining room for the Orléans in their exile and enjoyed views across the Thames. *The Ionides Collection*

Below: The tomb of Charles, Duc de Penthièvre; the fourth son and eighth child of the Orléans. He was born prematurely and died in his eighth year. Sensing his death near, he murmured 'moi mourir - moi mourir'. He lies beside his sister Françoise, in the Royal Chapel of Saint Louis at Dreux. Their sculptor, Jean-Jacques Pradier, was renowned for his delicate work in marble.

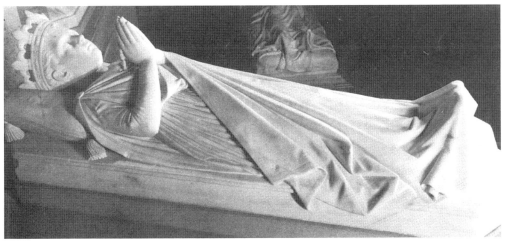

Top: King Louis Philippe, with Queen Victoria, visiting his old home, in exile; Orléans House, Twickenham, October 10th 1844. The Queen's favourite greyhound, Eos, accompanies them. *Coloured lithograph by Edouard Pingret. The Ionides Collection*

Above left: In this house, high above Honfleur, in the Val de Grâce quartier, Louis Philippe and Amélie lay low, from February 26th to March 2nd, 1848. Their benefactor was Monsieur de Perthuis, a kinsman of Général Dumas. It proved their final refuge before their 'hair-trigger' escape to England.

Above right: Claremont – a spontaneous gift from Queen Victoria. High above the rural town of Esher, with rolling green land below; where no fear of riots or assassination plots lurked, and Louis Philippe lived in peace, with his family and friends around him.

20

Louis Philippe's considerable inheritance of land and property, left him by his mother, now represented a huge new challenge. He had already spent eleven million francs on the restoration of Palais Royal, and relished the time and fulfilment in such enterprises. Along with his patronage and presidency of learned and literary societies, and his raised military commitments, he would discuss the defence and patriotism of France and her liberties. He took little part in court life under the reign of Louis XVIII, preferring to busy himself with his own chosen associates and charitable affairs.

The growing children were seen to be intelligent, handsome and polite. Their daughters had been taught by Madame Mallet, especially recommended by Madame de Genlis. The Princes, thrown in at the deep end of a public school, had been given the added opportunity of 'studying mankind'; a chance that their father in his roller-coaster youth had found beneficial. School prizes loomed and the Orléans parents lurched themselves into a session of long speeches. Chartres won second prize for his Latin composition, to the loud applause of his classmates. It was the summer holidays and the whole family left the heat and dust of Paris for cool, green Normandy. Louis Philippe's formidable array of acquired chateaux – Bizy, Anet and the farming lands of Aumale, with the nearby thermal waters – begged a visit. Finally, they would stay at Château d'Eu to explore its immense domain, set high above the Normandy coast. The party first set off for Château Bizy, close to the town of Vernon, beside the Seine. They travelled in a long, large 'voiture' with twelve seats. It had been custom-made by Louis Philippe for their family holidays. A type of itinerant menagerie, it took six horses to pull. The courier would ride ahead to fix the hire of fresh relays. Trotting through the ancient forest of Bizy, a fine avenue of lime trees led them to the Château, where they dined and slept. Louis Philippe was relieved to see the stables and outbuildings in excellent shape. The water basins, fountains and statuary with the vast areas of chestnut, oak and beech beyond, also appeared in good order. In the morning the Duc and Duchesse, together with their children, walked in the town. The poor and the old who had known and loved Penthièvre and his daughter crept out from half-timbered houses and up the tree-lined avenues. They had tears in their eyes as they shook hands and stared. 'Even during the Revolution they looked after us,' they murmured.

Leaving Vernon at midday, they passed through ravishing open country and reached Rouen late afternoon. The ancient Normandy streets fascinated the children as they scampered in and out of the quaint corners. But Louis Philippe was up against time. At seven o'clock, they arrived at a good, clean relay post house. In later years, Joinville took up his pen to describe these holiday ventures. At each relay, horses were up and harnessed, whinnying, lashing out and at the ready. The relay master would yell – 'Let go! Speed ahead!' The postilions, in their beribboned hats with hair powdered and plaited, would stream ahead. The horses would gallop through roads and villages to the noise of the bells and cracking whips; knowing the route, they were determined on the finish. If other carriages approached, the postilions roared ahead to make way. Any collision resulted in a torrent of swearing and shattered glass from coach lamps. Any horse that edged off the highway would lurch and topple the '*voiture*' into the ditch. Any such incident would delight the children; it was the sudden disorder of things that amused them. Joinville wrote to his school friends: 'We overturned in one place and crashed in another.' Occasionally the family took the '*voiture*' through the Auvergne, to stay with Aunt Adélaïde, at her castle, Randan. They always dreaded the journey over the mountains and through the villages of ambling white cattle. They proceeded with pain and difficulty along narrow roads, past villagers in wide hats, steering horses through the crops with their long poles. The '*voiture*' slipped and wobbled in alarming protest over the muddy lanes.

Reaching Château d'Eu on August 28th, 1821, the family was met by the Mayor, the Garde Nationale and civic authorities. Seeing the ancestral home mounted on its plateau, high above the town, momentarily stunned Louis Philippe. He remembered his last moving visit when he had effectively bade his grandfather '*adieu*'. Thirty years had passed and now this rambling old edifice, with its imposing turrets, was set to become the favourite family home. The tally of five boys and three girls would soon run through the same ghostly passages in the darkening evenings, just as he and his siblings had done; with the same fear and excitement at the menacing portraits that seemed about to step out of their frames. The storms over Tréport would still rattle the old windows and howl around the walls. The same seagulls would whip up a frenzy until dawn, when the sea quietened. Louis Philippe thought back to the old happy excursions; to *comédie operettes, bals, orchestres, troupes* and picnics on the broad, white pebble beach.

On that late August visit to Château d'Eu, Louis Philippe asked for a divine blessing; he wanted to take possession. The priest came at ten o'clock the following morning. After a glum, damp start, the weather cleared and the family went down to Tréport, to walk beside the sea along the jetty. The ancient Eglise Saint-Jacques, perched high up on the cliff, faced the harbour. They saw the lock gate opened with its torrent of water and everywhere the local wines and baskets of oysters were pressed upon them. Chartres went out on a fishing boat.

Alas, Château d'Anet had fallen into a state of such destruction and pillage from the Revolution that Louis Philippe felt he could not handle it. A process of state demolition was mercifully in hand. In June 1795, Diane de Poitier's funerary mount – placed in her chapel in 1577 – had been desecrated by the rabble, her body buried in a roughly dug grave in the parish churchyard. The black marble sarcophagus was seized by a local farmer and used as a pig trough. It was not until 1840 that Anet's formidable restoration was started. The ten-day tour of Normandy ended and 'we arrived at our dear and tranquil Neuilly'. Marie-Amélie was well aware that her hands were full: 'more salons, more stairs, more passages and more parties'.

On October 6th, it was Louis Philippe's forty-eighth birthday; always a jolly family celebration at Neuilly. Each child was led up to their adored father by Marie-Amélie, to give him some special present. Joinville was dressed for the first time as a grown boy and after lunch Louise played the harp and Marie the piano in an excellent duet. In the evening, there was a joyous dinner with the children and their tutors and governors and people of the household. The Orléans had an exacting study programme: geography, grammar, Latin, arithmetic and literature, as well as art and drawing lessons with Ary Scheffer, the fashionable painter. They were all talented: Louise took her painting and musical skills with her when she became Queen of the Belgians;

Marie became an inspired sculptor; Chartres and Nemours produced competent watercolours of their battles, on the hoof. Joinville had a serious ability for drawing and writing, as illustrated in his *Vieux Souvenirs*; a rare collection of watercolours from his sea voyages remains. The Princesses, with four-year-old Clémentine, would work one hour a day at their embroidery, sitting quietly with Marie-Amélie around a large table; stitching cushions, chasubles, pinafore dresses and tapestry work was *de rigueur* for a French girl's education. Gymnastics, dancing and riding had their regulated slots. Monsieur Amoros, a retired Colonel, became physical instructor to Chartres, Nemours and Joinville. He concentrated on their physical training and their judicious development of courage and resistance to challenge. The dancing Professor from the Opéra amused the children with his extravagant bow with his hand on heart and his stylish leaps. Clémentine and Joinville paired well and danced the minuet so stylishly that their proud mother had costumes made in the eighteenth-century style. They gave several little performances. Invited to a fancy dress ball at the Tuileries, Joinville, complete with sword and tricorn hat, picked a quarrel in the arrival queue. The accosted boy drew his sword and they engaged in mock thrusts. '*Arrêtez, méchants enfants!*' screamed Marie-Amélie. On another later occasion, dancing with Joinville, the ravishing Clementine caught the eye of Charles X. He led her over to Louis Philippe, confessing that had he been forty years younger, he would have asked him for his daughter's hand to make her Queen of France.

At the end of January 1822, Marie-Amélie gave birth to her fifth son; he was christened the Duc d'Aumale and his sharp blue eyes followed the family's every movement. '*Petit* Aumale' was also to distinguish himself in the field, making his mark in Algeria. His subsequent writings led to his membership of the Académie Française.

Stretched out on her *chaise longue* in unalloyed lassitude, the Duchesse d'Orléans felt her age from the demands of a ninth labour. After two weeks she squeezed into a corset, reportedly regaining her figure in three days. Louis Philippe was always anxious for her return to the marital bed. When showing visitors round the rooms at Palais Royal, he would indicate its voluminous dimension and say proudly, 'You see – I sleep with my wife.'

In the uneventful last lap of the reign of Louis XVIII, the Orléans reflected a happy and bourgeois family. Bourgeoisie was soon perceived a viable ethic under the example of the Orléans. Domestic happiness with solid joys and the rewards from well-educated children was accepted as a *'juste milieu'*. Class divisions were imperceptibly breached. *'Je me moque absolument de l'étiquette,'* declared Louis Philippe. But, fuelled by envy and boredom, criticism was ready to pounce. To crown their prodigious inheritance, the dying old Prince de Condé had finally left Chantilly and its glorious trappings to the little Duc d'Aumale. With memories of his own footsore and hungry wanderings, Louis Philippe was anxious that his children should never know poverty. He continued to restore his properties and heeded the familiar advice from his faithful old mentor, Général Dumouriez. 'Take plenty of exercise, especially on foot, go in for even a little manual or tiring work, in order to avoid corpulence, to which you are prone. Love your old friend and write to him as often as your affairs will allow.'

Troubled news came from Spain in the autumn of 1822. Upheavals had led to Ferdinand VII, the cousin of Marie-Amélie, to be seized by religious rebels. They had since gained ominous control of the country. Louis XVIII, always ready to uphold a Bourbon, considered going to war. He feared that a successful revolution in Spain would fire up the French Republicans to similar action. On 12th December, Louis Philippe received the Duke of Wellington at Palais Royal. On his way back to England from the Congress of Verona, the Duke divulged the opinions of the three great powers. They were unanimously behind France; a coup for the King. He declared war. In March 1823, 80,000 men with the Duc d'Angoulême in chief command, arrived in Spain. They were welcomed with huge relief by the pious and peaceful citizens who had been terror stricken by the zealous heretics. The heroic French had saved them! Angoulême forged on to Madrid, only to find that the Royal Family had been seized and imprisoned in Cadiz. In September, the French army attacked and captured the key south port. There was delirious dancing in the streets of Paris, where the people's vanity still smarted from their defeat at Waterloo. For the Duc d'Angoulême, who had spent a comparatively colourless life in the Bourbon backwaters, it had been a significant triumph. He was to become the Dauphin the following year, when his father succeeded to the throne as Charles X.

At the beginning of July, a strange event had crossed Louis Philippe's path. He had been startled to read in *La Quotidienne* the account of his 'suspicious' birth:

At Modigliana, a small town in the Appenines, the Comtesse de Joinville gave birth to a son on 16th April 1773. I now seek in France one named Louis and his father, Comte de Joinville. If these two personages are still alive and presuming they are able to prove their identity, would they make themselves known to La Baronne de Sternberg, at Hôtel Bellevoir, Rue de Rivoli: she has something of greatest interest to communicate to them.

Not a little intrigued, Louis Philippe was anxious to call on La Baronne Sternberg. Or should he send along Abbé Saint-Fare?

Charming, a man of the world, comfortably obese in his puce soutane and sleeves of lace, the *Abbé*, clutching his *Quotidienne*, entered the rue de Rivoli. Accompanied by two valets, he was hoisted up to the Baronne's salon on the fifth floor. They saw a middle-aged woman with dark, elegantly coiffured hair and a hooked nose. Her piercing brown eyes had a befuddled expression.

'*Monseigneur*,' she addressed Abbé Saint-Fare, 'the Duc d'Orléans was born in Modigliana 15th April 1773?'

Replied the *Abbé* briefly, 'Born the same year, but in Paris, October 1773. The Comte de Joinville was a name that the Duc's father often travelled under. It is probable that the Comte was even with an *amour* in Italy that same year.' La Baronne left France for Italy, and wrote her memoirs – *Accidents de Cours* – on the illicit exchange of herself (of the highest birth) with a boy from the lowest social order.

In the late autumn of 1823, a lull of inactivity rolled over the throne. Louis XVIII appeared mentally spent and inexplicably shocked by his admirable victory over Spain. He was strained and insecure, dithering his way through Court functions. In October he was seen to fumble with his prayer book, dropping it repeatedly in the Thanksgiving Service at Notre Dame. It was clear that the King was shuffling to his grave. He struggled heroically and stubbornly through several months. When in July 1824 Marie-Amélie gave birth to her tenth child, Antoine Duc de Montpensier, the King paid her a token visit at Neuilly. Creeping paralysis of the dorsal spine led to collapse with syncopal strokes. His large head dropped to his knees. Occasionally, he would rise up in a rage, complaining of all the fuss. Excessive somnolence set in and the family gradually took their leave.

On September 12th, the Duc d'Orléans, on holiday with his family at Château d'Eu, was summoned to Paris. He left at eight o'clock in the morning, arriving within fourteen hours. At Palais Royal, he changed into military uniform and drove through the night streets to the Tuileries. Theatres and bars were closed, silenced; the churches were lit up for praying. The Comte d'Artois, whose days as 'Monsieur' were clearly numbered, assured Louis Philippe that the King was dying. 'Pity me, dear cousin; my heart is torn; but I hope that *Dieu* will give me the strength, of which I will perhaps have great need.' Stubborn and imperious to the end, the Sovereign had refused to take the last sacrament; he had persuaded the *abbé* it was too soon. Hours passed, with the *abbé* more and more disturbed, when somebody suggested that the Comtesse du Cayla might tend her devoted admirer. The King finally complied and was heard to mutter, 'I did not think, Madame, that you would be the one to announce my end.'

A telegraphic dispatch from Paris arrived on Saturday September 18th for London's *Morning Post*: 'The King was relieved from his earthly sufferings at four o'clock this morning with the debility of all the functions.' A codicil to the dramatic news made interesting reading: 'His brother's accession to the Crown does not hold any disturbing factor for the people. For sometime the King had closely associated his brother with his Government and any transactions.'

After the obsequies with funeral crêpe and solemn grandeur for the one brother, it was the time of splendiferous enthronement for the other. The consecration of Charles X at Rheims was succeeded by a state function *par excellence*, in Paris on June 7th, 1825. Instigated by George IV, it was the investiture of the new French King with the highest of English Orders – the Knight of the Garter. The ceremony was held at the Tuileries, with the Duke of Northumberland and the British Ambassador monitoring events: Charles X observed the scene intently. At nearly seventy years, he was a sensation.

Tall and slim, with his engaging smile, he was dressed on this auspicious occasion in white silk tight breeches with a large bow at the left knee, and a white close-fitting flared coat and white shoes. His whole stature was even more embellished with the bonnet of the Order. It was surmounted by an enormous cluster of four-foot high white ostrich feathers; so striking was it that one courtier imagined a whole bird had been placed on the King's head. The Orléans' *équipage* on such sovereign occasions surpassed all others. It was noted for its finest horses, particularly when the grown sons pranced alongside their father. Louis Philippe himself was described as a Pharaoh with his gold Bourbon tunic and his ducal crown. Marie-Amélie beside him shimmered in white satin, stitched with sumptuous jewels. To see Charles X established on the throne was a relief to Louis Philippe; it improved his standing in the court. He was soon sent for and he and his family were raised to the rank of 'Royal Highness'. Unlike his deceased brother, Charles had no great intellect or political *savoir-faire*. Instead, he made a dazzling figure-head with his superb bearing on a horse, his charm and quixotic spirit. His wild and youthful ways, with that rogue seducer Prince Jules de Polignac, had been subjugated by his reforming mistress, Madame de Polastron. On her deathbed, she had urged him 'to live only for God'. The King's new recognition for the Church was exploited to full advantage by the growing power of the clergy. The death penalty was inflicted for profanation, violation and robbery of churches. Despite this ruling, Charles X was to hear 'Down with the Jesuits!' intersecting the cries of '*Vive le Roi*', as he rode in procession to the Republican parade ground, the Champ de Mars.

At the start of his reign, Charles and his cousin Louis Philippe maintained a good relationship. The King would speak candidly; he appreciated the delicate position of the Orléans succession to the throne in view of his four-year-old grandson, the Duc de Bordeaux. But in the event of the boy's untimely death, he professed glibly that there would be no reason or difficulty in Louis Philippe himself or young Chartres becoming kings of France. Charles X respected Louis Philippe but warned his cousin of the calumny and bad reports sometimes associated with him. Louis Philippe assured him that he had no ambition except the continued happiness of France with their King on the throne.

Charles X spent his days in seclusion at Château Saint-Cloud, dwelling on his preferred systems of arrogant Government; notably the extinction of the people's prerogatives and the increase of the Sovereign's absolute supremacy. His Chief Minister, Jean, Comte de Villèle, encouraged some constitutional mischief with this indolent King. The Garde Nationale, who had effected prodigious protection to National Liberty, were deprived of their privilege to elect their own officers; next came the invidious destruction of the freedom of the press. The disciplines of this nonchalant King were confined to early morning prayers in the Chapel, a walk with his dog and gun after breakfast, a meagre lunch of soup and chicken, and then off to Rambouillet to his horses. In the evening, it was cards or the chance minuet with his frisky daughter-in-law, the Duchesse de Berri. He treasured his grandson, the Duc de Bordeaux, who would be brought to him each morning, together with his camomile tea. The child, throwing his arms around his grandfather, would chatter ceaselessly, keeping the tutors and his lessons waiting.

In the relative calm of Charles's reign, and before his repressive and autocratic rule became too dominant, Louis Philippe took his eldest son, Chartres, to England. He had not seen George IV since his succession in 1820 and felt a need to keep in touch, and to meet again his old political friends and even make some new ones. It would be a chance indeed to introduce his handsome son into English Society; to curb his youthful appetite for the seamy side of Paris. There had been rumours of the dazzling young Chartres seeking out night spots of *louche* repute. His mother prayed for him; his father warned him not to live too fast too soon. The eighteen-year-old duc reminded his parents that he was his own man. His looks and manner certainly charmed London Society. Louis Philippe was horrified to see the change in the King of England; he had become grotesquely fat. *The Times* berated him for his reckless drinking and gambling; such excessive spending! And despite his publicized debts! His gargantuan gorging could only compare with a starving carnivore. The Duke of Wellington, now less suited to his placement as Prime Minister, recalled sittings at breakfast to include 'two pigeons and three beef steaks', supplemented with champagne, port and brandy and liberal doses of laudanum.

Despite the rapport between old friends, there was unrest in the English Government towards Charles X; notably, his slack regime and inability to quell the opposition. The rumoured threat that he was to appoint his lightweight playfellow Polignac as his next Chief Minister would severely damage any English confidence in the French Court. It was also being suggested by the European powers that in a bid to revive his popularity, Charles X was flirting with adventure; the conquest of Algeria no less. The French Consul in Algiers was accused of refusing to pay a debt to the Ruler, the Dey, who had let fly with his peacock feather whisk and swatted him on the face. Charles X apparently now judged an annexation of the barbaric Algerians a good enough revenge. Any altruistic pose of freeing the Mediterranean coasts from menacing plunder and piracy left Wellington thoroughly sceptical. After these open exchanges, the Duke looked on Louis Philippe as an informer and steady advocate through any storms ahead. Louis Philippe and Chartres next set off for Twickenham to visit his dearest friends – Mrs Forbes and her daughter, Lady Elizabeth Hay.

Lady James Hay
 Jalkes Hotel
or Mrs Forbes

Saturday 16th May 1829
Isleworth
Middlesex

Arrived last night: I am anxious to know when I can find you at home at Isleworth. I propose to be at your door tomorrow, Sunday, at twelve o'clock, or half-past twelve. If you will admit me with the Duke Chartres and my fellow travellers. From your house as the roads are not quite new to me, I propose visiting my dear Twickenham and coming home by Richmond and Hammersmith bridges. My joy is great at the thoughts of seeing you again, but time is wasting to say more at present, and remain, most affectionately,
     Ever yours
     L P D'Orléans

It was his brother Montpensier who had loved Elizabeth Forbes. In August 1813, she married Sir James, six years after Montpensier's death. It had been a gratifying trip for father and son, travelling together to England.

And Louis Philippe was especially pleased to have heard from Dumouriez, who, on receipt of his pension, was now thankful to keep a horse and carriage in his old age.

The last six years, between 1824 and 1830, had run smoothly for Marie-Amélie; within the treasured confines of her children's upbringing and the engaging company of her husband, she had cherished the happiest of times. Now trouble loomed; even their idle King could perceive cracks in his reign with the people's rumbling aggression at his suppression. Charles X had become disaffected with Louis Philippe and his sister Adélaïde. He had heard rumours of their conniving with disgruntled agitators; even legitimists were bowing out to liberal Orléanists. On May 31st, 1830, there was a ball planned at Palais Royal for the King of Naples, the brother of Marie-Amélie. He was to be accompanied by his third wife, a Spanish Princess. Charles X refused to accept; it fell to his senior daughter-in-law, the Duchesse d'Angoulême, to remind him firmly that they were all of one race and one blood. Cuvillier-Fleury, one of Louis Philippe's devoted Aides-de-Camp, commented after the event: 'The Queen was very ugly and made a grimace when we were presented.' The King's appearance also drew startled comment. 'His face was smothered in white hair, which made him resemble a white bear and nearer seventy than fifty.'

With an overture of drums and fireworks, the orchestration of this whole event was magnificent. Coloured lanterns swung gaily through the gardens, where stealthy shadows lurked. There was a sense of suspicion about this ball. The pride of Louis Philippe was transparent as he walked through the dazzling salons among his guests, past the décolletés robes and magnificent jewels. It was the King's arrival he was anxious for. At eleven o'clock, Charles X, heralded by outriders, gardes and drummers, made a brilliant entrance with his Neapolitan guests. Smiling and charming, he bowed his way through the crowded Palace and affected not to notice a strong force of the Opposition. He instead applauded Louis Philippe for the superb renovations to his fine courtyards, by their shared architect, Pierre de Fontaine. He kept to himself his disturbance at espying Lafayette, Guizot and Thiers, all of them key Orléanists and talking in groups. Twelve-year-old Joinville remembered this Spanish ball vividly. The night was hot and the garden brilliantly lit. The 'Anti-cour', opening on to Rue Saint-Honoré and the central Cour d'Honneur, were closed but the people still infiltrated. The crowd grew and strained to see the party. Joinville himself ran ahead of the King to clear his way to the Terrace. The boy admired his upright figure and his Royal bearing. Charles X sniffed the air. 'A good wind for my fleet to Algiers,' he cried out proudly. A force of 37,000 had set sail that very night. Charles waved his hand several times to the crowd below. There was no response. His people shuffled and swelled below him. Silence fell as they gaped at their King. '*Bonjour mon peuple!*' And he left the ball.

Immediately, the palace garden mob set fire to gardens, chairs and benches; this vehement act of arson stirred up uneasy memories of 1789. At dawn, the troops were called in and the garden evacuated. It was the first riot of that eventful year, 1830. For the Orléans children, it was their first sight of disorder. They were angry and astonished. Soon after, on July 9th, Algiers was annexed to France. Considered an action of National pride and political courage. Charles X had triumphed. He had even succeeded under the old white flag. However, the press soon resurrected the *tricolore*. Recalling this snide volte-face in later years, Joinville commented: 'The Press, the most dominant instrument of destruction in modern times, had done its work.'

From his cold and arrogant stance towards the bourgeoisie and his stubborn disregard for its rising power, Charles X had relegated any such irritable concerns to his Ministers. He had quite enough to do exercising his personal stamp of Absolute Monarchy and his repression of the populace; the honour of the Bourbon regime was paramount and so indeed was each decree that came to his mind. He had also seen fit to blanket the entire country with the Catholic faith. Priests had been forcibly attached to each regiment and were received with unanimous scorn. Charles X's First Minister, Villèle, had attempted to balance favours between the populace and the Royalists; he had been known for his adroit touch. His successor was the sycophant Martignac, who had proved woefully conducive to the King's indolence. It was, however, his close friend Polignac who Charles X finally championed. Devoid of political acumen and disinterested, this imbecile Prince paved the way for another Bourbon downfall. Général Comte de Rumigny noted witheringly in his *Souvenirs* that neither Louis XVIII nor Charles X were happily inspired in their choice of ministers.

21

France was bored again. The burning hot summer threatened dismal harvests. Food prices in Paris rocketed and employment dropped. The King lolled and dallied at Saint-Cloud. On Monday July 26th, *Le Moniteur* published a damning cascade of autocratic new ordinances drawn up by Charles X and his ministers. The editor, on reading them, exclaimed that he had lived through the worst days of the Revolution and that he now resigned in profound terror. Louis Philippe, at Neuilly, was incandescent with scorn: 'They are mad. They will get themselves driven out. I have been in exile twice and want no more. I shall stay in France.' His sons, Nemours and Joinville, setting off for college, had never seen their father more furious. The ordinances had been secretly contrived by Polignac and the King's ministers, late the previous evening. The newly elected Chamber had been dissolved; liberty of the press was abolished; the entire franchise of the electoral vote was banned. Had Charles X thrown in the towel? The King had listened to the reading, which had included a new bid of power to the ultras and a clean sweep of any bourgeois initiative.

In an agitated state, his face flushed and breathing hard, he had signed the document. Within an hour of the morning press notices, Paris seethed in heat and anger. Demonstrations erupted in the gardens of Palais Royal, but for the Orléans, at Neuilly, the day had passed calmly. Mrs Forbes, the elderly friend from Twickenham, was staying. Louis Philippe had been showing her round the château and the garden. Guests joined the family for dinner. Comte Molé, with his distinguished record in French politics, added valuable weight to the table talk. He even raised the possibility of legal resistance to the ordinances.

On Tuesday 27th, the crowds worked their way through the traditional paths of revolution and plunder. Guns and weapons were seized from the Arsenal quarter. Trees were felled as the rabble streamed down boulevard de la Bastille and rue Saint-Antoine. Barricades were raised throughout the city. Fighting and shooting sprang up, leading to fraternising between troops and rioters. '*A bas* Polignac! *A bas les aristocrates!*'

It had been another comparatively quiet day at Château Neuilly. In the evening, the family and the household gathered round the billiard table where few spoke. Louis Philippe sighed deeply from time to time; Marie-Amélie, her head bowed in misery and fear, muttered her prayers. She had been informed through a commanding officer that the Duc could be arrested if the troubles continued.

The remorseless days of blazing sun were unabated. The romanticist Stendhal, thoroughly disillusioned with Paris and its blasé boredom, was nevertheless 'enraptured by those July days ... I shall never forget the lovely sunshine and the first sight of the *tricolore.*' On Wednesday July 28th, the ubiquitous white flags were torn down and dragged in gutters; the *tricolore* hung out everywhere. Barricades of tree trunks, cobbles, broken up carts and tables manacled the city. Street lamps were pulled down, adding to the chaos. '*Vive la République!*' And even '*Vive l'Empereur!*' was a popular cry.

In vain had Maréchal Marmont, Duc de Raguse, alerted Charles X at Saint-Cloud. 'This is no longer a riot, it is a Revolution ... I await with impatience the orders of Your Majesty.' The King, seemingly oblivious to the din of gunfire over the Louvre and the Tuileries, chose to resume his game of whist. His grandson's governess stepped in. She urged the toppling Monarch to climb the tower and observe the tumult through a telescope. In the rue de Rivoli, pianos, chairs and tables were landing on the Garde stationed below. As the tocsin swung from the bell tower of Notre Dame, the alarm and turmoil mounted. The insurgents stirred up a triumphant rampage through the troops and helpless citizens. Coffee houses and reading rooms had been closed by the police; all news was unreliable and the journals were seized. 'My happiness is finished,' moaned Marie-Amélie. In her accumulating agitation, she feared for her husband's life and the safety of their eldest, Chartres, heading his regiment at Joigny. By Thursday July 29th, the younger Ducs, Nemours, Joinville and Aumale, sixteen years, twelve and eight respectively, were thoroughly initiated in the chaotic violence and bloodshed of a revolution. A cannon ball had been fired into the park at Neuilly. Six soldiers were wounded. The château staff were sent to retrieve them and any other soldiers menaced by massacre, sheltering by the park gates. They were fed and given plain and unidentifiable clothes. Joinville and his brothers put them on a boat, under the Seine bridge at Neuilly, to drift towards the great willows of Asnières.

'Poor Paris! Poor France! I have tears and blood in my heart.' Louis Philippe sat with friends and family on the sloping lawns, sobbing unashamedly. On that same day, at noon, the great Talleyrand, always a cool spectator of imminent events, had stood at the window of his Hotel in rue Saint-Florentin. From his commanding view over the Place de la Concorde and the rue de Rivoli, he had pronounced that the elder branch of the Bourbons had ceased to reign. Meanwhile Aunt Adélaïde had galvanised her nieces into a frenzy of cockade making. She had ravished her wardrobe for red, white and blue.

Again, there were rumours that the Duc d'Orléans could be seized; even murdered. Urged by Marie-Amélie, he rode off at dawn over the fields to the secluded Château de Raincy. Alone with his horse, he blessed the peace and comparative safety from the mob. He remembered that dire December morning in 1792, when his father had also sought obscurity at Raincy; bound for the guillotine, here he had said his tearful *adieux* to Louis Philippe and Adélaïde.

On Friday July 30th, the Orléans children were taken to Villers-Cotterêts, another close haunt and favourite Château of their grandfather, Philippe 'Egalité'. At daybreak, Paris had finally collapsed in a frenzy of mob hysteria. The Tuileries and the Louvre were extravagantly ransacked and vandalised; portraits, tapestries and furniture were ripped through and smashed; jewels and priceless dresses were clasped to ugly bodies. If Louis Philippe had chosen to stand back from the bloodshed and revolutionary zeal, his supporters were now fired into decisive action. Two editors of *Le National*, Adolphe Thiers and François Mignet, had printed up placards and already plastered them on the walls of Paris. Namely listing the attributes of the Duc d'Orléans and his qualifications for imminent tenure of the crown. The documents, worked on overnight, held stark messages: Charles X, guilty of shedding the people's blood, must never return to Paris. A Republic would cause further division. The Duc d'Orléans bore the people's *tricolore* flag in the Revolutionary wars of Valmy and Jemappes. The white cockade must be forbidden; the *tricolore* to be the only National Standard. The Duc d'Orléans should accept the Charter as understood by the people of France. 'It will be from the people of France that he will hold his crown. This last to signify that Louis Philippe would not come to the throne by divine right, but as a Constitutional Monarch.

Despite his acute intelligence, Louis Philippe was prone to hesitation and indecision in a crisis. It was to his sister Adélaïde that he would turn, for her calm and decisive counsel. She had always believed in a modernised Monarchy in tandem with a representative government; her ultimate ambition was to see her brother astride a constitutional throne. While Louis Philippe's zealous protagonists had scattered their seed round Paris, their role model had frowned and fretted through the small hours, alone at Raincy. Louis Philippe was now judged the one viable amalgam of Royalty and Republic. Or was he just the last ditch for the survival of the French people's crown? He wondered. It was morning. Where to go? The two horsemen who cantered up the avenue at Château Neuilly just howled in disbelief when told he was not there. The agitated men, Thiers and the artist Ary Scheffer, had the gravest news. France was on the brink of Terror. Thiers, who was no horseman, had been similarly placed; having settled for the smallest pony, he had been in difficulty coaxing it over the barricades. Various mobsters had lifted both him (astride,) and his startled pony over the monstrous piles. A mounting consortium was streaming up the avenue. Captains of the Garde Nationale sent by Général Lafayette, leading politicians and journalists pressed unceremoniously into Marie-Amélie's salons. They refused to believe that the Duc d'Orléans was absent and menaced his nervous wife with insistent questioning.

Thiers took the floor. The Duc must return to Palais Royal or France was lost. Madness had seized the city. Charles X had become an object of vilification to the country. Général Lafayette could not long contain the people's fury; his stand at the Hôtel de Ville was losing its grip. He was being urged, in desperation, to proclaim a Republic. Marie-Amélie showed little sympathy toward this rough and vociferous crowd before her. Strangled with sobs, she chose to impress on her impromptu audience the goodness of King Charles X who had treated them so generously. What a shameful return if the Duc d'Orléans were to press his suit in such a roughshod manner. The motley group was hushed a moment as it gazed on this transparent Bourbon. Her voice rose above the ensuing babble: 'They will call him a usurper; he, the most honest of men.' Madame Adélaïde, however, had no love for the *passés* Bourbons. She turned to Thiers, who now held the core of the drama. How could she help? Replied the little, rising politician in desperation: 'All authority is gone … Anything can happen. Only hurry!' Always decisive, she sent word to Louis Philippe to set off for Palais Royal immediately.

Louis Philippe had valued the dawn hours spent alone at Le Raincy. Now in his fifty-seventh year, he had recalled the atrocities meted out to the Bourbon throne. A King and Queen beheaded; his father's same fate to follow; the final fate of a ferocious Emperor; his own three unceremonious flights to exile; and now his cousin's Abdication. To such betrayals of a throne was it not madness to sacrifice his beloved wife and children? To marginalise his concerns for their achievements, for the volatile fray of politics? To set aside the restoration of their homes and palaces, and forfeit family privacy and happiness?

On receipt of Adélaïde's summons, he in fact reached Neuilly at dusk. Together with his wife and sister, he sat in the torch-lit garden summerhouse, reading the Chamber's resolution, expedited from Paris that afternoon. The brief statement urged the Duc d'Orléans to return to the Capital and accept the Lieutenant-Généralcy of France. It stated that he should retain the National colours, that in the next sitting of the Chamber of Peers, the complete command of the Charter should be guaranteed to France. The document was signed 30th July, 1830, by forty-two distinguished ministers, seven of whom were to serve in Louis Philippe's future ministries; namely, Jacques Laffitte, François Pierre Guizot, Général Horace Sébastiani, André-Marie Dupin, Alexandre Dumas (*fils*), Benjamin Constant and Casimir-Périer. Louis Philippe exhausted from lack of sleep, the stifling heat and the week's disturbances, sat silent between his wife and sister. Marie-Amélie clung to him but Adélaïde pushed – '*Marche en avant!*' As she spoke, Lieutenant-Colonel de Berthois stepped through the gloom. He had word from Monsieur Thiers: that the Duc's presence at Palais Royal was imperative. The two men, in rough coats, strong boots and Adélaïde's own approximation of a cockade pressed into their buttonholes, set off on foot for Paris. They headed for the Etoile. After stumbling over several barricades, they neared Palais Royal. They entered, dazed and dirty, by the back entrance at 216 rue Saint-Honoré, giving on to the 'Anti-cour'. There had been calls of "*Vive la Charte!*" on their way. It was midnight. Louis Philippe collapsed fully dressed on a sofa and tossed through another night on little sleep. His own cousin! How could he renege on the loyalty he had shown? At seven o'clock, he sent a messenger to the seasoned old Prince Talleyrand. Should he accept the Lieutenant-Généralcy? *'Ou'il accepte'* was the succint reply. At eight o'clock, twelve deputies from the Chamber descended on him. A proclamation had been drawn up. A copy of this concise document was read to him on July 31, noon.

> Inhabitants of Paris! The deputies of France, at this moment assembled in Paris, have expressed their wish that I should repair to this city to exercise the functions of Lieutenant-Général of the Kingdom. I have not hesitated to come and share your dangers, to place myself in the midst of your heroic population and exert all my efforts to preserve you from civil war and anarchy. On re-entering Paris, I wear with pride the glorious colours which you have resumed, and which I have myself for a long time worn.
>
> The chambers are now about to assemble; they will advise you as to the best means of securing the reign of your laws, and the maintenance of the rights of nations. The charter will henceforth be a reality.
> LOUIS PHILIPPE D'ORLEANS.

With Louis Philippe's approval of this decisive statement, it was immediately exposed around the city. At three o'clock, together with the President of the Chamber and deputies, Louis Philippe left Palais Royal for the Hôtel de Ville. Resplendent in his Général's uniform, with its wide *tricolore* sash, he was accompanied by his aides-de-camp, Général de Rumigny, Général Gérard and Lieutenant-Colonel Berthois. The court artist, Horace Vernet, depicted the scene; Louis Philippe's mare, Clio, is seen delicately straddling the piled up cobbles at the Saint-Honoré gates of Palais-Royal. Rumigny later described the people lifting Louis Philippe and his mare bodily over barricades. Clio had complied like a lamb and did not once kick out. There was a sustained and joyous applause from the thick throng lining their route.

'*Vive le Duc d'Orléans! Vive la Liberté! Vive la Charte!*' Their humble faces were entranced as they blew kisses to their Prince. 'He has not betrayed us, or abandoned us, that one!' Louis Philippe was received at the Hôtel de Ville by the dapper Général Lafayette. He embraced Louis Philippe at the foot of the stairs and led him up to the pillared Council Chamber.

Again the acclaimed document was waved and read before him. Louis Philippe replied to the effect that as a Frenchman he had lamented the wrongs of his country and the blood that had been shed; as a Prince, he was happy to contribute to the restoration of his country's rights and happiness. Whereupon the Republican demagogue, Général Dubourg, stepped before him. 'Sire, I hope it is your intention to observe your oaths. if you forget their obligation, you know the consequence?' Standing tall and stern in his order of the Légion d'Honneur, the Duc gave a withering reply: 'Learn, Général, that I have never, during my life, failed to do so.' Concluding this brief and dry ceremony, Lafayette had led Louis Philippe out to the balcony. He thrust a *tricolore* flag into his hand. The old Général was triumphant and determined to be the one to create this Republican King. He was at his zenith. Next, in a gesture of gross familiarity, he kissed the Duc on the cheek. The wild fervour in the Place de la Gréve below was tumultuous – *"Vive le Duc d'Orléans! Vive le Général de Lafayette!"* The screaming ovations were sincere and the crowd enormous. Any assassination could have been possible, with no police or Garde Nationale on parade, noted Général Rumigny.

On their return to Palais Royal, the Orléans party and their horses were again jostled interminably by the rapacious masses. A crazy man, half nude and twirling a halberd, leapt out before Rumigny and Berthois and effectively led their procession. He danced and sang, throwing out his limbs in frightening gestures. As Louis Philippe passed between his people, reassured by their cheers and their apparent homage, his ADCs were also aware of hurled insults and shaking fists. A few had even pointed their muskets at the Duc. Arriving safely at Palais Royal, Rumigny observed that never had such a brave and positive '*démarche*' been effected by a Prince; his aplomb and his confidence in his people augured well for the country's future. And was it Louis Philippe's enduring sense of duty and patriotism that had hurled him into this affray? To still the waves of anarchy that now engulfed France? Buoyed up by the sounds of a jubilant Paris ringing in his ears, the Duc d'Orléans sent for his family.

At nine o'clock, on the night of his triumph, his wife and children arrived from Neuilly in a modest omnibus. Joinville remembered the whole city lit up 'as light as day'. Flags and *tricolores* in every window. The poor, sad Champs-Elysées strewn with rubbish and sawn-up tree trunks. The milling rabble shouting and singing. When each refrain ended, gunshot had rung out. Men and women, smothered with gigantic cockades in their hair and hats, strolled along, waving guns in the air and shouting at will. In the comparative quiet of rue Castiglione, the Orléans descended from their unlikely conveyance and walked the short distance, along rue Saint-Honoré, to Palais Royal. Nobody had recognised them.

They were shocked to see the grand entrance doors wide open. The beautiful marble staircase exuded sweat and ugly screams, as seething bodies were slumped akimbo. Marie-Amélie's treasured salons were crammed with ruffians, singing and yelling as bullets rained on the padded silk walls. The gross disorder and confusion slowly debouched into the cool and peace of the garden.

Joinville was especially disgusted to see a young girl, dressed as a man in tight black trousers, carried up the stairs by students from the Ecole Poly-téchnique. A heroine of the barricades, they howled, who had tended and blessed the wounded! They wanted to introduce her to the Duc. Whereupon Marie-Amélie, despite her shock over the outrageous abuse of her Palace, stepped in to allay matters; she praised the girl and encouraged her in her work. The children caught sight of their father in his cabinet and were sent off to bed. He had been talking with André Dupin, his hard-headed legal adviser, and with Général Comte de Sébastiani, his new Minister for foreign affairs.

On that same hot, wild night, Charles X and his fragmented family – the Duchesse de Berri, her daughter, Mademoiselle, and her ten-year-old son, the Duc de Bordeaux – had hurriedly left Saint-Cloud for Chateau de Rambouillet. The Duc d'Angouléme, his elder surviving son, had chosen to hold out at Saint-Cloud; with a depleted Garde his efforts had ended in disaster. He fled to Versailles and on to Rambouillet. His wife, the Duchesse Marie-Thérèse, had been taking the waters at Vichy and was returning to Paris with difficulty. The King's household, comprising a Royal complement of aides-de-camp, Garde, valets, butlers, chefs, coiffeurs, doctors and tutors, were preceded by numerous wagons of horses, guns, bullets and shells. The formidable cavalcade reached the Chàteau at around ten o'clock. They were not expected. Nobody had thought to bring food and everybody went to bed hungry. As the King ate his breakfast, on Sunday August 1st, he read a paper on the explicit news of the Duc d'Orléans' appointment to the Lieutenant Généralcy. He noted with surprise that the drama had taken effect the previous day at the Hôtel de Ville. Not even a passive and indolent King such as Charles X could have wished for continued violence and agitation between his army and his people. He approved his cousin's promotion to high office and hoped that he would establish the tranquillity of France. In order to expedite his own departure, Charles X even sent the Duc d'Orléans a formal notice of Abdication:

Rambouillet, 2d. Aug. 1830

My Cousin, I am too deeply distressed at the evils which afflict and threaten my people ... I have in consequence resolved upon abdicating the crown in favour of my grandson. The Dauphin, participating in my sentiments renounces his rights also, in the Duc de Bordeaux's favour. You will, therefore, in your capacity of Lieutenant-General of the Kingdom, have the accession of Henri V to the throne proclaimed ... I renew to you, my cousin, the assurance of those sentiments with which I am your affectionate cousin.

Charles Louis Antoine.

Louis Philippe at once consigned this letter of Abdication to the Archives; if only to recall how an innocent child had become embroiled in the wrecked Monarchy. Louis Philippe took serious note of the King's desire for his grandson, in his majority, to become Henri V. He called immediately for Lord Stuart, the English ambassador, and asked him whether Colonel Caradoc, the trusted officer, could convey an important message to Charles X. The Colonel, on the night of August 2nd, travelled '*poste*' through the plains of Normandy, towards Cherbourg, in the wake of the fallen King's exile. The officer had a brief note from Louis Philippe, concealed in his coat lining. It read: 'Believe, Sire, all that Colonel Caradoc will tell you on my behalf. Louis Philippe d'Orléans.' The Royal party had halted for the night in the small town of Merlurault. Charles X received Caradoc eagerly and questioned him on the state of Paris. He seized the journals from the Colonel, who in turn handed to him Louis Philippe's concise note. The King read it in the candlelight. Colonel Caradoc next outlined to him the urgent plan devised by Louis Philippe; namely, on how to advance the proclamation of his grandson as the future Henri V. The King should now first entrust the Duc de Bordeaux to the Colonel's care for the return journey to Paris. The presence of the ten-year-old Duc de Bordeaux at the Chamber of Peers, sitting beside the Lieutenant-Général, would stir up every promotion for the young king-in-waiting. Colonel Caradoc was persuasive and wished to take away the favoured boy back to Paris. The King sent for the Duchesse de Berri and explained the situation. He admitted he was inclined to accept the plan. The Duchesse was vituperative with her objections and claimed vehemently her son was never safe without her; and what, she enquired, could happen to him, sitting on the knees of the Duc d'Orléans at the Hôtel de Ville? The luckless Colonel was subsequently scolded by the Duke of Wellington for his interference in such French concerns.

Was it sour grapes that made Charles X throw a spanner into his abdication? Or the flourish of a posthumous prestige card? A last-ditch wave of the white silk cockade in his elegantly raised hand?

Twenty years later, the Prince de Joinville summarises in his *Souvenirs* an assessment of the July monarchy. The principle of Monarchy had become an anathema to the people; it had emerged as a vital encouragement for revolution. His father, desperately sad for France, had seen the approaching outcome with the deepest misgivings. When Charles X relinquished the throne with no attempt to protect it, the continued bloody uprisings were left unstaunched. Charles X's insistence that his grandson should succeed to the throne was not a viable option. The Duc d'Orléans stepped in to save France from the ignominious fate of a Republic; of a dictatorship or of invasion and any diminished territories. 'And so for eighteen years he was chained to his destiny in peril of his existence. That will be his honourable place in history – at the price of man's injustice.'

On August 3rd, Louis Philippe addressed the Chamber of Peers. An assembly of state officials, councillors, ministers and keepers of the peace, (including the diplomatic body) was convened to judge the newly appointed Lieutenant-Général. The summer convulsions in Paris had appalled the citizens. It had left them morbidly sceptical of any future authority. Would this Orléans Bourbon offshoot be able to unshackle the straitjacket rule of his elder cousin?

Louis Philippe rose and with his customary command addressed the Chamber:

My Lords and Gentlemen – Paris, disturbed in its repose by a deplorable violation of the Charter and the laws, defended them with heroic courage … During this absence of all public power, the wishes of my fellow-citizens were turned towards me; they have considered me worthy of co-operating with them in saving the country … I am placed in order to re-establish the empire of the laws, save the menaced liberty, and render the repetition of such great evils impossible, by securing forever the power of that Charter.

Yes, Gentlemen, this France, which is so dear to us all, will be happy and free; it will show to Europe that, intent solely on its internal prosperity, it cherishes peace as well as liberty, and only desires the happiness and repose of its neighbours.

The following days brought a modicum of calm; roads were repaved and carriage circulation re-established. The reappearance of soldiers and the civic garde induced a sense of order and security. The more turbulent rioters were corralled into the military and dispatched to Algeria. Despite precautions, an intrusive rogue garde assumed positions at Palais Royal; night and day the garden and arcaded galleries resounded with a racketing tumult. Screams of '*Mort à Louis Philippe!*' rang out in the nearby streets. The civic sergeants gave chase with thundering steps, their bayonets glittering in the night glare. The family and household were shocked to see Marie-Amélie so drawn and pale and sad-eyed. She was profoundly depressed by the bedraggled hubbub in her own home. Each day a new batch of dirty mothers and children thrust their way up the Grand Staircase, all clamouring to kiss the Duc and to sing with him the 'Marseillaise'; shouting and drinking and collapsing, they would finally slump into sleep. How appalling and disgraceful it all was, thought

Marie-Amélie. She and Adélaïde escaped when they could to visit and help with the wounded in the hospitals; each establishment was painfully over-stretched by the remorseless upheavals.

On August 7th, 1830, the Duc d'Orléans was declared Louis Philippe ler, King of the French. But this proclamation needed a more visible and marked ceremony. On Monday morning, August 9th, Louis Philippe was driven alone, across the Place de la Concorde, over the Seine, to the lofty portico of Palais Bourbon. His wife and sister, his three daughters and five sons were waiting for him in the Chamber of Peers. The audience rose as he entered. He seated himself on the throne, a simple throne, adorned with the arms of the Orléans–Bourbons, and swathed with *tricololore* flags. The insignia of the elder Bourbons were cunningly concealed.

The new King signed documents and listened to declarations and reminders of the Constitution. With ringing calls of '*Vive le roi, vive la reine et vive la famille royale*!' the enactment was over. Louis Philippe ler, King of the French, rose from the throne and lifted his hands high to the standing assembly in a gesture of profound acceptance. Hardly the full-scale Cor-onation as mounted by his stagey cousin Charles X at Rheims, but sensitive to the day. Walking slowly from the Chamber, in his self-conscious majesty, Louis Philippe mounted his horse and trotted with his sons back to Palais Royal.

22

The London *Times* was swamped with express reports from its Paris correspondents. The proceedings in France had been paramount to all other news. On August 11th, 1830 one report read: 'In point of politics, we are in the most perfect calm … Every face seems cheerful and happy, proud of the past and confident in the future.' Another correspondent commented on the discordance in the people's calls: '*Vive la République! Vive le Duc d'Orléans, à bas les Bourbons!*' He continued: 'I endeavoured to explain to them the nature of a republic and that if they were favourable to such a form of government, they must give up all thoughts of the Duc d'Orléans as King.' This didactic informer had further pointed out to his London readers: 'It appeared to me to be rather inconsistent on their part to cry "*à bas les Bourbons*" and in the same breath "*Vive le Duc d'Orléans*", he being a Bourbon himself.' On August 12th, he concluded: 'France is restored to the most perfect tranquillity'.

In the space of three days there had been a remarkably rapid exchange of the throne of France, from one King to another. A hefty proportion of the nation had favoured a Republic; Napoleon II had even been fancied as a sovereign hero. Yet it was the prompt action of Louis Philippe, in the face of mad and inexorable anarchy, that had saved their country and gained the throne. 'You ask me for news,' resumed a further reporter, 'and the only news I have to give you is that I have seen a King of France walking yesterday with an umbrella under his arm in the rue St Honoré …' It also transpired that Louis Philippe had subscribed 100,000 francs 'for the relief of the brave men who were wounded on the momentous days of July 27th, 28th and 29th'. At the foot of this exposé, an insertion was squeezed in, to the Editor of *The Times*:

Sir, Enclosed is the amount of the subscriptions of forty four friends, meeting at 'The Two Angels and Crown', Little St. Martin's Lane, being a token of their admiration of the heroic bravery displayed by the Parisians on 27th, 28th and 29th July…

Despite these reports of goodwill and calm, there were sickening revelations of the deported King and his son, the Duc d'Angoulême. Again on August 12th *The Times* divulged that Charles X, playing cards at Saint-Cloud on that memorable Wednesday night, the 28th, 'had smiled and looked more cheerful at each discharge of the cannon, which consigned thousands of his good people of the good city of Paris to destruction.' On August 11th, an earlier disturbing incident sent from a courier, published in the Paris papers, had reached *The Times*. 'The Duke of Angoulême ordered ten men of the Garde Royale to be shot, in the park of Saint-Cloud, even at the time when there was no hope of the success of his party, on the night which preceded his flight.' An even more damning account of the wretched Angoulême's erratic behaviour had been printed in *The Times* on Friday July 30th. In the heat of the succession fracas, he had berated the Duc de Raguse, who held the military command of Paris. He had failed to direct the troops! He had failed to quell the mob! Angoulême demanded Raguse's sword and, seizing it himself from the scabbard, broke it into pieces. His hands were so cut up and bleeding that his alarmed attendants wondered if the wounds were self-inflicted. The tormented Duc d'Angoulême, a deposed Dauphin and childless, was to gravitate to insanity and finally to his death in 1844.

With comparative calm over Paris, Louis Philippe turned his mind to forming his ministry. *'Et que pensent les Anglais de nous?'* asked the French. 'What will be the result of the new order of things? ... How shall order be established with so many perturbations?' queried the English. *The Times* finally licked its lips: 'When we see his list of Ministers, we shall be able to form a more correct judgment of the real strength of the constitutional, as opposed to a merely republican, party.' It was understood that although the Duke of Wellington was not overjoyed with such a dramatic turn-about, he was happy with the exit of Charles X.

On August 16th, the exiled King had left Cherbourg for a new home. Holyrood Palace in Edinburgh had been lent to him and his family by the British Government. Palatial, gloomy and cloistered, it included a throne room, a morning drawing-room, an evening drawing-room, antechambers, dressing-room and closets. The ex-despot hunkered down with his two daughters-in-law and his customary etiquette intact; with his 'whist' each evening and the dutiful Duchesse d'Angoulême embroidering alongside. The

Duchesse de Berri, after months of excruciating boredom, marched off to Brittany to join the provincial wars in La Vendée. For forty years, the peasants, nobles and priests had united in a ferocious rebellion against Central Government in Paris. The Duchesse had chosen this fractious rural zone to contest her little son's position as the true King of France. This defiant slap in the face at Louis Philippe and her fond aunt, Marie-Amélie, was tacitly ignored.

The new King of the French was quick to form a ministry. 'An administrative Monarchy,' Adolphe Thiers described it; not to be outdone by Lafayette's sobriquet of 'a republican monarchy'. Général Laffitte headed a loyal and competent cast; to include Comte Molé, Maréchal Gérard, Casimir-Périer, Dupin and Thiers. The perennially exultant Général Lafayette was given command of the Garde Nationale. When Dupin, days earlier, had praised Louis Philippe fulsomely on his Royal office, he had replied: 'My dear Dupin, have no illusion, do not congratulate me so much. This crown of thorns, of which each needle will pierce my head, I will never discard if I do not save the country from the anarchy that menaces it.'

The formidable Prince Talleyrand was made the Ambassador of the French to London. He was soon sending incisive dispatches to Adélaïde; and Louis Philippe felt boosted by his canny envoy's off-the-cuff advice and speculation. There was a mutual confidence and ease between the three of them. Guns at Dover had saluted the Prince. 'I travelled through beautiful England and so peaceful.' He was well received by his old associate, the Duke of Wellington, and the Foreign Secretary, Lord Aberdeen. Much had changed since he last stayed in London; expelled from his first exile there in 1794, he had sailed from the Thames to America with an introduction to George Washington. As he sat now, in White's Club bow window, a renowned addition since his last visit, and completed in 1811, he noted the passing fashions. It was all markedly modified for his exuberant taste; no more knee breeches, no wigs, and everywhere nankeen trousers, frock-coats and top hats. Gratified to be the first distinguished foreign Ambassador to be made a supernumerary member, Talleyrand would sit long and comfortably in White's bow window, at No. 37 St James's Street. Quick to appreciate any hint of feminine allure, the old Prince had noted that feather boas were in vogue. They were described as 'faithless', due to their swivelling around the ladies' necks and always wanting to escape. He kept a particularly keen eye open for any such boa sightings.

He was disconcerted that the British government lasted out the new French ministry for only a few weeks. The Tories were succeeded by the Whigs. Earl Grey became Prime Minister and Lord Palmerston, his Secretary of State for Foreign Affairs. In the discreet seclusion of his Howick estate in Northumberland, Grey pronounced Talleyrand 'one of the greatest rascals in the world'. But the old maestro never let his irritations disrupt his dextrous manipulations. He kept his own counsel on the clever Palmerston, described just over one hundred years later by the charismatic diplomat, Duff Cooper, as 'this flamboyant Harrovian with his dyed whiskers and striped pantaloons'.

It was a roller-coaster life at Palais Royal that marked the first months of Louis Philippe's reign. Holding to his endemic beliefs of peace, prosperity and practicalities, the confident King strode through the Paris streets, shaking hands indiscriminately with 'friends' and 'comrades'. This open familiarity often provoked contempt. Inwardly cringing, Queen Marie-Amélie would occasionally take his arm. Worse was to come when Adélaïde hatched the idea of informal supper parties at Palais Royal. Self-invited guests from every creed and class were ostensibly welcomed. The children found these latest social departures an appalling embarrassment; did their 'bon papa' have to stoop so low? These ploys to bridge the social gap were rooted in Louis Philippe's early days of army command. His inherent desire to be liked had led him to sweep out the stables, at the crack of dawn, alongside his troop. Ironically, his disparate subordinates would prefer to give deference to his position rather than accept his pandering to theirs. An attitude later reported by an officer Général who commented that he felt totally at ease with the King, as though an equal. But with the Queen, it was a different thing. Whenever he had to reply to her, he was lost for words, standing before her like an imbecile.

A rumbling turbulence still seeped through Paris, encroaching on the precincts of Palais Royal. Général Comte de Rumigny was woken one midnight by his valet: 'Général – two sinister-looking men demand to see you.' Consigning two pistols in his fireplace, he asked them to enter. They were from '*Les amis du peuple*'. Bearded, cadaverous, their shirts streaked with blood, they exclaimed: 'We are fighters. And we have not troubled to change our garments because all is not finished. We need to see the King – immediately. His life is in danger, and the repose of France. After a revolution like ours, the people demand a renewed society.' Rumigny, knowing the King's habit of reading into the early hours, guided the ruffians to the Royal apartments, warning him of their imminent arrival. Louis Philippe listened attentively to the burden of their song and then reasoned with them. 'You insist that society is dissolved? What do you know of the opinion of the people? Our society has been shocked and shaken up, but it exists. It cannot be improved or changed within a twinkling of an eye. You are brave young men, seduced by some theory which you have nourished a long time.' The vagrants left, not a little impressed by their King's sang-froid and reason.

Palais Royal was soon rocked again by frenzied mob aggression. There was yelling for 'Death to the ministers of Charles X! Death to Polignac!' 'The head of Louis Philippe Ier!' would reverberate around the windows. The mobsters were dispersed without force. But the evening of October 18th brought shudders of fear to the Royal Family as they relaxed in their salons. A bellowing roar like a mounting sea surged towards the Palais. The officer at the gate shouted to the rabble: '*A* Vincennes!' It was there, in the garrison, where the ex-King's ministers were imprisoned. The mob retreated, but there was a sting in its tail. At two o'clock in the morning, the King and Queen were woken by the same ruffians charging up the Grand Staircase. 'The King! We want the King!' The Garde closed in quickly on the crazed mêlée. Louis Philippe resumed sleep, but Marie-Amélie lay in a strait-jacket of fear, staring at the dark with clenched teeth. She had never guessed such horror could breach the preserves of Royalty. 'God knows what next year will bring. I will fulfil the needs in which I am placed.' Each day of her life had become a weight that had to be borne; happiness and tranquillity were for others. Another blow to those first disturbing weeks was Général Lafayette's resignation. She was appalled at such a loss; and Europe quaked at the possibility of a new French Revolution. Considered a '*poseur*' by Louis Philippe's ministers, and they were relieved to be rid of him. His top-dog bearing and his demand for free control of the riot faction, had grated. His jealousy at Laffitte's dominant position as head of the Government had consumed him. Louis Philippe did not dissuade his overriding Général, and gave him a National funeral on his death four years later.

Three months into Louis Philippe's reign, Paris remained resolutely in chaos. 'One dare not go into a shop to buy anything when the streets are full of agitators!' exclaimed Dupin, the Legal Minister. Churches were kept locked and mobs were regularly curbed by troops who were stationed night and day throughout the city. Cobbled streets were abandoned to verminous filth and left swimming and clogged in sewage. There was no drainage system except for random flooding from heavy falls of rain. The labyrinth of high-fronted, dim, old, narrow streets were crumbling in the damp, stale air. The habitual household privy had no water, and waste was thrown from the window, a practice blatantly adopted throughout the finest living quarters. The twelve-year-old Prince Joinville, whose bedroom at Palais Royal over-looked rue de Valois, would tell the time by the lady in black, opposite. Each morning, at seven o'clock precisely, she would rest her night pot on her sill; when nobody was looking nor '*en passant*', she tipped it into the street. Starving dogs and rats scoured the food markets, scuffling over rotting meat and vegetables. Underground sewers belched out evil gases. Louis Philippe asked that something be done. 'There is no remedy,' he was told. The comment of his early hero, Jean-Jacques Rousseau 'That noisy smoke filled muddy city' appeared a prize euphemism. It was not until 1851, in the reign of Louis Napoleon, that Baron Haussmann effectively 'ripped open the belly of old Paris'. Gutting the accumulated Mediaeval squalor, he next blanketed whole areas with rigid stone avenues and an awesome industrialised order.

23

It was ten years before France settled to the regulated prosperity that Louis Philippe and his government had doggedly championed. He balanced his adopted bourgeois stance with an authoritative crack down against any threats to his policy and position. When harangued by civic dignitaries, mayors or military officials on his National politics, he would silence them abruptly. He was 'not prepared to listen to them on subjects that were beyond their competence'.

On the morning of February 14th, 1831, Marie-Amélie prayed fervently that her 'Dieu' should 'send peace and religion back to the people of France'. It was Shrove Tuesday, the day of fun and feasting. A Remembrance Mass for the Duc de Berri, assassinated eleven years earlier, was about to be held at the Church of St Germain l'Auxerrois. A tumultuous crowd was collecting on the Quai du Louvre; it was a cruel, vindictive mob, bent on savage destruction and gratuitous plunder. The porch, dating from 1434, was opened wide for a stream of ultra-Royalists, for a fervently Royal ceremony. The magnificent interior spanned five centuries, with radiant stained-glass windows set in its ancient walls. The service began. A wild cry went up from outside. The rabble charged. Hurling themselves at the altar, they flung caskets, cups, candlesticks and sacred regalia at the treasured windows above. The radiant Rose window of the transept was smashed, as the congregation fled. The gleeful rioters romped into the vestry; donning the clerical robes, they careered through the streets to rampant applause.

Through February and March, rioting became the accepted sport and fashion on the streets. A wide choice of cheap and easy revolutionary movements simmered and suppurated through Paris. Contiguous European powers felt threatened; should they intervene? It was a gloomy Wellington who had recently warned: 'A democracy once set going must sooner or later work itself out in anarchy.' In the summer of 1831, Louis Philippe engaged a fresh staff of secret police (Cabinet Noir), and made a significant shuffle of his ministry. Laffitte had to go; his financial management had careered out of control and his nous for politics had proved negligible; although his advice to his King to eradicate the fleur-de-lis from the Royal arms had proved pertinent. He and Lafayette had both become besotted with their own brilliance.

Eight months into the new reign, France was rife with stagnant industry and trade. A spate of screaming for 'bread and work' erupted outside Palais Royal; stones were hurled at embassy windows; ecclesiastical rare tomes from the thirteenth-century Archbishop's Palace were flung into the Seine. Louis Philippe had necessarily gained the throne through brutal barricades and revolution; he now paid the penance of this decision by the masses. Yet he had promised them prosperity; industrial progress, propelled by technical advances. France was still fabricating wooden rail cars, when England and other European neighbours were running iron models. Louis Philippe knew that he had to call on the dynamic Casimir-Périer to become his First Minister. He did not like him; he knew that he would monopolise all vestige of governmental power, which he, Louis Philippe, had liked to nominally share.

In that troubled March of 1831, it was categorically argued that Casimir-Périer was a fine choice. His ability, energy and subtle diplomacy would restore the dignity of France and restore confidence in Europe. In his didactic manner, he first excluded Ferdinand, the young Duc d'Orléans, from all Cabinet meetings, on the pretext that he had 'visionary leftist leanings'. Louis Philippe himself would be eased out of the Cabinet during debates, to be merely asked for his signature to unanimously agreed measures. He tactically busied himself with dispatching a posse of trusted Générals to London, Austria, Russia and Germany. They each carried an appropriate message from the new King; namely to assure the potentates that any hesitation on his part would have flung France into irreparable upheaval. Talleyrand had meanwhile cajoled London and Europe in his own succinct turn of phrase: 'I think that the Duc is now quite convinced that the movement of the French in July was entirely caused by the state of general dissatisfaction; that there was no single intrigue; that the Duc d'Orléans was forced to become Lieutenant-Général of the Kingdom and subsequently to accept the crown; that in so doing, he has fulfilled a duty; and that in fulfilling this duty, he has rendered an essential service to the whole of Europe. The King has many admirers here and many who love him.'

The cunning old Maréchal Soult, the Duc de Dalmatia, had been retained in the War Office. Louis Philippe was always a mite suspicious of this military maverick with his cadaverous features; there had been a shady rumour in Cadiz in 1810 that Soult had been plotting to shoot the young Duc … Now, twenty years on, with the frontier shenanigans brewing between Belgium, Holland, Russia and Poland, Louis Philippe gave his ministers their head. He fully appreciated Casimir-Périer's moderation and resistance to peripheral bellyaching between the European powers; such incitement was not an option. It was France's own, civil war that gripped the King and his Ministers. Casimir-Périer controlled the summer rioting with an iron hand. Trials, heavy fines and fire hosing were effective deterrents to the raging rabble; but the relentless smashing up and looting spread clamour and fear throughout Paris.

After a rare lull from mob intimidation, Palais Royal was again targeted on September 17th, 1831. Louis Philippe, Queen Marie-Amélie and their sons and daughters were hosting a distinguished dinner, to include Lord Granville, the one-time English Secretary of War and consecutive Ambassador to Russia, Holland and France. There was a rumbling and tramping in the corridors below. The conversation faltered; Louis Philippe and the family continued eating. A thunder of feet up the main staircase as the hooligans were chased by the Garde; a crazed lunatic crashed into the dining-room, lunging at the King with a villainous knife. The thrust was parried by the King's son, the Duc d'Orléans, who, flinging himself at the demented rascal, dragged him off his father. After this murderous intrusion, the Royal Family was urged to take up residence at the Tuileries. It had become impossible to guard them at Palais Royal. The outer courtyards and numerous colonnades and the garden flanked with shopping arcades had always lured a dissolute crowd. Casimir-Périer assured Louis Philippe that he would be regarded by his people as a real King in the Royal and ancient Tuileries. (And he, the prestigious First Minister, would clearly feel more suited to be tending him there.)

The Orléans family had loved their joyous, bright Palais Royal. They were devastated to leave it. The Tuileries loomed before them as a grim, dark fortress, waiting to share with them its sagas of grief and defeat. Louis Philippe had a moat dug under the windows, with an iron balustrade and a deep bank of lilies. 'I do not want my wife exposed to the horrors that Marie Antoinette had to listen to for three years.'

The Royal Family's precautionary move was soon flouted. On the night of February 2, 1832, a ball was held at the Tuileries. There was a conspiracy afoot by the grumbling Carlo Legitimists to assassinate Louis Philippe and his wife and children. The case for the 'minor' son of the Duchesse de Berri to succeed to the throne as Henri V had necessarily been in abeyance; but he had now reached twelve years and his chances of becoming the next King were being stirred up by his mother. She herself was scheming to pose as his Regent. Général, Comte de Rumigny noted witheringly in his *Souvenirs*: '*La Duchesse de Berri fait encore du bruit*.' Judged a loose cannon by Louis Philippe and inwardly indulged by Marie-Amélie, the Duchesse's spleen was finally snuffed by her second marriage, to a Sicilian Count.

On the night of the ball, it was the minor officers in charge. A gang had seized their few weapons and unlocked the Tuileries gates. Flinging themselves into the thick of the ballroom, they attempted to lay hands on the Royal targets. The dancing was not interrupted, and continued until five o'clock.

Louis Philippe was well equipped to address the daunting vicissitudes of the French throne. Matured through twenty-one years of exile, where tough times of danger and destitution had stalked his every step, he was now steeled to every calamity. And he had always entertained magnificently. Those first winter months at the Tuileries were transformed from the dull, dark nights of the *Ancien Régime*. Louis Philippe hosted gala dinners, concerts and more grand balls for the glittering thousands – and the bourgeois mingled between.

His personal disciplines were precise; he rose at seven o'clock and lit his own fire. He would scan the most urgent letters. At nine o'clock, in his grey redingote that dropped to his ankles, he was joined in his dressing-room by his wife and children. They all chattered with abandon as he shaved himself, and Richard, his *coiffeur*, pinned on the newly acquired toupee. He happily answered questions from his youngest children only. He next took infinite care cleaning his teeth, which were exceptionally good. Once he was dressed, his ADC on duty would bring the English papers, notably *The Times*. He read them briefly; he preferred their impartial views. The French papers either criticised his Government or praised it, and taught him nothing. He breakfasted frugally on boiled rice, a croissant or waffle and a glass of water; such abstinence surely harked back to Mme de Genlis' dictum: 'Gluttony is the true avarice of children.'

An especial pleasure, if his day permitted, was a stroll with his architect, Monsieur de Fontaine, through the various building sites. Restoration work on the Tuileries, the Louvre, Palais-Royal and Versailles was constantly underway. Louis Philippe was to eventually lavish on Versailles 23 million francs out of his private purse. As he talked with the builders, praising their handiwork, he would fondle their trowel, explaining how he still cherished his early building days. They none of them suspected they were talking with the King. On his return to the Palace, his clothes were smothered in dried plaster. As a patron of the arts, Louis Philippe spent his life honed to the details of upkeep and embellishment. Any maintenance costs for Saint-Cloud, Fontainebleau and Neuilly were funded by his own resources.

From midday, he and Adélaïde would usually head a Cabinet meeting. He liked to know about everything and everybody and to size up the state of the country. Masking his close attention with a certain nonchalance, he would cover his papers with fanciful pen drawings; his aquatic birds were particularly admired by his ministers. At the end of any long debate, Thiers would stick out his short neck and growl: 'I am finished.' Louis Philippe would caution him: 'I am more so than you, but I do not say so.' An afternoon carriage ride to Saint-Cloud or even a walk to Neuilly would refresh his busy day. Striding out vigorously, his legs swinging at a youthful pace, he would knead his affable image. Observed Charles Greville: 'He is too complaisant to the rage for equality, and stoops more than he need do; in fact, he overdoes it.'

On Wednesdays and Fridays, dinner was strictly '*en famille*'. Louis Philippe would be served his own selection of soups, which he would mix together to his own taste; this was followed by roast meat, vegetables, his favourite macaroni and a glass of Spanish wine. The family was offered a wider choice of food and wine. By ten o'clock, Marie-Amélie and the Princesses were settled in a salon with sewing and conversation. The Princes lingered with their father as they sifted through newspapers laid out on a drum table; they read out loud extracts from political reviews and any sarcastic comments on the family. Creeping out of the room, they would go off to play billiards, leaving their father to doze a little. After a brief siesta, Louis Philippe might receive a small consortium of Ambassadors, Maréchals, Générals and Ministers. He would then join his wife and daughters. The Comte de Rumigny describes these united moments of talk and laughter as unforgettable; delightful. The tireless King would next shut himself in his study, with state papers and problems, into the early hours. He kept a special notebook of criminals waiting on death penalties. (His future would-be assassins were to be given his most merciful consideration.) Attempts to assassinate Louis Philippe would continue throughout the next seventeen years; every day now police reports were sent to his Cabinet for his perusal. A lamp burned by his bed all night and two loaded pistols lay ready in the event. Marie-Amélie lived each day in fear for her adored husband. Despite her real concerns, the Orléans Court were riding all threats and dangers with equanimity.

In March 1832, the year-long suspected outbreak of cholera heaped pestilence on the filth of Paris. Such a scourge of horror had never been known before. By April 1st, citizens had succumbed in every quarter. Hospitals, bursting with tatterdemalion corpses, dropped them into passing carts; piled high, they were toppled into ditches and slaked with quicklime. The Orléans stayed put in their Palaces. The Princesses were denied their popular outdoor activities; hospital visiting, attending military reviews and all court gaieties with their two elder brothers. Marie-Amélie worked obsessively collecting clothes and money.

On April 4th, the twenty-two-year-old Duc d'Orléans, together with Casimir-Périer, paid a visit to the Hôtel-Dieus, a rambling seventeenth-century hospice across the Seine from Notre Dame. Louis Philippe's ministers were aghast at such contact. Orléans and Casimir-Périer taking the hands of the feverish and dying! Their words of compassion and assurance were jogged by the incessant removal of the dead. No medical help or prayer could allay this plague. The Opposition of Casimir-Périer's Ministry denounced him and the young Duc for visiting the cholera wards, suggesting that they had merely wanted to have a closer look at the people's agony. By April 1832, 12,000 had died in Paris. Casimir-Périer himself was now sickening; he felt increasingly ill, tired and disillusioned. What had his hard year's work achieved? he asked in despair. On May 16th, he died, screaming. A few days earlier he had murmured to a friend: 'I am very ill, but France is more ill than I!'

Casimir-Périer's death threw Louis Philippe's government dangerously off course; his balance and authoritative pace had given France a renewed directive. Although the King had envied his First Minister's power and success, he accepted that affairs of state were not his prerogative; he had effectively spent a year under Casimir-Périer's thumb. He now seized his chance and immersed himself in the details of administration, for which he had more enthusiasm than ability. Yet, with his clear thinking, his courage, the experience of his Généralship of the Republican armies, his genetic lifeblood from Louis XIV and his renowned energy on four hours sleep, he grasped the challenge.

On May 28th, thirty-four Opposition deputies applauded the death of Casimir-Périer with furious warnings of revolutionary uprisings in the nearest future. His 'wicked policies' at home and abroad would be broadcast through leaders of the Secret Societies, to include 'Les Droits de l'Homme'. Next, on June 2nd, the rebel Bonapartist and Republican Général Lamarque died of cholera. His last words repented his failure to afflict reprisals on France for the infamous treaties of 1815. His colossal funeral on June 5th was the perfect trigger for more savage street rioting. Général Lafayette accompanied the hearse, hustled by a hundred thousand workers. 'Long live the Republic!' was their jubilant cry. 'Down with Louis Philippe! He will die on the scaffold like his father!' The procession tumbled into the Place Vendôme, with its towering central column; once the hallowed seat of their hero denuded by Louis XVIII in 1818 when it had been topped instead by a vast bronze fleur-de-lis. There was now Imperial insistence that the hearse be trailed round the Place three times. Lafayette, appalled at the disorder under his command, fled the scene in a fiacre to the Tuileries; he had overheard mutterings of a conspiracy to throw him into the Seine. Maréchal Soult moved in on the ferocious turmoil with more troops, more guns and the Garde Nationale.

The Royal Family had established itself at Saint-Cloud for the summer; distanced on its hillside overlooking the Seine, it gave comparative calm with cool air and space. Even so, the screams and shots in Paris wafted up to them. Général Hymés arrived on horseback, and advised Louis Philippe to enter the fray. He turned to his wife: 'Amélie, there is trouble in Paris. I am going.' 'I am coming too,' said his Queen. The Royal carriage reached the Tuileries in the early evening of June 5th. There was immense applause. The troops and the Garde Nationale were heartened that Louis Philippe had joined in their danger. Marie-Amélie watched him head off with a beating heart. It was a reckless bid for recognition and acclaim. She found it hard to approve his resolution, and the protests resumed when he had passed. Lafayette's successor, Maréchal Comte Georges de Lobau, had established a firm hold and cleared the outer city of the worst rioting; but the centre streets were still under savage insurgents.

Louis Philippe rode around the Tuileries and the Place du Carousel, exhorting the Garde Nationale with every encouragement. The night quietened, but the fighting started up again at dawn. The straggle of rebels was soon quelled; boulevards were cleared. News of the King blazing a trail along the *quais* stirred up new respect and goodwill in the people. Genial, unperturbed, praising officers and privates alike, for maintaining civic order, his calm authority even impressed the enemy. Louis Philippe's ardent desire to be liked had been granted. Marie-Amélie's joy was immense at her husband's safe return; she had suffered two tortured days of reported bloodshed.

A few months earlier, the two elder Orléans Princes had together been commanding manoeuvres through the shambles of savage street battles in Lyons. Depression of trade, redundancy, and lethal pay disputes, had driven silk workers to the abyss. A burning barge was floated down the canal to enflame the wooden piers of bridges. The cherished old church was blown up. There were over a thousand casualties. The silk strike was successfully crushed under the forces of Maréchal Soult.

24

The Prince Royal, Ferdinand, Duc d'Orléans (or Chartres, as the family still called him) was now twenty-two years old. He had a dichotomous persona. Tall, distinguished-looking and handsome, he could be aloof and arrogant towards his peers, his friends and his temperate father. He had developed marked Republican leanings. He would provoke and openly criticize Louis Philippe, claiming his rule was 'floating on the breeze'. As the heir apparent, he was detested by the Legitimists, but nicknamed 'Beauty' by his fond siblings. Notwithstanding his cool and severe determinations, the Duc d'Orléans had wit and knew how to charm. Arriving one day at Ary Scheffer's studios, he was not recognised by the Concierge, who asked him to run up with the Royal portrait painter's trousers; only to be quick about it as Monsieur was expecting the Duc d'Orléans. 'Give them to me – I will hurry,' said the Duc. He raced up the stairs and greeted Scheffer: 'I have come two steps at a time, to bring you your trousers in which you are to receive me.'

In contrast to the Prince Royal, the Duc de Nemours was painfully shy, stammering out his answers and in dread of any public performance. However, his sweep of blond hair and dreamy eyes turned heads. With his distinguished reserve, Nemours was the son who reflected the air of a true aristocrat; he was likened to his striking ancestor, Henri IV. Marie-Amélie was particularly close to her diffident son; he had always been painstakingly attentive to his mother's religious leanings.

The younger Prince Joinville had been allowed to leave Collège aged thirteen, much to his relief: 'I was doing no more good there.' In the spring of 1831, he had embarked on a naval career with his father's blessing. Travelling with his valet, Auguste Trognon, by post-chaise from Paris to Toulon, he feasted on the passing scene – Lyons, Orange, Avignon, Aix and Marseille. Pleased with his Captain, his uniform, his boat, *l'Arthémise*, with her 52 cannons and tall, voluminous sails, the aspiring schoolboy sailor coasted into Algiers. Crossing the Mediterranean, back to Toulon, Joinville's maiden voyage floundered in stormy seas. 'Man overboard!' A lifebelt was thrown in; the man seized it, but was swallowed up in the demented waves. Thirty men fell on their knees before Joinville, their junior command. 'Let us save our friend. We cannot abandon him.' Confided Joinville: 'I gave in.' Twelve men set off, lowering the lifeboat with difficulty. 'We saw them capture the victim, when an enormous wave capsized the boat, leaving three men clawing at the keel.' Joinville made to go to them, but the midshipman on board waved *adieu*. Thirteen men had drowned. Joinville cursed his feebleness in command; it had been all his fault for the sake of one; he felt cruelly punished. His Captain put a hand on his shoulder: 'You will command one day, young man! This memory will recall for you the inflexibility of duty!'

Joinville's first testing campaign had proved a salutary experience. He returned to his adoring parents and siblings from whom he had never before been separated. His father entered him into a naval school, to acquire every technique of his chosen career. Joinville always reminded Louis Philippe of his own father, Philippe Egalité; they were two irrepressible charmers, flamboyant, nonchalant and careless of their audience. Tossing his thatch of dark hair and adopting a careless swagger, Joinville added drawing lessons to his curriculum. The renowned landscapist, Nicolas-Alexandre Barbier, helped nurture his cherished talent. Remarked Alphonse de Lamartine, the provocative politico/poet: 'The sons would have been eminent as citizens if they had not been princes...' Clever, laconic, and snide, but a Liberal backer of Louis Philippe, Lamartine was angered by the class divisions of the aristocracy, who held firmly to their kind.

Joinville and his younger sister, Clémentine, had always been paired as children, and remained close. They developed an interest in the old historic Paris, inspired particularly by the genius of Victor Hugo. They would enjoy strolling through secluded streets, exploring churches and monuments and picking up the traces of their family's turbulent past.

The next treasure to slip from her mother's shielding arms was Princesse Louise, the eldest daughter and the adored angel of the family; a giver and a doer with nothing to fear except for the long shadow of a suggestion that she should marry the widowed Prince Leopold de Saxe-Cobourg. She was twenty years old and he was forty-two.

Louise, well aware of her father's disappointment if she refused, had pleaded for time, and more time. She dreaded this fate; she had felt intuitively that this severe and handsome stranger yearned still for his long dead wife, the Princess Charlotte. Louis Philippe was inordinately proud that his lovely, clever Louise; her rosy face framed in golden curls, was to become a Queen. Leopold had recently been made King of the Belgians.

On August 9th, 1832, the wedding took place quietly at the Château de Compiègne. Louis Philippe had felt the joyous celebrations should be distanced from Paris, after the months of sickness and rioting. The Château, secluded in its forest, had an exquisite chapel, ablaze with gilded chandeliers. But it was with tears and sobbing that the family let their darling go. Louise, exquisite and resigned, stood proudly at the altar; a compliant victim, a political pawn. Her father had pondered long and hard on the obvious advantage of this marriage. What an alliance! France, Belgium and England: to be cemented threefold. And then at her leaving, he shut himself in his study and wept. Turning to Trognon, who stood beside him, he confessed that he should not have allowed this sacrifice.

Louise tried to cheer her spirits as the berline whisked her away to Belgium. She stifled a sob. Her King sat silent with pursed lips as he looked out on the endless Normandy plains of harvested corn. Their honeymoon! She hung her head and passed the hours revising her mother's list of instructions: 'Satisfy the wishes of your husband. Endear yourself to his family and his country. Don't make hasty judgments. Refrain from spontaneity. Never laugh in public. Be neither haughty nor familiar. Never forget that you represent France...' It was a long list.

Her younger sister, Marie-Christine, was dark haired, witty and vivacious. She had quickly become an acclaimed sculptress. Her marble statue of Jeanne d'Arc was judged *'une œuvre de premier ordre, pleine d'idéa'*. Stalwart and proud, hands crossed over her chest, it was placed in the gallery of the statues and tombs of the Kings of France, at Versailles. In October 1837, the Princesse Marie married Duke Alexander of Würtemberg. Remarked the young Queen Victoria: 'He is somewhat colossal, I own, but well-proportioned and good-looking, I think.' A healthy son was born to them; but his mother's life of twenty-six years was cut short with galloping consumption. Little Prince Philippe was a special comfort to his grand-mother, Marie-Amélie, who was always devoted to him.

The Comte de Rumigny remembered a quixotic encounter with the doomed Princesse. He had lived on intimate terms with the Orléans family, watching the children grow up around him. One night, at Château Neuilly, he had heard a strange noise on the stairs. He leapt up in his scanty nightwear and, taking a pistol, dashed off to bar the way. A feeble light was reflected on the wall: 'Who goes there?' he cried. There was a laugh and a familiar voice came back: 'Do not worry, Général, put away your gun. Since you are there, come and help me straighten up Jeanne d'Arc. She is listing to one side.' Rumigny joined the Princesse. She smiled at him under her nightcap, and led him to her studios. She explained how she could not sleep; she had been worrying about her '*chère* Jeanne', who was tilting and could even collapse. Rumigny agreed that the exquisite heroine had lost her aplomb. The nocturnal Princesse and the gallant knight secured the damsel's balance. As they returned to their respective rooms, Princesse Marie said to the Comte: 'Thank you, my friend, you have saved my heroine. I will make you a gift of my scale model.' She kept her word.

Her own tomb in the Royal Chapel at Dreux, is sculpted by the versatile Lemaire. Raised on a pillow, Princesse Marie's head is turned to the right and to a replica, *en petit*, of her cherished Jeanne d'Arc; her long ingenious fingers touch her scalpel.

Although Louis Philippe could never compete with the artistic talents of his progeny, he shared an acute appreciation of all the arts. His hero, Henri IV, who had ruled two and a half centuries earlier, had also enjoyed a powerful penchant for the trowel. Paris had positively pulsed under his embellishments. His equestrian bronze statue was mounted on Pont Neuf, his favourite bridge, tactically close to the people. Melted down for the Revolution in 1792, it was speedily replaced with the Restoration.

Returning from his twenty-one years of exile, the then Duc d'Orléans, on October 20th, 1814, had written from Palais Royal to Abbé Montesquiou. Appointed to the new Secretary of State, the Abbé was in charge of the recovery of personal effects. Having listed various family items of value and sentiment that the Abbé would be kind enough to give him the pleasure of restoring, Louis Philippe added:

Allow me, my dear Abbé to add another request which I hold close to my heart; of which you talked with me on the first days of my arrival in Paris this last May. It is of a statue in white marble of Henri IV by the sculptor Prieur. This statue alone was exempted from the sale at Saint-Cloud by my grandfather; he had it removed from the gallery at Saint-Cloud, where it had stood between the two windows ... I repeat, there are few objects I desire to achieve as much as that one.*

By October 1832, Orléans and Nemours were again in battle, in the vanguard of Maréchal Gérard's incentive against Antwerp. An army of 70,000 men, with an Anglo-French agreement, succeeded in routing King William of Holland's stubborn siege. In the thick of the fighting, a bullet skimmed over Orléans' head; raising his hat, he exclaimed: 'One must be polite with new acquaintances.' Nemours sent his mother a close report of their skirmishes at Antwerp. She replied, December 1832,

Mon blond petit chéri.

Yesterday at midnight, I received your letter giving such a clear account of your '*baptême de feu*' ...

And later in the month she wrote:

My dear and beloved sons,

Yesterday your father brought a letter from Chartres (sic) to my room; he read it to me for I was so agitated that I could not read it myself. Continue to write frankly to him and give him all details. You cannot imagine how greatly confidences from you please him, your excellent father, who has such need of consolation ...

Adieu my beloved ones. I embrace and love you from the depth of my heart.

In your letters, address me not as Queen, but as mother; it is the title I prefer.

Marie-Amélie.

---

* Barthélémy Prieur had in fact carved this statue of Henri IV in alabaster. It is now exhibited in the Louvre. Prieur died in 1611, just months after his king's assassination in May 1610.

Louis Philippe had next seen fit to renege on his zeal for direct and personal government. He invited his long trusted adviser, Dupin, to take command. The offer was a thankless task and repudiated. Dupin, with his legal proclivities, preferred to sit on the fence. The Prince de Broglie, the shrewd and authoritative aristocrat, complied. He had always shown a firm sense of duty and shared Louis Philippe's trust in the *'entente cordiale'* with England. Maréchal Soult was persuaded to join the Cabinet; his position was nominal, he was no politician. But the final Minister, the young Adolphe Thiers, was fast becoming a brilliant speaker. De Broglie finally proclaimed that he could only agree to serve if François Guizot was included in the Ministry; an academic, a diplomat and another eloquent speaker, Guizot was further embellished by his enduring love affair with the sexually rampant Russian Princess Lieven. Having acquitted himself of his sole command, Louis Philippe rode out to the opening of the Parliamentary session at the Palais Bourbon with a light heart.

It was the morning of November 19th 1832. The King and his cortège crossed the Seine by the Pont Royal and stepped out on to the Quai d'Orsay. A shot rang out. Louis Philippe ducked over his saddle and then promptly stood in his stirrups. He saluted the cortège and the crowd of onlookers. There were huge cheers. A man had pushed out from the rue du Bac; levelling his muzzle, just yards from his target, he had fired. His pistol lay smoking on the ground, beside soldiers lining the route. The culprit, named Bergeron, was seized, but later released through lack of evidence. Louis Philippe entered the Chamber of Peers to deliver his opening address, his demeanour as calm and confident as always. This first attempted assassination of their new King passed almost unnoticed in the ubiquitous civic turmoil; but the incident incurred admiration throughout France. Louis Philippe's courageous spirit and sense of purpose was a fillip to his command.

The year 1833 was comparatively stable for France. The new ministry was recognised as an intelligent and competent body; the throne was in good repair. Prosperity appeared tangible, and was encouraged by Guizot's rousing call of *'enrichissez-vous!'* The fabric of Paris was being repaired and restored under Thiers' supervised works, on the Etoile, the Madeleine and the Place de la Concorde. Holding to his notion of trying to please, Louis Philippe had resurrected Napoleon on his column in the Place Vendôme, on July 25th. The occasion had been respectably attended, including the Royal Family. A remarkable reflection on the renewed calm of the city and a sanguine acceptance of 'slings and arrows of outrageous fortune'. But peace in Paris was always an illusion. At the December Parliamentary session, Louis Philippe delivered his warnings; disorder was fermenting from the 'Sociéte des Droits de l'Homme'. 'An increasing vigilance is still necessary; insensate passions and culpable manoeuvres are at work to undermine the foundations of social order.'

Godefroy Cavaignac, a genetic regicide whose mother had famously claimed him '*un Brutus*', was the ultimate rabid Republican. Such exacerbating rallying cries as 'The forty-second year of the French Republic'. 'Those who usurp sovereignty should be killed by free men'. 'Liberty must be watered with blood, not tears' were passed exultantly through the streets; but the Parisians, bored at last with old arguments, now turned aside from trouble. Yet the cancerous subversion of the secret societies was spreading; ringleaders were arrested, their archives confiscated. Meanwhile regular police reports of assassination plots to the King and his family left Louis Philippe shocked and dismayed.

In the spring of 1835, the two Ducs, d'Orléans and Nemours, were invited to London. With their upright and handsome bearing, they were enthusiastically welcomed by the English Royals and aristocracy. Their distinguished manners immediately dispelled the hackneyed notion that the French Monarchy was bourgeois. Bourgeois? The Orléans Court at the Tuileries? The livery and *équipage*: magnificent! The King: '*un grand seigneur*', with such style; a true Monarch of the day! His Queen: well versed and accomplished. Such exquisite Palace entertainment.

Nemours wrote to Marie-Amélie in colloquial style: 'Received everywhere *à merveille*, petted and fêted ad lib.' They were invited to Windsor Castle by King William IV and then to meet the Princess Victoria at Kensington Palace. In her sixteenth year, Nemours described her to his avid mother as small, but with beautiful eyes. Lord Palmerston, who lost no chance to deprecate the French, was constrained to write most favourably of the Princes to their mother.

Despite his pride in his children, the King was still plagued with civic disorder. It spread a rash across the country; worse still, surreptitious death threats were left constantly on his desk. His Cabinet had engendered more upheaval with their bickering and irritations. Guizot and Thiers, both petulant and provoking, were eased out of office. Maréchal Soult left his post in tears; de Broglie resigned. Louis Philippe approached the well-attuned Comte Louis-Mathieu Molé and, once again, Soult. Prince de Broglie next agreed to be both Prime Minister and First Minister. 'Why do you need a Prime Minister?' queried Louis Philippe. 'Are you not in agreement with each other? And am I not in agreement with you?' Louis Philippe then voted in Maréchal Mortier, Duc de Trévise, his old friend from the days of Dumouriez's army. Incapable of public speaking, he was removed within weeks. Guizot meanwhile had flourished on his polished speaking; even though Thiers had assured selected audiences that 'In politics, Monsieur Guizot is stupid'. Exasperated with such puerile shenanigans, the Monarch looked back on his six months of shrewd self-rule with amazement. How he missed Talleyrand with his concise synopses. His Ambassadorial term had ended the previous November and he was now happily ensconced in his Paris Hôtel with his long distance love and companion, Dorothea de Dino; the forty-year-old Duchesse with her eighty-two-year-old Prince.

Derision walked hand in hand with the King's hard-earned achievements. The earlier familiarity of his street walkabouts and the spontaneous hailing and handshaking had since regurgitated in a stream of sarcastic caricature. Had Louis Philippe gone pear-shaped? 'Down with the Sleepy Pear!' Portrayed with a portly stomach, bandaged in a white waistcoat, luxuriant side-whiskers curling down his wobbly chin, his toupee awry ... any startled reader should turn to a portrait of the real King. Ary Scheffer, in 1835, depicts Louis Philippe in his sixty-third year; reassuringly handsome, with his distinguished features firmly in place.

Always kindly disposed, the King one day came across a ten-year-old boy at Neuilly. He was attempting to draw, on a park door with a piece of chalk, the face of the King. It was caricatured as 'a sleepy old pear'. Louis Philippe approached him and, gently taking the crayon, said, 'You are holding it wrong – try it this way,' and he completed the drawing. Turning to the confused and blushing child, he put into his hand a silver coin, clearly engraved with the 'pear'. The thrilled boy squealed loudly '*Vive* Louis

Philippe!' In his final exile, the unsung hero would quote: 'During my reign, I was victim of that weapon which Voltaire called "the printed lie" … a weapon which inflicts wounds that never heal, because they are poisoned.'

As he sat contemplating and sifting his troubles and solutions, in the early summer of 1835, Louis Philippe also listed his blessings. His cherished family, his wife and their restored homes. Marie-Amélie with her soothing words, her affection and sympathy could not always help or advise, but was swift to console him. To stay her recent nerves, she had twice visited their angelic Louise at Château Laeken in Belgium. The first-born son had died, a cruel blow. For King Leopold it was the second tragedy of a lost son. Now, in April 1835, another Leopold – Leo – *le petit trésor*' – was born. A joyful Marie-Amélie was truly enchanted by their first surviving grandchild.

And now, this handsome parade of their five sons riding out from the gates of Versailles profoundly recompensed all doubt and tragedy. The magnificent painting had just been completed by the acclaimed Horace Vernet. The proud King on his grey horse, with Orléans and Joinville to his right; Nemours on his left, with Aumale and the youngest, Montpensier (his father's 'Ton Ton'). A dazzling display in their military uniform: chests sashed in red, epaulettes gilded; their bicorne hats emblazoned and tasselled, worn front to back.

'*Le père*' or even '*l'excellent père*', they called him. They were all survivors. He bowed his head in relief and thanksgiving. The great military review was to be held on July 28th, the fifth anniversary of the Revolution. And Louis Philippe inwardly steeled himself.

25

Morbid wavelengths from the subversive secret society, 'Droits de l'Homme', had sent signals through the streets of Paris. It was July 1835. Exacerbated by the rejoicing and splendid military preparations for the fifth anniversary of the Revolution, the scars and reprisals were set to burst. Prince Joinville remembered Thiers, Minister of the Interior, thrusting into the 'Salon des Tuileries', on the morning of the parade, Tuesday July 28th. It was a perfect summer day. He beckoned the three Princes into a corner. 'He emphasised we would be protecting our father's life. He talked to us sternly, staring hard above his glasses. He cautioned us: "We have had advice from all sides. It is a question of a deadly machine, near to the Théâtre de l'Ambigu, on the Boulevard du Temple. This morning we have visited houses in the area – nothing!"' Should the King cancel his review? His three sons agreed he should be told, and, as to be expected, the King would not hear of any postponement. '*Veillez bien sur votre père*,' Thiers urged again; always uneasy on a horse, he was gravely disappointed not to have persuaded the Princes to abandon the procession.

The King, Princes, Aides-de-Camp and ministers rode out from the Tuileries at nine o'clock. Louis Philippe was tightly surrounded by the Royal party, severely on its guard. The accompanying Maréchals de France and Générals in full uniform and the civic dignitaries made a glistening cavalcade. Their assassins were ready, waiting at their post. At midday, the parade would pass below the half-shuttered window, into thunderous devastation and carnage. The murderous côterie – Joseph Fieschi, Pierre Morey and Theodore Pépin of the 'Droits de l'Homme' – were further labelled with prison sentences, Republican insurrection and a violent loathing of Louis Philippe.

Fieschi, a Corsican immigrant, had hired the third floor of an inconspicuous house at No. 42 Boulevard du Temple. Together with his one-eyed mistress, he had lain doggo since April (the month that Louis Philippe and his family would reserve for picking violets at Neuilly). The machine of death was now poised for its quarry. Twenty-five barrels of explosives were ready, mounted on an organ-like structure, to be discharged by a single match; this lethal contraption was subsequently referred to worldwide as the 'infernal machine'. The previous night, Fieschi and Morey, experienced in artillery, had placed it in the half-shuttered window. The invidious Morey had even adjusted it to ensure that Fieschi himself would be blown up.

The Royal procession trotted briskly through the purlieus of rue de Rivoli, Place Vendôme, the Madeleine and rue de la Paix. The crowds had been ecstatic, cheering and waving flags; it was a family outing and everywhere the children squealed and clapped. The long, thick line of troops had stood attentive to their Royal inspection. It was approaching noon. The sun blazed and sucked relentlessly on the torrid air from the overcrowded streets. On the boulevard du Temple, the usual bustling footways with the grocer, the wine-merchant and 'Le Café-Bar Fetti' was hushed by the heat. The majestic cavalcade headed slowly along the Boulevard Saint-Martin and towards its appointment with death. Louis Philippe, hedged around by his loyal Garde, called to them: 'You can be certain that if there is any danger it will be from a window and not from the street.' As they trotted up the rising ground of the Boulevard du Temple, the riders looked up fearfully at the passing windows. A sinister puff of smoke escaped from a third floor. '*Voilà, pour moi!*' cried the King to Joinville. And then it came: the explosive cluster of guns detonated with a shattering impulse over the procession and bystanders. Projectiles hurled down twenty feet to the ground from the smoking black window. '*Je suis touché,*' yelled Louis Philippe as a spent bullet grazed his forehead. His horse reared; it had been hit in the neck. Maréchal Mortier, his dearest friend, had been shot in the left ear; he fell dead, with his horse slain beneath him. Joinville seized his father's horse by the bridle; Orléans and Nemours followed, their swords swinging. Through the chaotic mêlée of death and panic, the howls of the dead and wounded, the riderless horses, the dust and smoke and the stench of blood, they made their way up the boulevard. Their first thought was that the gunfire would continue.

Louis Philippe stood in his stirrups and waved his plumed hat above the dazed and milling crowd. '*Me voici! Me voilà!*' His frenzied people pressed forward to touch their King and his horse. One young man in a red cap hissed loudly; the Comte de Rumigny slapped him to the ground with the flat of his sword. Thiers came upside, his white nankeen trousers covered in blood. Maréchal Mortier's blood, he assured them; he had fallen alongside, his hands lifted up, in silence. The Prince de Broglie, fastidiously removing a spent bullet from his cravat, agreed with the King's command that the procession should move on. The prescribed route for the Review continued for its full two hours. The renewed applause '*Vive le Roi!*' was immense. This was not a time of mourning.

The London *Times* correspondent sent a 'second express' from Paris, July 30th, 1835.

His Majesty's providential escape may fairly be ascribed to the circumstance of the diabolical engineers having neglected to make allowance for the King's not riding in the centre of the road, but keeping considerably nearer that side of it in which the line was stationed which happened to be under his immediate inspection.

Marie-Amélie had waited anxiously in her study at the Tuileries with her two daughters, Princesses Marie and Clémentine. They were set to join the King and Princes at the Chancellery in the Place Vendôme. The door burst open. It was Colonel Bayer. 'Madame – the King was fired on – he is not wounded – nor are the Princes – Maréchal Mortier is killed. The Boulevard du Temple is covered with the dead.' Marie-Amélie ordered her carriage, exclaiming: 'What horrible people! What a frightful Nation! We are surrounded by assassins!' The Chancellery was awash with sobbing and hysteria. The wives and sisters of the King's cortège gathered round Marie-Amélie in mounting panic, their festive clothes and headdresses awry, crushed, forgotten. The fear of the unknown had gripped them all, as they waited in wild circles for news of the dead and alive. And then, a distant rumble; it was the thunder of applause as the King approached, and finally dismounted. Marie-Amélie rushed to him. Strong and calm, he bent to embrace her and then wept on her shoulder. She touched her three sons again and again to check if they were wounded. She wrote to Aumale and Montpensier, staying at Château d'Eu: '*Tombez à genoux mes enfants, Dieu a sauvé votre père.*' The Royal Family, under her persuasion, held a funeral service on August 5th for the victims, at the Church of Saint Invalides. Eighteen were reported dead, a girl of fourteen, and twenty-two wounded. The Queen personally received the coffins at the portal door and later accompanied them to the vault.

Fieschi, Morey and Pépin were decapitated on February 19th 1836. It is recorded that Fieschi, even though gruesomely wounded, revelled in the drama of the trial. The terraced house, No. 42 boulevard du Temple, was demolished and subsequently resurrected. From 1856 to 1869, it was lived in by Gustave Flaubert, where he wrote his acclaimed *L'Education Sentimental*, the study of an ineffectual anti-hero. Today's honey-stone façade is embellished with a simple stone plaque, to commemorate the *'cher maître'*.

Two successive assaults on Louis Philippe by lunatic loners do not even appear in the indexes of his biographers. On June 25th, 1836, Louis Alibaud made his attempt, afterwards claiming he had wished to rid his country of a tyrant King. At six o'clock in the evening, Louis Philippe, together with his wife and sister, had left the Tuileries in their yellow berline, with its newly adapted armoured panels. The six horses reached the causeway by the Pont Royal, when a ruffian stepped from the crowd and thrust a gun, disguised as a cane walking-stick, on to the carriage door frame. He discharged it at the King and narrowly missed. On their destined arrival at Neuilly, wadding was found burrowed in the Royal toupee. The annual July review was cancelled. Louis Philippe did not desist.

Always sensitive to European reaction, he was dismayed by a sharp put-down from Vienna. Both the Archduke Charles of Austria and his chief adviser, Prince Metternich, pronounced an end to any marriage project between the Duc d'Orléans and the Archduchess Theresa. Orléans and Nemours had just completed a rapturous visit to Vienna, charming the Royals and eligible Archduchesses with their looks and breeding. The Archduchess Theresa had been openly attracted to the dazzling Orléans; until the formidable Archduchess Sophie, the matrix of the family, had taken her aside. Theresa was duly warned of the Orléans regularly being fired upon in their carriages by ruthless regicides. The appalling terrors endured by Marie Antoinette and her plain little niece, Marie-Louise, were also detailed to the dismayed Theresa. The Archduke Charles, on hearing the news of Alibaud's attempt on the King's life, bade the two Princes a gracious rebuff, salving their humiliation with a gift of a fine horse each.

Louis Philippe, looking old and tired, took a month's holiday in September, at Château d'Eu, with his family. The verdant open spaces and peace of Upper Normandy cast a balm. They had no visitors and took long walks by the sea and in their surrounding beech glades. The anguish of lurking dangers receded from Louis Philippe's mind. In the evening it was charades, the favourite family game. Marie-Amélie, with her Neapolitan blood, astounded her children, the aides-de-camp, tutors and valets with her vivacity and mimicry. The idyll soon ended. The Duc d'Orléans was called back to Mascara, in the barren deserts of Algeria. To his mother's grievous distress, he was first shot in the thigh and next contracted dysentery and nearly died. Her sons were all to be captivated by Algeria. Their mother shuddered; she imagined the heat and suffocating sands, the tortuous, winding little roads crowded with negresses touting their wares, the ramshackle cafés, thronged with those strange men in huge turbans...

Despite being curiously admiring of and even amused by Adolphe Thiers, Louis Philippe saw his advance over six months as negligible. The economic recovery had trundled along since the end of 1833, but no mooted tax reductions had been implemented. He had no quarrel with Thiers sucking olives in Cabinet and spitting out the stones in his presence; but the small man's crass initiative in wheedling an Austrian or even a Spanish bride for the Orléans Princes spelt Thiers' dismissal.

Comte Molé, at fifty-five years of age, became Louis Philippe's new Prime Minister in August 1836. He was described by Disraeli as 'A grand *seigneur*, of the highest breeding, excellent talents, very general information, a complete political culture...' Marie-Amélie had always liked Molé; he had dignity and listened to her. He was to hold a stable pole position in Louis Philippe's Cabinet until 1839. Derided by his peers for having no policies, he pursued a pragmatic course of prosperity at home and peace with Europe; the very ideals held by Louis Philippe, who kept his distance from the workings of this able Minister. He had heeded Thiers' earlier prognosis that he, Louis Philippe, was constantly rocking the boat, getting up and seizing the rudder and upsetting the constitutional balance. But he had been urgently assured that Europe would be happier with his hand on the rudder than that of the hotheaded Thiers.

Molé sized up to his first session of the Chamber on December 27th. As

Louis Philippe and his three elder sons crossed the Quai des Tuileries, a pistol shot was fired into their carriage. They arrived at Palais Bourbon, spattered with blood and splintered glass. Loud cheers. The resolute King read his speech from the throne. It was these assassination attempts that injected fresh loyalty and enthusiasm for the Orléans Monarchy. A young ruffian called Meunier was arrested. He justified his crime with an unexpected literacy: 'What I have read has taught me that the Orléans have always made France unhappy.' Louis Philippe saw fit to commute his death sentence and had him exiled to America.

With the issue of the twenty-six-year-old Prince Royal's marriage still pending, a bride was finally found. Madame Adélaïde, through her determined forage among European Ambassadors, had been offered the perfect choice for her nephew: the Princess Hélène de Mecklemburg Schwerin. Intelligent, graceful and cool, she made her debut at Château de Fontainebleau on May 29th, 1837, for preliminary marriage rites. It was only Marie-Amélie whose heart secretly rebelled against her son's alliance with a German Protestant. Louis Philippe was delighted with the procedures, as each civil, Catholic and Protestant ceremony followed the next, in the chapels and great drawing-rooms of Fontainebleau. His only gripe had been that he had declaimed against Napoleon's bed, finding it too soft.

On June 4th, in brilliant sunshine, to the cheering of an unusually exultant Paris, the dazzling wedding cortège headed down the Champs-Elysées. Louis Philippe and his sons, together with the newlywed Prince Royal, rode on horseback. The Queen and the newly acclaimed Duchesse d'Orléans, with the Princesses, followed in an open carriage; the young girls' heads were elegantly framed in delicate straw hats and swaying white marabou feathers. It was barely three weeks earlier that Louis Philippe, walking in the Botanical Gardens together with two Ministers, an ADC, and the Prefect of Police, had been jeered at close up by mocking bystanders. Their leering faces, so full of evil intent, had shocked the small Royal entourage.

It was at Versailles, on June 10th, that the Prince Royal and his elegant Duchesse finally appeared at a banquet for 1,500 people. They enchanted all with their vivacity and their friendly greeting. There was a performance of Molière's *Le Misanthrope* in the magnificently restored and gilded theatre. The entire Palace glittered with lights and candles and women emblazoned with jewels. Louis Philippe's restoration work was not yet fully achieved; but the State Rooms were sumptuously completed. His personally orchestrated 'Gallery of Battles' and the 'Gallery of Busts, Statues and Tombs' had been reconstructed from the wounds of the Revolution. Indeed, he had been working on Versailles since 1833; not only had he spent 23 million francs from his own purse, but had the grace to suggest that any imperfections on his part might be remedied by future aspirants. He adored such projects; although his removal of a livid red marble fireplace with bronze rococo decoration from Marie Antoinette's bedroom was deplored.

'I hate war,' he had once declared to Guizot. 'I do not care for either gambling or hunting, and I have no mistresses ... All I want to do is to give employment to workers; to encourage the Arts and to leave beautifying monuments behind me for France.' To this effect, he oversaw plans and estimates often late at night. He never felt a more worthwhile 'fellow' than when talking with artisans who would lean down to him from their ladders. Indeed, at this time, at his dazzling son's wedding, Louis Philippe stood unquestionably high in public opinion. The stalwart survivor of the Fieschi débâcle! The King of the French was held a hero.

Several now commented on how strongly Louis Philippe resembled Louis XIV, his Bourbon ancestor; in their respective age and maturity, their facial traits had fused. The high forehead, the pronounced Roman nose, the quizzical gaze and the firm, hard lips denoted their genetics. Louis Philippe's maternal grandfather was, after all, the Duc de Penthièvre, the illegitimate grandson of Louis XIV. The acclaimed English diarist Charles Greville would always refer to Louis Philippe's fine head and this close resemblance. But the Comtesse de Boigne added her sour note to this occasion. She pointed out that Louis Philippe had sat beneath a large picture, inscribed in gold letters: '*Le roi gouverne par lui-même.*' On that particular night, he reigned triumphantly.

26

It was next the turn of the Orléans' fourth son, the gallant Henri, Duc d'Aumale, to step into the limelight. Like his elder brothers, he had developed a passion for Algeria: the arresting drama of the deserts; the guerrilla tactics through the gorges and the danger of the unknown. Aumale was also captivated by girls; and notably the delectable Parisian actress, Alice Ozy. She would disguise herself discreetly as his younger brother, Montpensier. Alas, loyal to her profession, she found another. Aumale, dumbfounded with grief, wrote poignantly: 'I love you more, since you love me no more!' He hared back to his beloved deserts, to resume action against the battling Emir Abd el-Kadr.

And then it was Joinville to hold court with his even more exotic persuasions. Having joined the Navy and distinguished himself in 1838, with skirmishes around the Gulf of Mexico, he next landed in Brazil, complete with glossy black beard. He asked for an audience with Emperor Pedro I, and later, during their conversation, had the unexpected chance of meeting the sister. The Princess Françoise was stunning. Joinville, staring into her voluptuous dark eyes, was rooted to the ground. He at once alerted his parents of his intention to marry the Brazilian beauty. Louis Philippe sent his Ambassador to the Emperor to formalise matters. When the precipitate couple arrived at Brest, Joinville, in hearty mode, greeted the Harbour-Master: 'I bring home the sailor's wife. She is attractive, don't you think?' They were finally to marry in Rio de Janeiro on May 1st, 1843.

Princess Françoise startled the Tuileries with her hot, silky beauty and further amazed the lunch table when, sitting on the King's right hand, she broke into song. At a banquet that evening, she made a surprise request for 'parrot broth', in preference to the chicken bouillon. Louis Philippe was enchanted with her native caprices, but inwardly hoped that Aumale would not bring home a girl from Algeria. The young Queen Victoria was exceedingly taken with the 'Little Chica' on their future meeting at Château d'Eu. She was to note in her diary: '2nd September 1843 – Joinville amused us considerably... His wife, Chica, is delicious and lively. She has a beautiful figure and large chestnut eyes.'

By spring 1839, Molé's ministry was strangled by his Peers and by both Legitimists and Republicans. The boredom factor had taken hold. He resigned on 8th March. Guizot and Thiers both fought to lead a new ministry, but neither could agree to serve under the other. Finally Maréchal Soult was called in to support Thiers; by March 24th, there was still no elected Prime Minister. The opening of the Parliamentary Session was delayed until April 4th. As the ministers wrangled for power, the streets of Paris overflowed with redundant workers; the banks were closed. Louis Philippe looked on his broken Cabinet in deepest gloom.

On Sunday May 12th, a shot was heard. Fanatics from the underground 'Société des Saisons' had clogged up the rue Saint-Martin with barricades. Smashing up a closed armoury shop, they went off to shoot a few soldiers at the Palais de Justice. The incident halted all the petty prevarications of Louis Philippe's unformed Cabinet. He turned to Soult, both for his Prime Minister and his Foreign Minister. This promising appointment survived only to the end of the year. The Maréchal had been bamboozled by the East Mediterranean manoeuvres of Mehmet Ali, the Sultan of Egypt. Soult's seasoned military tactics had proved incompatible. The Anglo-Russian alliance and Anglo-French alliance were becoming dangerously stretched and beyond the old soldier's understanding. Meanwhile Thiers bored after the summer of enforced leisure and his historical reading, framed up once more to Louis Philippe. Thiers was always an experience; described by Lord Melbourne as 'a strange quicksilver man'.

Casualty, defeat, more wounds and blood; Louis Philippe looked to Thiers for a smidgen of deliverance. His bumptious Minister often had some improbable solution. Thiers, with his active passion for Napoleon, did indeed have a surprise suggestion: to send Prince Joinville off on his frigate to St Helena and collect the Emperor's corpse for burial in Paris. A venture that Thiers guessed rightly would sweep away the prevalent boredom of the people. An enduring affection for the dead warrior could still unite a disparate country. Consent was given by the British government for Napoleon's remains to be entombed beneath the massive dome of the Invalides.

On July 7th, 1840, Joinville set off on *La Belle Poule* with his friend and agent, the English officer Viscount Chabot. He was amazed to be assigned such an adventurous mission; although he complained to his father that whereas his brothers were winning glory in Algeria, he himself was acting as a humble undertaker. Rather by sea than rail! Despite the growing railroad mania, progress could prove accident-prone. Charles Greville had noted on his first trip from Birmingham in 1837 that his initial nervousness from 'a feeling of being run away with' had soon subsided. Despite the few stinking puffs, he was comfortably seated in a sort of chariot and found the speeding panorama delightful. In that same year, Marie-Amélie had taken her first rail journey from Paris to St Germain; it was considered too dangerous for Louis Philippe. Rail accidents lurked. The tragic rail disaster on May 8th, 1842 was to shake the Nation. On a fast return trip from Versailles to Paris, forty-eight passengers were burnt to death. An axle had snapped; the inner doors of the compartments had been locked and set fire to by the mob. A pleasure outing for 700 Parisians to see the glorious fountains had ended in carnage.

Joinville and his crew sailed down the Atlantic Ocean, passing Tenerife, where they took on food and water. With a west tack, they headed to Bahia on the Brazilian East Coast. Joinville looked out keenly for the mouth of the Conceição River; he had heard talk of game in its tropical vegetation. With a few officers, he took the '*vapeur*' up the waterway. They could see no trace of life. Then, suddenly, toucans and parrots swooped above. In the light of the moon they next saw the dense forest bristle with guns and sabres. Their little party was surrounded. (Joinville recalled the attack on Captain Cook by cannibals.) Seized and disarmed, they were dragged into a clearing. With their guns discharged, it appeared the savages deemed them unworthy of attack. The captain of *La Belle Poule* mustered his crew for an uninterrupted crossing to St Helena, marooned in the far South Atlantic.

An albatross escorted them as they neared the towering black volcanic rock; battered by monstrous high winds, the stark and forested isle was covered with a permanent cap of snow. Joinville docked his boat at the modest jetty. It was October 8th. The Governor was ill; his place was taken by the Commandant of the troops, Colonel Trelawny, who had a passion for genealogy. An emotional crowd had collected to watch the tomb lowered down the mountain. But the body had first been exhumed and allowed open for two minutes. After nineteen years it had remained perfectly preserved. To the roll of drums and a funeral march, the British infantry stowed the tomb in the longboat of *La Belle Poule*. The troops lined up along the shore in a motionless salute, as the parting boat fired its cannon. The women of St Helena had wept to see their hand-stitched *tricolore* tent sheltering the Emperor's resting place. A spectacular sunset had blazed on the scene. The crew in white with black crêpe armbands, set sail for France. Dusk fell – and a deep quiet. Disembarking at Cherbourg, after five months at sea, there was consternation over the 'official catafalque'. Joinville found it unacceptably ugly; he had the whole recovered in a mourning drape of purple velvet.

The awesome ceremonial to mark the tomb's arrival at the Invalides took place on the morning of December 15th. The people, nursing memories of their quixotic warrior, had waited in eight degrees of frost. Victor Hugo's aperçu that the whole of Paris had 'flowed to one side of the city, like liquid in a leaning vase' captured the compulsive drama. It was noted that Queen Marie-Amélie was not present. Had she succumbed to a diplomatic fever? Her reticence towards the reckless ups and downs of the Emperor's fortunes still held.

A huge and silent crowd pressed relentlessly down the Champs-Elysées to the esplanade of the Invalides. Lone cries of '*Vive l'Empereur*' floated on the freezing air. Finally the funeral chariot, drawn by sixteen horses, smothered in cloth of gold and nodding white plumes, halted before the great dome. There was a muffled salute of rumbling guns and deadened drums. Joinville stood before Louis Philippe with a formal salute.

'Sire! I present to you the body of the Emperor Napoleon.'

'I receive him in the name of France.'

The Emperor's sword and bicorne hat were laid on the coffin. The obsequious embellishments of this questionable hero continued for another twenty years. A sarcophagus of red porphyry was eventually placed on a massive pedestal of green granite, hewn from the Vosges Mountains; the whole was displayed in a specially designed circular crypt. The ultimate detail of the emperor's burial involved securing him in six contiguous coffins; the first to envelope his body in tin, the second in mahogany, the third and fourth in lead, the fifth in ebony and the sixth in oak. Was there a lingering hope of preserving the body into eternity? Or an unspoken fear that the wily rascal might escape again?

Had Thiers' grand idea been merely a brilliant spectacle to divert the people from the winter cold? Louis Philippe was pleased; Europe would be impressed. This homage to Napoleon, now revived. It had proved a successful gesture. But there emerged a Republican undercurrent of disapproval; why had the Monarchy showered the ceremony with gold and tinsel? A simple parade would have been preferable.

His dumpy figure, hat in hand, Thiers would walk around the tomb, contemplating his hero's greatness; the very compassion of the man! He recalled that perceptive letter written to the widow of Admiral Brueys; he who had been killed on his quarterdeck by a cannon-ball. Leading an expedition to Egypt and the disastrous battle of the islet of Aboukir, Brueys had cried out: 'An Admiral ought to die giving orders.' From Napoleon's 'confidential correspondence', Thiers had read the moving letter written after the Peninsular War.

'...I feel warmly for your grief. The moment which separates us from the object we love, is terrible; we feel isolated on earth ... We press our children to our hearts; tears and more tender sentiments arise; and life becomes bearable for their sakes. Yes, Madame, they will open the fountains of your heart; you will watch their childhood; educate their youth; you will speak to them of their father ... After having resumed your interest in life by the chord of maternal love, you will perhaps feel some consolation from the friendship and warm interest which I shall ever take in the widow of my friend.'

From 1836 to 1840, Molé, Thiers and Guizot had jockeyed in turn for prime positions in the King's Cabinet. It was Guizot who had finally headed the political seesaw through the last seven years of the July Monarchy. Louis Philippe judged him the fundamental command of political management; he was the star of the podium, with his fighting delivery and his voice – arresting, eloquent and remarkably resonant. Louis Philippe and his accomplished Parliamentarian were in transparent cahoots over the mission for prosperity at home and peace abroad. Stendhal had already praised the progress of country development under Louis Philippe: wide ownership of land, houses being built in towns and villages, and the boon development of local branch roads. Political reform with universal suffrage was not in the King's remit, with his suppression of revolution the ultimate concern. The contract between the King and his Ministers and their established conservation policies was locked in their agreement. Their dictum of peace and prosperity was imperial and not to be disturbed. It was noticed that the poet politico Alphonse de Lamartine was agitating for '*La Réforme*'. He complained aloud and vociferously that France was 'bored to death'. Nothing had been achieved by the King and his Minister with their duo dictum of conservation. '*Rien, rien, rien!*' screamed the Opposition, writhing for a fight. But Guizot had his majority. 'The people yearn for events,' he said dismissively.

The Prince Royal, the Duc d'Orléans, relayed his acute concerns to Ary Scheffer in 1840. 'The present epoch is prosperous and peaceful, but it is too dull not to become soon stagnant and consequently corrupt; innumerable vulgar and mean little interests seethe under an apparently united surface, which can only be disturbed by the most violent upheavals.' The underworld of Paris was already rife with secret plotting, provocative pamphlets and plans for riotous action.

Louis Philippe, nearing seventy years of age, was comfortably set in his ways. A vigorous defence of property and family was the basis of a strong society, and he held them both firmly under his watch. Universal suffrage! Springing from the womb of dishevelled democracy! It made him shudder. The social changes, the alteration of laws and powers; the instability, the uncertainty, the flood of disorder! He would remain the last of the Enlightened Despots. He was reported by visitors to the Tuileries to have a youthful energy that defied the years. He moved his large frame with ease and his conversation was lively, flavoured with wit and tact. His anecdotes and observations of the human predicament were particularly entertaining. His devoted sister, Adélaïde, with her own political acumen, would sit with her little dog and a parrot, in an adjoining room, tending his correspondence. His family circle had been completed by two gratifying grandsons: the Comte de Paris in 1838 and the Duc de Chartres in 1840.

It was on July 2nd, 1842, that the mother of these young Ducs, Hélène, was escorted by the Duc d'Orléans to Plombières to take the waters. Having settled her, Orléans returned to the Tuileries and then to Saint-Omer to take up a command. On July 9th, he dined with Marie-Amélie and his father at Neuilly. The next day, he returned with an enormous bouquet for his mother. It was her birthday. 'From all the family,' he said. Marie-Amélie scrupulously noted her son's last precious visits in her diary.

11th July – Again came to lunch and spent the evening with us. Very busy with his command.

12th July – He arrived at 4pm. We talked about Hélène and her health, about which he was tormented ... on the elections and other matters – always he ended – 'Well we always finish in agreement on the important issues.' We walked in the park – him, Victoire, Clémentine, Aumale and me. He had never been so gay, so brilliant, so affectionate to me. 'Come,' I said and took his arm. We entered the salon – a lot of people to dinner. He stayed talking until ten o'clock and came to wish me goodnight. 'You will come and see us tomorrow before you leave?' '*Peut-être!*' he replied.

The following morning, July 13th, the Duc d'Orléans ordered a low and speedy phaeton with two young horses; purportedly not fully trained in traffic, they were to drive him from Paris to Neuilly. Orléans was not convinced by the équipage, but time was short. He was anxious to please his loving mother, and to take leave of his father, on his way to inspect regiments at Saint-Omer. In he jumped with a little groom on the dicky seat behind him. At the Etoile, the horses grew restive; a few paces ahead, at the Porte-Maillot, the postilion's horse took fright and galloped off; the phaeton and pair raced ahead. Orléans stood up in the open carriage. Were the horses out of control? 'No, *Monseigneur* – I am still driving them.' Could he hold them back? 'No, *Monseigneur.*' The Duc, with his knees held fast together, jumped impulsively on to the footway of the Avenue de la Grand Armée. The little groom was aghast; the Prince Royal lay crumpled and motionless; he was carried unconscious into a humble grocer's shop. An ironic twist of fate: a grocer had come to the questionable help of his despairing forebears, Louis XVI and Marie Antoinette.

The Royal Family, waiting at Château Neuilly for Orléans, and the family lunch, were alerted: "The Duc had fallen and was slightly hurt." A cruel euphemism; the Duc lay unconscious on a straw mattress in a windowless storeroom. His skull was fractured; noted Victor Hugo in his journal: 'Broken under the skin, like a plate'. The Queen, sensing the worst, started on foot for Paris. Louis Philippe caught up with her in the carriage. They drew up at a scene of horror. With a blunt razor and goblets grabbed from a beer parlour, their dying son was being bled. Marie-Amélie fell to her knees, weeping and praying at Orléans' side. Monsieur Trognon, the sons' old tutor, stood by helplessly. He would always remember this mother in her darkest hour. As Marie-Amélie waged with her faith, she called out in anguish: '*Je ne dirai pas c'est trop, mais c'est beaucoup.*' Louis Philippe stood motionless, his eyes fixed on his doomed and precious heir. '*Si c'était moi au lieu de lui!*' he exclaimed through his gasps and sobbing. State dignitaries and officers squeezed through the hot and crowded room and finally the Curé of Neuilly. He administered the last sacrament. It had taken the Prince Royal six hours to die. The Queen kissed her son's lips. She wished his soul might pass into her own; it had always grieved her that his faith was not as strong as she would have preferred.

Their second son, the Duc de Nemours, was shattered. Chartres had been more than a brother to him. Their elder sister, Louise, Queen of the Belgians, wrote a long and emotional letter to her niece, the young Queen Victoria. 'He was the *head* and the *heart* and *soul* of the whole family.' Mourning for the Duc d'Orléans, Ferdinand Louis-Charles, was widespread throughout France and Europe. Ever the sceptic, Lord Palmerston deemed Orléans' irreparable loss 'a calamity for France and Europe'. The proud and devoted younger brother, the Prince de Joinville, made the poignant reminder to all compatriots that for a decade they had seen Orléans as the '*chef de domain*' – 'the leader of the great days to come'.

A few weeks later, the Government proposed that two statues should be raised to Orléans; one in Paris and one in Algeria. There was considerable debate on where in Paris the Duc should be best placed. The Queen was asked for her opinion; a statue in Algeria certainly, where he had given plenty of service in battle. However, her son had been left too little time to expand his qualities around Paris. In her opinion, a position could not be fully justified. Her impartial reasoning and distaste for exclusive flattery was appreciated. Despite her diffidence, a fine bronze figure of Orléans on his prancing horse was placed in the Louvre courtyard. Sculpted by the Italian Baron Charles Marochetti, it was removed in 1848 to Versailles at his father's discretion. Finally, it reached a terrace of the Château d'Eu, where it has remained, facing the South Wing.

Another solemn quandary was next confined to Louis Philippe's study, with his former advisor, Thiers. It concerned the issue of the Regency for Orléans' son and heir, the Comte de Paris. His mother, Hélène, Duchesse d'Orléans, was a German, a Protestant, and now a widow, tasked with the care and upbringing of her two sons. Yet she had always expected to be Regent for her four-year-old son in the event of his father's death. In 1840, Orléans had the foresight to leave a testament, principally that his son and heir should be brought up a Catholic and that he was strongly opposed to any woman being appointed Regent. He added: 'The Head of the French Nation should always be ready to mount his horse within a quarter of an hour.' Thiers assured Louis Philippe that he should put forward the Duc de Nemours as a good and competent Regent. The shy and diffident Duc had already been constrained to marry; in wrath and torment, he had broken with his dancing girl for Victoire, Princesse de Saxe-Cobourg, described as clever, charming and as fresh as *'un petit bouton de rose'*. Their marriage had taken place on April 27th, 1840, at Saint-Cloud.

Meanwhile, Marie-Amélie played lovingly with her three bereft grandsons: Louis Philippe, Comte de Paris, Robert, Duc de Chartres and Prince Philippe of Würtemberg, their four-year-old cousin. The boys were seemingly unfazed by their great loss; except for Philippe, son of the tragic Princesse Marie, who came sobbing to Marie-Amélie: 'Isn't it true, Grandmamma, that Paris has no Papa and I have no Mamma?'

A refreshing stay *en famille*, at Château d'Eu, was called for. Louis Philippe's custom-built, charabanc rolled through the peace and green swathes of Normandy. Still, the soothing balm of the open country could not allay the Orléans' shock and sadness. At Eu, the King had become profoundly morose; his mood irritable and even angry. He was prone to fits of temper and to uninterrupted monologues before his family, his staff and his officers. A distinguished guest, the Comte de Saint-Aulaire, the former Ambassador to

Vienna, was talking companionably with the Royal couple in a room adjoining the Galérie de Guise. The doors were open to the orderly officers. Louis Philippe suddenly stood and called loudly to Marie-Amélie, who was sewing in a corner: 'There are some who regard me as a usurper; but you know, don't you, that I am not a usurper!' The Queen, tears welling up, went and shut the doors to the orderlies. Her precaution and silence aggravated the King and he wrenched the doors open, forgetting his usual tenderness and respect to his wife. He protested at the top of his voice: 'And why do you not wish me to say in front of our officers that I am not a usurper? I insist upon saying it and I insist upon everybody hearing me. No, I am not a usurper!'

Louis Philippe had always found Saint-Aulaire a rewarding sounding board. The consummate diplomat was a good listener and knew of the King's strong aversion to European intrigues and skirmishes in the Mediterranean. The ultimate pacifist, he had once confided to Saint-Aulaire on the provocations of his Minister Thiers. 'You must be aware that I will not allow myself to be carried too far by my little Minister. Basically, he wants war and I don't; and if he leaves me no alternative, I will break with him rather than break with Europe.'

The poet Alfred de Musset – a close friend of Duc Ferdinand since childhood – was to evoke the scene with his poem, *Le Treize Juillet*.

Le Treize Juillet

*Ces stances ont été écrites pour l'anniversaire de la mort
(d'un accident de voiture à Neuilly) du duc d'Orléans, fils
de Louis Philippe, qui s'était produite le 13 juillet 1842.
Elles ont été publiées dans la Presse le 18 juillet 1843. Le
duc d'Orléans avait le condisciple de Musset au Lycée
Henri IV. Il mourut à l'âge de trente-deux ans.*

XVII

*Hélas! mourir ainsi, pauvre prince, à trente ans
Sans un mot de sa femme, un regard de sa mère,
Sans avoir rien pressé dans ses bras palpitants!
Pas même une agonie, une douleur dernière!
Dieu seul lut dans son cœur l'ineffable prière
Que les anges muets apprennent aux mourants.*

XIX

*Il aimait nos plaisirs, nos maux l'ont attristé.
Dans ce livre éternel où le temps est compté,
Sa main avec la nôtre avait tourné la page.
Il vivait avec nous, il était de notre âge.
Sa pensée était jeune, avec l'ancien courage;
Si l'on peut être roi de France, il l'eût été.*

XXI

*Certes, c'eût été beau, le jour où son épée,
Dans le sang étranger lavée et retrempée,
Eût au pays natal ramené la fierté;
Pendant que de son art l'enfant préoccupée,
Sur le seuil entr'ouvert laissant la Charité,
Eût fait, avec la Muse, entrer la Liberté.*

XXVI

*Neuilly! charmant séjour, triste et doux souvenir!
Illusions d'enfants, à jamais envolées!
Lorsqu'au seuil du palais, dans les vertes allées,
La reine, en souriant, nos regardait courir,
Qui nous eût dit qu'un jour il faudrait revenir
Pour y trouver la mort et des têtes voilées!*

XXV

*C'était là que la Mort attendait sa victime;
Il en fut épargné dans les déserts brûlants
Où l'Arabe fuyant, qui recule à pas lents,
Autour de nos soldats, que la fièvre décime,
Rampe, le sabre au poing, sous les buissons sanglants.
Mais il voulut revoir Neuilly; ce fut son crime.*

215

27

The Duc de Nemours now had to forego his exercises in Algeria. His place was beside his father, taking up his brother's role at receptions and military reviews; promoting himself and his lovely Duchesse, Victoire, as popular assets to the citizens of Paris. Joinville and Aumale also resumed their duties. Embarking at Brest, they sailed together on *La Belle Poule* to Lisbon, where they separated: Aumale to command at Tittery, a province in Algeria; and Joinville to continue down the Ivory Coast to Rio de Janeiro where he married his Chica, the beguiling Princesse Françoise de Brazil. A tremor of jealousy darted through Europe; the Orléans had spread themselves everywhere!

Aumale next found himself caught unawares in the middle of the desert by the ace warrior Abd el-Kadr. The young Duc hurled his troops into a rash and brilliant cavalry attack on the Emir's headquarters. This daring raid set the Presse alight. Aumale was promptly awarded a Lieutenant-Généralcy. His father wrote assuring him that the Nation and the Army were 'electrified'. He enclosed three articles, which he had found the most striking, with the added compliment: 'On this occasion I have set aside my rule of not reading them.'

On his subsequent leave at Neuilly, the young hero insisted on treating the family to an Arab feast of roast sheep and conserves. Louis Philippe was not won over. 'Aumale, I prefer my own dinner. I am for civilization.' He fell to pondering on Algeria and the advantages to France of its annexation; notably trading profits and an excellent training ground for French officers. The tribe wars largely curtailed; justice and safety introduced; and productivity increased. Algeria had benefited by its conquest; but as his Minister, Guizot, would point out: 'It requires the constant presence of a French army.' To include all the King's excellent sons.

Despite the tragedy of their adored brother's death, life rolled on for his siblings. On April 28th, 1843, the beautiful Princesse Clémentine married her sturdy Prince Augustus de Saxe-Cobourg and Gotha, at Saint-Cloud.

Happy reverberations next rolled in from Prince Joinville and his Princess Françoise in Rio. Another unexpected departure had evolved through sister Louise and her close friendship with the young Victoria. The two Queens had been hatching a plan for the English Queen to stay at Château d'Eu. Her Prince Consort would accompany her in the steam yacht, the *Victoria and Albert*. They would first make visits along the English coast, at the end of August, and then continue from Plymouth across to Normandy.

Victoria was extremely fond of Louise's husband Prince Leopold of the Belgians; he was her uncle. His sister was her mother, the widowed and ill-humoured Duchess of Kent. Victoria had little love for her. Staying with her Royal niece at Buckingham Palace, Louise wrote to Marie-Amélie:

> July 10th, 1843
>
> I will tell you in strictest confidence that Victoria is counting on seeing you and 'the *Père*' at Eu. It is important you understand that this plan to visit would be a great satisfaction for the 'excellent *Père*'; that he knows nothing in advance and that it should be a real surprise.

A month went by; there had been grumbling imbroglios between the English Ministers over Ireland and Spain. Again Louise wrote from the Palace:

> August 13th
>
> The voyage appears almost certain. It should be necessary perhaps to advise the 'excellent *Père*' on several points. He should not talk politics; Victoria never talks politics.

Indeed her recently retired Prime Minister, Lord Melbourne, had also warned her not to talk politics, with the French King; although he had greatly approved of her visit. Sir Robert Peel, her new Prime Minister and younger Minister for Foreign Affairs, Lord Aberdeen, were also intrinsically happy that under the young Queen's own initiative, the visit to Eu should be arranged for September 2nd.

Louis Philippe was totally entranced that the Queen of England was to stay in his historic family home. A triumphant turn! The very '*entente cordiale*' that he had long nurtured. The Prince Consort was not so convinced by his impetuous young wife's latest idol; this old King, overflowing with repartee, had clearly taken her fancy. And he, Prince Albert, had only just snuffed Victoria's romantic penchant for that old rogue in the Caucasus – Shamil, the Imam of Daghestan! His letters to Victoria – 'O honoured Queen' – described how he was at war with Russia; endless invaders besieging his valleys; of wives and children with no food; of no respite from the bitter cold. 'O Queen, bring us aid.' It is doubted that Victoria was ever privileged to open and read Shamil's rousing spiels.

Louise, the architect of this much-vaunted rendezvous at Eu, developed more niggling fears for her father's deportment towards the young Queen. She reiterated to Marie-Amélie that he should be natural, without ceremony; like he normally was. Louise impressed on her mother that it was the *Père* whom Victoria wished to meet most.

The *Père* was now constrained to make Château d'Eu especially comfortable for the esteemed visit. Sixty extra beds were ordered from Neuilly; more silver, more porcelain, more pictures and more carpets arrived from the Royal repositories. An Eudois hotelier, August Lecarbonnier, offered to retain rooms at a modest rate, in the event of an overspill of guests. Queen Victoria and Prince Albert were to be accompanied by a formidable suite, headed by Sir Robert Peel and Lord Aberdeen. Both now mollified towards the Anglo-French '*entente cordiale*', they made a more courteous and compliant duo after the imperious former Foreign Minister, Lord Palmerston. The party of family and friends included the Wellesleys, the Cannings, Lord Liverpool, Lord Cowley, General Anson and Lord de la Warr, Queen Victoria's Grand Chamberlain. She had chosen her maid of honour from one of Lord Ravensworth's eight 'Liddell' daughters. Sir James Clarke, her mother's dependable doctor, completed the party. The Commander of the steam yacht – the *Victoria and Albert* – was the Lord Adolphus Fitzclarence, one of the ten children fathered by William IV with the actress Dorothea Jordan; as a peripheral member of the Queen's family, he had willingly charged himself with his niece's voyage, to follow on from his father – 'The Sailor King'. At Cherbourg, it had been arranged that Joinville should be taken on board to accompany the Queen and her Consort up the French Coast. Dressed in his best uniform, the Prince noted that nobody seemed ready on the yacht deck, nor even dressed. He did not cut an especially good impression himself; Lady Canning set down her first sight of him, from her porthole. 'The Prince Joinville does not look in good health. He is very stooped, very big and tall, has good features and an abundant beard.' Joinville himself was induced to portray their Captain, the Lord Adolphus as: 'a good boy – but a ruddy complexion type, with an eye he has trouble keeping open'.

Around five o'clock on Saturday 2nd September, 1843, the *Victoria and Albert* neared Tréport. Guns fired to herald the Queen's arrival and an eager crowd swelled along the sides of the outer harbour. Louis Philippe, on standby with his twelve-seater *'voiture'*, drawn by eight horses, had been busying himself with the details of the receiving tent. His Queen, Marie-Amélie, his sons and daughters were amused to see his complete joy of the moment. A whale boat of twenty-four oarsmen took the King alongside where he leapt aboard with the agility of an eager young man. The little Queen, glowing in purple satin, a straw hat with yellow ribbons and a nodding white ostrich plume, happily accepted Louis Philippe's embrace. A correspondent from the English Press suggested that Her Majesty was pained by the King's embrace. Their marked cordiality had caused frowns in her entourage. In their eyes, King Louis Philippe had mounted the deck like an old pirate, ready to snatch their precious Queen. When Victoria stepped ashore, there was even more kissing; dearest Louise and Clem and Chica. She was excited and overjoyed to be in France for the first time. 'The dear King!' 'The dear Queen!'

Victoria wrote up in her formidable diary her own impressions of her arrival in Tréport...

I was more and more agitated ... Tréport is in a little creek with cliffs here and there and an old English church. I saw the King's boat. He came alongside. The good King was standing ready and extremely impatient to board. He mounted as quickly as possible and embraced me tenderly. It was a moving scene and I will never forget the emotion that it caused me.

Queen Victoria was finally whisked away beside Louis Philippe in his *'voiture'* to Château d'Eu. The footmen, the harness handlers, the huntsman and coachman were all in red. The postilions wore high boots and blue livery. The party set off at a gallop in clouds of dust; but the narrow roads of Normandy were always difficult to manoeuvre. On this august occasion, Joinville was the cause of leading the coachman astray. Victoria explained:

We nearly had an accident. As we passed through the outer gate, only half the horses obeyed; the others refusing and the *voiture* went crossways. Said the King: '*Cela me désole.*' After several attempts we finally passed through and arrived at another gate.

Noted Joinville: 'Father fumed. Queen Victoria laughed out loud but the coachman gave me a furious look. I had dishonoured the most important undertaking of his career.'

Victoria was captivated by her first '*coup d'oeil*' of the Château; set back from an elegant garden, the imposing rose brick façade with its towers and windows was ablaze in the setting sun. She was greeted on the vast front court by a glittering display of cavalry. The Garde Nationale, with their breastplates gleaming, stood in the soft evening light.

A banquet at eight o'clock, to be redefined as '*un petit dîner en famille*'. Victoria was placed between Louis Philippe and Joinville the 'sailor prince'. Always interesting and well informed, he kept her highly amused with his commentary on everybody present, the only trouble being his deafness, which made him talk too loud. She found Marie-Amélie completely charming, poised between a natural grandeur and her kindness. She still had a young and remarkable supple figure but why had her hair gone grey? She later learned from Louise that both Louis Philippe and their mother had turned quite white with Orléans' death. Victoria herself looked superb in a scarlet evening dress, with the Order of the Garter – '*Honi soit qui mal y pense*' – across her shoulder. Her emeralds and diamonds completed the picture. Louis Philippe gazed on her admiringly, repeating to her ceaselessly how happy he was with her visit; how attached he had been to her father, in England. The Prince Consort had also made an excellent impression. 'A fair and handsome man, a little pale.' With his unassuming poise and dressed in tails with a wide cummerbund, he had won them over.

The following morning Victoria and Albert were shown around the

Château; the rooms were at their most illustrious after the King's extensive restoration. 'I do like these dear people and feel so gay and happy in their company ... I feel completely at ease, as if I was of the family ...' After previous references to 'my sad childhood' the young Queen was clearly relishing the happy bustle of a large family. She had certainly blossomed since Charles Greville had seen fit to describe her, at ten years old: 'Our little Princess is a short, plain-looking child ... However if nature has not done so much, fortune is likely to do a great deal more for her.' The young Queen, on her first trip to France and now twenty-five years of age, was to be unanimously hailed as 'adorable'; not pretty but gracious and dignified.

After '*le luncheon*', Louis Philippe offered her his arm and proposed a '*promenade en voiture*'. Victoria was again placed beside the King, who seemed determined to keep her close. The party of two charabancs passed softly along the bridle-paths of the Forêt d'Eu, where stag and wild boar roamed. The vast beech glades were turning ruby and gold and Victoria admired the plantations of silver birch. Peasants darted out of the thick copse with fruits and bouquets of flowering shrub. But the hilly roads down to Tréport were the worst she had ever seen. 'In truth they were not roads and we were horribly jolted. The surrounding country resembles Brighton.' As they approached the Port the '*voitures*' caught people's attention – '*Vive la Reine d'Angleterre!*' Victoria was enchanted with the headdresses of the women, their shawls and coloured pinafores. She concluded happily: 'It is the people as well as the country; their physique, their dress, their manner, everything.' It was all so different from England.

On Monday September 4th, Louis Philippe, with his talent for creating a scenario, had arranged a luncheon in the forest – a '*fête champêtre*'. A vast oval tent had been erected in a clearing; the interior, hung with gilded garlands, was to seat seventy-two guests at a long table. A fine velvet carpet had been laid throughout. Twelve *maîtres d'hôtel* presided over a hundred footmen in Royal livery. A grand spread, *à la mode Anglaise*, of pâtés, meats, chicken and patisseries, was served, with the total consumption of forty carafes of wine. Victoria confided to her journal: 'It was a charming *fête champêtre*; "just like in Germany," Albert said.'

By six o'clock, they were returned to the Château where an evening concert was in store. Artistes from the Opéra-Comique performed a range of work from Beethoven and Gluck. Victoria was sitting between the 'dear Queen' and Louise. The heavily panelled Galerie des Guise became insufferably hot. All three escaped down the stairs at each interval, to breathe some air.

Albert left early on the morning of September 5th, with Aumale, to inspect the mounted Frontier Garde. Victoria enjoyed a leisurely breakfast in bed. At ten o'clock, Hélène, the widowed Duchesse d'Orléans, entered her room. The Comte de Paris, her five-year-old son, came along too. The subdued Hélène talked with tears in her eyes, of Victoria's sympathy for her sadness; the young Queen, a mother herself, admired Hélène's obvious spirit and sense and her show of much courage and force of character. Victoria was next ushered in to see '*La Tante*', Madame Adélaïde; she had already judged her a curious old lady and a difficulty for Queen Marie-Amélie to put up with; nothing was done without consulting this ubiquitous presence.

The day brightened and Victoria was taken on an intimate stroll with Louis Philippe in the walled gardens. A blaze of golden peaches caught her eye. Louis Philippe picked one for her. How should she peel it? To her surprise the King drew a knife from his pocket, with his time-honoured quote: 'When one has been like me, a poor devil, reduced to living on forty sous a day, one keeps a knife in one's pocket; I could have lost the habit many years ago, but I preferred not to; one never knows what may happen.' Victoria looked on her hero with a compassion and tenderness. She took the peeled peach and ate it with the aid of her kind host's lace handkerchief.*

September 6th, the last day. Again Albert had got up early, to go bathing from Tréport's white pebbly beach. Marie-Amélie came to Victoria's room with a ravishing bracelet; a sapphire embedded in diamonds. Victoria had planned to show the family round her yacht. It was a beautiful morning, but a strong breeze had put up in the Channel. The idea had to be abandoned. During the five busy and beguiling days, the Lords Aberdeen and Liverpool had played Box and Cox to secure any discreet exchanges; with Guizot usually popping up between.

---

* It could be supposed that this same knife was the very one given by Marie-Amélie to their ten-year-old grandson, Robert, Duc de Chartres on Louis Philippe's death in 1850. It was later sold at Christie's, Paris, in 2008; with a pliable silver blade and mother-of-pearl handle, it fetched 937 euros.

One afternoon Guizot and Aberdeen had asked for a reprieve from the afternoon's activities and walked alone for two hours in the park. They discussed their Governments, their respective trading interests and relations with the Orient, Russia, Greece and Spain. Guizot found Aberdeen sound with a liberal judgement. The two Ministers returned to their countries confident in the '*entente cordiale*' initiated by the twenty-five-year-old Queen with her seventy-year-old 'pin-up' King. Who could foresee the disparate issues on the horizon soon set to rock the apple-cart?

The five-day visit had proved a triumph of fond exchange and laughter. Victoria had enchanted Louis Philippe and his entire family and household. Yet snide ripples had run through the French Press. *Le National*, 3 September, 1843 commented: 'Naturally the young English Queen has wished to visit France; but what good has this Royal caprice done the country? What are we to gain from the excursion of a woman bored with London life? Is it a political ploy? Should we fear the price of our hospitality?'

Again on 3 September *Le National* lanced another barb, with the suggestion that the next budget should include a reference, entitled '*Visit of the Queen of England* – it would be hard on the poor farmers who scarcely have bread and on the miserable sailors who earn their livelihood exposed to the English bullets, to have to pay; and on the musicians that play "God Save the Queen" and the forty cooks who prepare dinner for the Queen, escorted by her ministers.'

On 5 September *Le National* jibes at the Queen's warm greeting to the Prime Minister, Guizot. 'Sire, I am charmed to see you again. Continue your work, Monsieur. Contribute as much as you can to make England the most powerful empire of the world. It is the greatest service that you can render to France. Your country is at risk.'

Finally *Le Constitutionnel*, the paper of Louis Philippe's calling, trumped these petulant protests with chivalry and sense:

5 September
Nothing honours France more than this spontaneous act of the Queen of a powerful Empire. We can speak freely because politics have nothing to do with this visit.

A mere month elapsed before the newborn '*entente cordiale*' was seized from its cradle. The Duc de Bordeaux, now twenty-three-years of age, son of the dogged Duchesse de Berri, had moved in on London. He had taken a house in Belgrave Square with the intent of proclaiming himself Henri V, the lawful King of France. A delegation of Legitimists, to include a handful of peers and deputies, ostensibly loyal to Louis Philippe, had crowded the Square and its respectable environs. There was considerable noise and *louche* behaviour. Charles Greville complained that '. . . the town has ever since swarmed with monstrous beards of every cut and colour'. Chateaubriand, the exuberant orator and the Duc de Fitzjames, eulogised 'the King' on the 29th and 30th November, 1843. Tumultuous roars of '*Vive Henri V*' reverberated around the fashionable residences.

Louis Philippe was furious that such a wild scene should have disturbed the Queen of England and her Belgravia. He need not have worried; Queen Victoria's loyalties were entirely with the Orléans and her dear good King of the French. She had refused to receive the young pretender, dubbing him 'a poor stupid boy'. He had not even asked her for permission to create such ludicrous brio!

Again the cradle was rocked in February 1844, when the sultry steam in Tahiti welled up into a sudden contentious brawl; the salient players comprised the Queen Pomare, who liked to roll her own cigars with a single pandanus leaf; her lover, George Pritchard, also acting as her British Consul, from Birmingham, and the compulsive French Admiral, Dupetit-Thouars. Tahiti had illegally been put under the protection of the *tricolore* by the Admiral. He had since moved fast to land soldiers and a consortium of French authorities and sentinels. Pritchard, whose consular duties had even extended to his role as the island's Protestant priest, the chief *accoucheur* and the general pharmacist, ranted hard against the newly installed regime. He was swiftly imprisoned by the French Admiral and expelled to England. His tale induced 'gross outrage' from Sir Robert Peel; while Louis Philippe and Guizot totally refuted Dupetit-Thouars' sedulous annexation of Tahiti. Inflammatory speeches from both sides of the Channel threatened to erupt into war. Pronounced Louis Philippe: 'I have no patience with the manner in which people so often magnify miserable trifles into *Casus Belli*.' Queen Victoria, revealing a new political aplomb with her open indignation over the 'pretender' in the Belgrave Square episode, later wrote admiringly of Louis Philippe to her uncle Leopold, ending ... 'He is determined that our affairs should go on well. He wishes Tahiti *au fond de la mer.*'

28

With these storm clouds dispersed, the young Queen Victoria confirmed her invitation to Louis Philippe to stay at Windsor Castle. Queen Marie-Amélie had graciously declined. She feared the rough October Channel crossings. It was unanimously decided that the Orléans' youngest son, the Duc de Montpensier, should accompany his father. 'La Tante' Adélaïde had not been invited. The King's eldest daughter, Queen Louise, exchanged confidences with her niece Victoria on Louis Philippe's habits when staying away without Marie-Amélie.

'Ma chère et bien-aimée Victoria...' The only prerequisites for his room were a large table for his papers and a hard bed with a horsehair mattress, resting on a board. He wished above all not to upset his hostess, but would find it difficult to present himself in good time for the family breakfast; the shaving ... the teeth ... the toupee... As he only took two meals a day, he would prefer to dispense with the breakfast; perhaps Montpensier might bring him bouillon. Louise was also at pains to point out Marie-Amélie's concern that the King was liable to play 'le jeune homme'; riding horses and taking every opportunity as though he was twenty years old.

At seven o'clock on the morning of Tuesday October 8th, 1844, Louis Philippe and Montpensier disembarked at Portsmouth, to be met by Prince Albert. Again the King was ready with a buoyant embrace for his 'cher cousin'; but the ever-correct Consort drew back a little and stiffened. After a display of civic ceremony, Prince Albert led them to the Royal train for the journey to Windsor. Louis Philippe had chosen to include the artist Edouard Pingret in his retinue; a pupil of David, the painter of formidable realism, and of Jean-Baptiste de Regnault. The resulting lithographs of this exceptional visit to Windsor Castle are a prized record and held in the Louvre. Pingret swiftly set to work on the Queen's coach; a cocoon of padded seats and walls, quilted in grey silk and bordered in a deep braid of scarlet and cream. From Farnborough they were driven in an escorted open carriage, arriving at Windsor at two o'clock. Louis Philippe bowed and waved with his accustomed gusto at the crowds, as Montpensier laughed happily beside him.

The Châtelaine Queen, waiting with her suite at the foot of the Grand Staircase, later entrusted his embrace to her journal, with his words: '*combien de plaisir j'ai à vous embrasser...*' She was immediately charmed by Montpensier and urged her ogling three-year-old, Bertie, to grow up like him. The elderly King tripped youthfully behind the Queen up the Grand Staircase to his bedroom; a veritable display of blue silk hangings and silver fringes, with a battery of portraits by Holbein, Titian, van Dyck and landscapes by Claude. Pingret felt properly challenged in his mission. When an eight-seater charabanc was presented to the Queen by her admirer, the artist lavished his attention on the silver door handles and pleated sunblinds.

A '*promenade en charabanc*', as Victoria referred to their excursions, was mooted for Thursday October 10th. It was a beautiful morning. The party comprised the Queen and Louis Philippe '*en avant*'; her mother, the Duchess of Kent, and Montpensier in the second banquette, followed by Prince Albert and the Countess of Gainsborough, Général Athalin and Alexandre Dumas (*père*), Lord Charles Wellesley and Colonel Bouverie, Commandant of the Horse Guards. The party, drawn by six horses, set off first for Twickenham to visit the King's old home, Orléans House, his much loved retreat in exile. The incumbents, Lord and Lady Mornington, accompanied the Queen and her favourite greyhound, Eos, down the garden to the river. Louis Philippe, immaculate in morning dress and black silk top hat, strolled happily across the lawn, noting familiar trees. The charabanc next rolled the party across Bushey Park to Hampton Court, where they were guided through Cardinal Wolsey's apartments. Passing out of the red salon, Bertie was rewarded with a little toy gun.

It was time for luncheon, and the party set out for Claremont, Victoria's childhood home in Esher. Did Louis Philippe sense a frisson as they clattered up through the green slopes to the imposing portico? '*Claremount*'! It was almost thirty years since he and Marie-Amélie had spent happy times there with a young and radiant woman, Princess Charlotte; now he was returned with another.

The following day the Investiture Ceremony took place in the Throne Room at Windsor Castle. After another good lunch and a hefty shower of presents – a splendid clock, a pair of Sèvres vases, magnificent material for a dress – Victoria retired to change, into blue velvet and a diamond tiara. Seated at the head of a long table, she received Louis Philippe ler, *Roi des Francais*; he was dressed in his uniform of a Lieutenant Général. She later remarked that 'He bowed deeply in most perfect style.' The Chancellor next read the passage nominating the French King a member of the Order of the Garter. The Garter was placed by Prince Albert on the left leg. As recorded by the young queen.

I helped fix it. The King then murmured to me: 'I wish to kiss this hand' – which he did and I embraced him. Uncle Cambridge helped me place the decoration on the King's shoulder; then I embraced him again. He then embraced Albert and turning to the table shook hands with each knight.

This time of gifts and kisses reflected charmingly on the fond attraction of a man and a woman, irrespective of age.

Victoria had invited a hundred to dinner; a banquet in the 185-foot long St George's Hall, with its pitched and ribbed high ceiling. The magnificent gallery rang out to the sound of bagpipes and Strauss waltzes. Louis Philippe, freshly emblazoned with his decorations, clearly relished giving the Queen his arm into dinner.

An afternoon with the Queen at Eton was particularly treasured. Signing his name, seated in a window of College Library, he added the lines:

'Encore ému de l'accueil qui lui ont fait les élèves de cet honorable Collège.'

Louis Philippe

The Queen, standing by his side, signed 'Victoria Regina', along with 'Wellington', himself an acclaimed old Etonian.

Pingret captured the scene: the Royal and distinguished clustered around the French King; the enfilade of galleried rooms with their carved Ionic columns clasping the leather spines.

The Queen guided him further through Cloister Court and into School

Yard. According to her journal, 'a veritable delirium' of boys cheered and crowded their way. At five o'clock, they crossed the bridge back to Windsor Castle with their carriage chased and surrounded by hilarious pupils. Louis Philippe's visit was perfection, wrote Victoria to her uncle Leopold: 'He is determined, he says, to see me every year.' But their close and cordial friendship was more distrusted than shared by her Tory Ministers.

29

Back in the Tuileries, Adélaïde, uninvited on the Windsor bandwagon, had busied herself with brides for the remaining nephews. She had found the perfect candidate for the Duc d'Aumale: the Princess Caroline of Naples, a favourite niece of Marie-Amélie. Louis Philippe was pleased to have a toe in the Sicilian dynasty and the Princess's looks and deportment were admirable; although Marie-Amélie secretly regretted her crossed front teeth. Adélaïde now had one more hurdle to jump: to find a bride for the youngest Orléans Duc of all: Montpensier. She tinkered daringly with the Queen Isabella of Spain; fifteen years of age already, a husband was clearly in need.

The British Government had already put forward Leopold of Saxe-Cobourg, a cousin of Queen Victoria. However, Louis Philippe, entering the prenuptial fray, remarked there were too many Cobourgs scattered around England, Belgium and Portugal; he advised on a Bourbon to represent the Spanish throne. To Britain's disdain, he hinted at his son, Montpensier. The Duke of Cadiz, the Duke of Seville, and even the sixteen-year-old Count Trapani, were swiftly put forward. Not to be thwarted, Louis Philippe made a quick compromise with Isabella's younger sister, the Infanta Luisa, to be Montpensier's bride.

Isabella detested all her putative candidates. It transpired that Trapani was backward, Seville was a rebellious Progressive and Cadiz effeminate and suspected of impotence. Isabella had developed a strong aversion to his voice and his hips. Her mother, Queen Christina, turned to the French Ambassador, the Comte de Bresson, for advice. He suggested that if the Duke of Cadiz's regiment was stationed in Madrid, Isabella would be seeing him constantly and would grow accustomed to his voice and hips.

By September 1845, Victoria, still hankering after a 'Cobourg' and generally fussed by the proposed Bourbon marriages for Queen Isabella and the Infanta Luisa, invited herself to Eu. Returning from Germany, on September 8th, she spent the night. Together with Louis Philippe, Guizot and Aberdeen, she talked through the eventualities of the Spanish marriages.

A letter from Aberdeen was promptly sent from Eu to Peel, stressing that *'until the Queen was married and had children'* the Infanta should remain her mere sister, with no question of marriage to a French Prince. Louis Philippe was accordingly happy that if the Queen had children, to seal the succession, the heir presumptive Infanta would be free to marry Montpensier. Aberdeen concluded his letter to Peel: 'I distinctly understood that it was not only a marriage and a child, but *children that were necessary to secure the succession.*' In April 1846, the precarious nuptials were poised for more intrigue and more argument. The Comte de Bresson was well aware that Queen Christina had finally accepted the Duke of Cadiz for her Isabella, with the infallible proviso that the Infanta Luisa was married to the virile Montpensier. Bresson chose to tell the Queen that the simultaneous marriages of her daughters would be favourable to the Tuileries.

Lord Palmerston, a perennial spanner in the workings of any Anglo-French debate, had just returned to the Foreign Office. He immediately undermined Aberdeen's deft arrangements and ordered the British Ambassador to Madrid, to reintroduce the Cobourg candidate. Whereupon the wily Guizot countermanded the order and exhorted the French Ambassador to finalise matters for the simultaneous marriages between the two Spanish sisters and the two Bourbon Princes. On October 10th, 1846, the double marriage was solemnised at the Royal Palace of Madrid in the Hall of the Ambassadors. The Duke of Cadiz soon dispelled all doubts of his virility and gave his Queen four children.

Queen Victoria was furious and felt grievously deceived by this sudden sweep of events. Her dear old King had proved unreliable. She regretted the time and effort she had spent embroidering him a fancy waistcoat. How dare the French poke their fingers, unilaterally, in the Spanish throne? She had written ruefully to Uncle Leopold:

7th September, 1846

My dearest Uncle,

The settlement of the Queen of Spain's marriage, coupled *with Montpensier's* is *infamous*, and we *must* remonstrate ... Originally they said that Montpensier should *only* marry the Infanta *when* the Queen was married and *had children* ... The King should know that we are extremely indignant, and that this conduct is *not* the way to keep up the *entente* which he wishes.

It would appear that Louis Philippe was reluctant to write to Queen Victoria. Aware that he had broken his pact, he asked Marie-Amélie to write instead; women saw things differently. He himself had seen fit to take decisive steps for a double marriage. It had seemed inconceivable that four young people should be corralled into an extended intrusion of their privacy.

The (French) *Presse* and *Morning Post* dabbled vociferously in their shared disdain of the 'Cordial Understanding'. An absurd illusion! The French and English would always be sceptical of such an alliance. And now it was defunct! *La Presse* revelled in the realisation that now France was united in a new '*entente*' with all the nations of Europe, against their common enemy: England.

The controversial young couple caused a stir on their return to Paris; fêtes were thrown in their honour and a magnificent gala was staged by the Spanish Ambassador. Inspired by this extravaganza, the Montpensiers themselves orchestrated a fête for June 16th, 1847. An elaborate marquee was set up in the woods of Vincennes. It was surrounded by treasured tents captured from the recently deposed Governor of Algeria, Abd el-Kadr, and one from Napoleon himself. With musicians, with singing and dancing and with the trees ablaze in rocking Chinese lanterns, Louis Philippe was proud that his youngest son had prompted such a scene. High Society, intellectuals, artists and diplomats; it was an eclectic *galère* after his own taste. Only Marie-Amélie was disturbed by this lavish exposé. There had been disastrous spring floods threatening the harvests; widespread hunger and destitution was already rumoured. Some of the guests on arrival had been booed and howled at; others had been showered with mud and pebbles. A glittering party was a signal to riot.

The summer of 1847 lurched on with a sinister sense of foreboding. The King looked tired and stooped; he walked heavily. Evenings at the Tuileries were quiet and empty; the bored and dutiful daughters-in-law read books aloud and embroidered. It seemed only Chopin could relieve the torpor; he himself, withered with consumption, took comfort in swathing the gaunt old rooms with his matchless playing.

At dawn on August 18th, 1847, Paris stirred awake slowly in its desultory discontent. News of a gruesome horror was poised to burst. The Duc de Praslin had murdered his wife. She was the daughter of the powerful Sicilian Maréchal Sébastiani, Louis Philippe's former Ambassador to London. The Praslin-Sébastiani family was closely linked with the Orléans in every social dependence. Fanny's murder was to prove a final nail in the July Monarchy's coffin.

Her blood-curdling shrieks had severed the silence of the first light. It was the heavy brass candlestick, brought down on her head with a single brutal blow, that had finally done for her. The night servants, Auguste and Leclerc, saw a thick column of black smoke drifting from the Duc's chimney. It was later discovered that bloodstained clothing had been burning and smouldering in his fireplace.

The Duc de Praslin had always been given a disparaging profile by his colleagues in the Chamber of Peers. A pale, sallow man, his ugly mouth always pursed to say something which he never did. His hands were coarse; he had no breeding. In October 1824, Théobald Praslin, aged nineteen years, had married the Maréchal's only daughter, the sixteen-year-old Fanny Sébastiani. Rich, highly strung, a little spoilt, a little lazy, she abided by the mores of her country: 'Dolce far niente'. They had inherited the magnificent Hôtel Sébastiani on 55 Faubourg St Honoré. Despite her indolence Fanny had produced, for her equally immature Théobald, nine children.

By eight o'clock on that morning of the rumoured crime, a questing crowd had pressed up to the closed gates of the family hôtel. The spreading swell of the curious onlookers alarmed the civic authorities; a mounted Garde was sent to control matters and barricades were raised. A rumbling of disgust soon reverberated through the city. The Praslin-Sébastianis who hobnobbed with the Orléans! The Duc de Praslin was equerry to the widowed Duchesse d'Orléans; he was her trusted and revered 'Chevalier d'Honneur!' It was even suggested the Duc had become her lover. Madame Adélaïde had long been the Duchesse de Praslin's close friend and confidante – 'My dearest Fanny'; and the Maréchal, the Comte de Sébastiani, a former Minister of Foreign Affairs, was Louis Philippe's long-standing and benevolent friend. The Royal Family was staying at Château d'Eu at the time of the crime. Louis Philippe recognised the serious implications for his own position and his Government. On August 19th he wrote a long consoling letter to Horace Sébastiani and throwing down his pen, his head in his hands, he exclaimed in despair – 'What a terrible mess! A machine which is always going wrong!'

By mid-morning the *louche* crowd at the Sébastiani Hôtel gates was becoming a mob, glutted with accumulating gossip. It waited, mesmerised, for news: a glimpse of the guilty party, an arrest, the broken knife flung from the Duc's window … there had been reports of the Duchesse's crushed head, her face no longer recognisable. The people waited and watched. What had happened to their ruling society? To the dignity of the Monarchy? The Orléans' close friendship with the Sébastianis was a travesty of judgement! They despised, feared and hated the guilty Duc, a privileged peer of France … And now they hated Louis Philippe.

The vestibule and ground floor of the Hôtel bulged with a civic Garde, the chief Magistrate crime detectives and the head of the 'Sûreté Nationale'. The *Presse* was inflamed with rumour and damning reportage. 'An appalling business,' pronounced the *Revue des deux mondes*. 'Must the ghastly murder of the Duchesse de Praslin take its place as one of the features in the general appearance of our time?' There was serious editorial reportage in London; deep concern was raised for the moral decline in the French upper echelons, fortified with warnings to England's own aristocracy.

Général Sébastiani, the Duchesse's uncle, the first to arrive at the hôtel, was hissed at when he left. He had fainted at the scene of his niece's mangled body. He had asked for a glass of water; the valet poured him some from the Duc's carafe. It later transpired the Duc had been rubbing bloodstains from his *robe de chambre* with the water in the carafe. The Maréchal Sébastiani, whose only child, his adored Fanny, had been wrested from him, was now to be dragged in the mire of hearsay.

As the crowd swelled before the Hôtel Sébastiani, a spirit of resentment for the aristocrats, and the conservative Orléanists, grew. Too many scandals had been sweeping Paris: government trafficking in money deals; the idle rich grovelling in marital murder. The military Sébastianis appeared always to attract death and disaster. The restless crowd pieced together the old story. As a young man, the Maréchal had fought for Napoleon and undertaken missions to Turkey from 1802 to 1806. He often told his bloodthirsty story.

Staying in Constantinople, having just repelled the English, he was invited by Sultan Selim III to choose his reward. Sébastiani, a full-blooded young man, asked his good-hearted host if he might see the harem. The Sultan guided him round the sanctuary, which included his wives. Had his guest particularly fancied a woman? 'Yes,' replied Sébastiani, indicating the one. (It is to be hoped that they exchanged a smile or some such recognition of their mutual attraction.) That same evening, Sébastiani was delivered the woman's head on a platter. The Sultan completed his gift from hell with the message: ... 'This way you can be sure that the woman on whom you set your eyes will never belong to another man.'

The Maréchal's son-in-law was presented no such heroics from the crowd that stretched across Paris. To the disgust and fury of all, the Duc's secreted vial of arsenic powder was to subjugate his trial at the Chamber of Peers. However, reports of his frequent visits to the '*lieu d'aisance*' drew howls of approval; further bulletins of colonic *lavements* 'and the anus to be leeched' – were greeted with gales of laughter and a sense of soothing justice.

The Duc de Praslin took six days to die, willfully ignoring the desires of a shopkeeper, overheard by Victor Hugo: 'Oh, how I hope that he doesn't die! It amuses me so much to read all about this case in the papers every morning.'

Louis Philippe was soundly shaken. *L'affaire* Praslin had quite wiped from his mind those two recent assassination attempts. What was a bad shot from an angry Fontainebleau gamekeeper to compare with a crazed husband striking his wife dead with a candlestick? And then that lunatic loitering behind a statue, aiming at him with a long-range pistol, as he had saluted from a Tuileries balcony?

In November 1847, the perceptive Joinville wrote to his elder brother, Nemours:

I am writing you a line because I am worried by all the events which I see piling up on every side ... The King has reached an age when he no longer accepts other people's observations; he is accustomed to governing, he likes to show that it is he who governs ... And worst of all I can see no remedy for all this ... You know my respect and affection for him; but I cannot help looking into the future and it rather frightens me.

Louis Philippe, pondering on imponderables from the comfort of his library chair, would look to Guizot for peace and sense; but his canny Prime Minister was listening to others. He dripped unpleasant information to his King like a mother ministering milk: more agitations for 'La Réforme', more fierce talk on revival of the political banquets, and recent publications on the grandeur of the Revolution, forty years on. Louis Philippe dismissed each serving like a sulky child, knowing full well that it would all be offered again. The 'soi-disant' banquets? A mere chance to welter in bouillabaisse and 'vins du pays', cheering along that Leftist Odilon Barrot and his fatuous waffle. 'Bon appétit to them!' It was of little concern to Louis Philippe. 'La Réforme'? He would reiterate to his friends and Ministers: 'I am not hostile to reform per se, but it would involve me first with Molé and then that would lead to Thiers. Thiers means war! And I am not going to destroy my policy of peace.' To the end of his reign, Louis Philippe presided over a 'juste milieu' constitution, elected by a substantial majority.

The King made his last speech at the Chamber of Peers on December 28th, 1847; a tired and inconsequential offering. Thiers had risen from the malaise to parade his provocative alternatives; he inspired no initiative from either side of the Chamber. At least, Montalembert, with his distinctive passion had given a two-hour address condemning the entire machinations of Revolution. But Guizot, his voice still frail from influenza, stayed silent. He saw the Throne and the Chamber in freefall. He was frightened; as Prime Minister he would bear all the weight. Could he? Should he resign? Despite this session of doldrums, the Prince de Broglie, in all his renowned superiority, wrote to his son at the beginning of February 1848: 'Things here are going slowly but splendidly. The majority is solid.'

After protracted bouts of asthma and a weakening heart, Adélaïde had died on December 31st, 1847. She had attended a banquet at the Tuileries the previous night and died at dawn. Louis Philippe had watched over her, stricken and alone, weighed down with memories; taking her hand at the end, he murmured his love and prayers. A resolute woman, she had achieved political coups for her brother's throne. She had initiated his sons' enlightened education, and their commendable marriages. She had exercised her skills and diplomacy with the chameleon Talleyrand and his charms. Adelaïde had been her adored brother's phantom powerhouse. Marie-Amélie, aware of her husband's indispensable need of her sister-in-law, had loved him too much herself to complain.

Madame Adélaïde was formidably rich. Her nephews and nieces were already anticipating their share of the will. But there was horror and aggravation when Adélaïde's entire estate was consigned to her brother, the King; to be divided after his death. Joinville, her favourite nephew, walked angrily across the salon to a window; he was joined by his brother Montpensier. They were all short of funds. Why did their father keep them on a shoestring? He hoarded all the family money!

Louis Philippe, at seventy-four years, was now an old man: with all the attendant bogies of nerve failure, fear of riots and bloodshed, and the rumoured desertion of the Garde Nationale. Above all he feared his capacity to command. Certainly Thiers, always ahead of the game, did not want bloodshed or barricades; he looked instead to the fall of Guizot, to a prompt volte-face of Ministers, and his comrade in Opposition, Odilon Barrot, as an effective member.

Louis Philippe sat through those bleak, damp February days of 1848, nurturing secret thoughts of abdication, of retirement at Château d'Eu, and even a rekindling of Queen Victoria's friendship. France was bored again and Paris restless. He again sensed danger, the vibrations of hate flexing for a fight. At dinner parties, hushed conversations were caught in corners. If Guizot was present he was cajoled for his opinions, but remained tight-lipped. At the opera and theatres, audiences would seize each other in the intervals. What was it to be? Riot or revolution?

Marie-Amélie glided through the dying February days, with her indomitable deportment; the Tuileries Salons drew her to the windows. She gazed down on the quiet, grim streets, running with the constant rainfall. Her pinched face framed with her white rigid curls, she would trace each of her children's trajectory.

Her Orléans! ... 'who I hoped would be the support of my old age exists no more!'

Nemours – her treasured confidant.

Joinville – his own man, her carefree one.

Aumale – the golden boy, now appointed the Governor Général of Algeria.

Montpensier – her ewe lamb, their 'Ton Ton'.

Their angelic Louise.

Marie, her lively imp, so soon deceased.

Clémentine, her blue-eyed '*belle*'.

The two lost angels: Penthièvre and Françoise.

And now a flow of '*petits-enfants*'.

Louis Philippe and Marie-Amélie would play 'Patience' late into the night, their comfortable chairs drawn up before a large fire. They were soothed by the constant drumming of rain. Muttered Louis Philippe: 'Those rascals hate water.' He believed that rain rather than a garrison could quell a riot.

30

On February 22nd, the following morning, the rain persisted and had put a dampener on any rioting. A Republican show of confusion and disorder had set in. A few armoury shops had been smashed and looted and barricades had been attempted. Bedraggled students made a half-hearted demonstration on their way to the Madeleine: 'Down with Guizot!' interspersed with yelps at the 'Marseillaise'.

By dawn, February 23rd, shooting was reported in the aggressive Temple area, where a force of regular soldiers had been spreading out; wet and hungry, cold and bored, it was decided the Garde Nationale should join the fray. Their Général Jacqueminor, now old and prone to languor, assured Général Tiburce Sébastiani, Commander of the Army of Paris, that his Garde Nationale was loyal. But Louis Philippe was profoundly sceptical over any merger of the Garde Nationale with the regular army; he remembered too many violent clashes between the two Forces.

The Garde Nationale took up positions in the Place de la Concorde early in the morning of February 23rd. A wave of insurgents moved towards them with provocative cries of '*A bas le système! A bas les ministres!*' and '*Vive la République!*' In no time the troops were mixing with these vociferous rebels and the Garde Nationale had allowed itself spasmodic calls of '*Vive la Réforme!*' and '*Vive la République!*' Général Jacqueminot's spurious report of loyal conduct had been misleading. Louis Philippe himself regretted that in the last years, since Orléans' death, he had failed to regularly review the Garde Nationale. He knew too well that the chronic erosion of an army's morale and loyalty spelt the ultimate collapse of the Monarchy.

With the disparate performance of the forces now nudging the Tuileries gardens, Louis Philippe's Ministers persuaded him that Guizot had to resign. An instant change of government was imperative. His most trusted Ministers stood before him in unanimous resolve: Montalivet, his military confidant; Duchâtel, Minister of the Interior; his aide-de-camp, Comte de Rumigny; Maréchal Gérard; the fearless Maréchal Bugeaud and Général Dumas.

241

Louis Philippe was shattered at this initiative, but the alternative of blood and battle between the Garde Nationale and the Army could not be countered. 'I have seen enough blood,' he muttered, and at 2.30pm called for Guizot.

The Prime Minister accepted Louis Philippe's command to resign; in an elegant show of diplomacy, he assured his King that he could never hold to his position without the support of the Monarchy. Louis Philippe was close to tears. Guizot entered the Chamber of Peers, head held high, to personally announce his resignation. It was a tumultuous triumph for the mob, the Garde Nationale and for the Republican representatives. At four o'clock, Molé was ushered into the Tuileries. It was in 1839 that he himself had been dismissed as Prime Minister; a pacifist like the King, he was an academic, with a simmering allergy to Thiers, who, in turn, had considered his Ministry a disgrace. On February 23rd, over that late afternoon, Molé attempted to form a Cabinet. Thiers had no inclination to help. Maréchal Bugeaud waited tentatively in the Palace for an order from the King to lead his men into attack.

By midnight Molé had abandoned his luckless exercise. By one o'clock, Bugeaud had his emergency call. It had needed a horror show of dead and wounded and his soldiers' panic, before the King had unleashed the old Maréchal. A heavy mob had moved in from the Place de la Concorde to the Place Vendôme, where the Garde Nationale was protecting the Chancellery. It was a single gunshot that had seized the furies; the Colonel of the Garde Nationale had been threatened with a torch shoved up to his face. 'I will light up your moustache!' shrieked the lunatic, stabbing his fire at his intended victim. Horses reared and the pandemonium mounted. The Colonel held his position and ordered: 'Cross-bayonets!' The Colonel's Sergeant shot-dead the burly ruffian. Shots and shouts and screaming spread into the Rue Cambon. A single horse, snorting at the stench of blood and cordite, dragged a cartload of twitching corpses off to the depository in the 4th *arrondissement*. The gruesome quarry was made to pass slowly and pause, in triumph, before the offices of *Le National* and *La Réforme*.

Bugeaud could not have inherited a more ferocious start: a welter of blood and bones just round the corner and a line of worn-out Staff Officers waiting on his orders. He marked out their final attack on four designated areas: the Hôtel de Ville, the Panthéon area, the Bastille and a contingent of reserves in the Place du Carrousel. 'It is now two o'clock. By four o'clock we must begin to attack everywhere. I don't want our force split up into little packets. What I want is four columns sweeping away the mob without waiting to be attacked.'

Guizot's dismissal had been bandied around the military with good effect but the substitute of Molé was not well received. Time was running out. The Chamber had next called for Thiers, and had urged him to assemble a Cabinet. In the early hours of February 24th, Adolphe Thiers proclaimed himself as the Minister of War and his voluble comrade Odilon Barrot as Minister of the Interior. The triumphant Barrot had accepted with alacrity and was seen at dawn to leave the Tuileries, anxious to show himself as the acclaimed redeemer.

Escorted to the stables in the Rue des Petits-Champs, he was promptly hoisted on a horse, which appeared agitated. The coachmen held the bridle to calm it and the apprehensive rider. Explained one, later, to Louis Philippe's Aide-de-Camp, Comte de Rumigny: 'Monsieur Barrot was half-dead with fear; his head fallen on his chest, he was pale as death. His hands did not hold the reins and each one of us held him by the arm to save him from falling to the ground. He was followed by hundreds of rogues who yelled at the top of their voices "*Vive la Réforme!*" We looked on him as a man heading for trouble. We led him back to the Ministry and helped him dismount.'

At the Tuileries, Louis Philippe and Marie-Amélie were sitting over breakfast with Thiers and a group of his favoured politicians. An officer rushed in. Maréchal Bugeaud had commanded a ceasefire. The Army was bored and disaffected. Units were splitting up, mixing with insurgents and drifting off to wine shops. The Reserve Contingent still manned the Place du Carrousel. The King turned to Thiers. The Tuileries were still defended? What should be done? This new Minister of War was concise; the safety of the Royal Family could no longer be guaranteed. They should leave immediately for Saint-Cloud. The Maréchal Bugeaud would then gain the city with the full complement of his forces. Another report came to the table. Conditions had calmed on the Place de la Concorde.

Louis Philippe was persuaded, and largely by Marie-Amélie, to ride out and review the remaining troops and Garde Nationale; to demonstrate encouragement and a degree of gratitude. In his Lieutenant Général's uni-form, flanked by Nemours, Montpensier, Bugeaud and a timid Thiers on foot, Louis Philippe faced a barrage of cries: '*Vive le Roi!*' '*Vive la Réforme!*' '*A bas le système!*' '*A bas les ministres!*' It was a courageous performance of Orléanist pluck and staying power, but he soon turned his sons and horses back to the Tuileries. Mercifully Joinville and Aumale were still stationed in Algeria. They had been spared these days of angry savagery; and the humiliation of their father. Worse was to come.

Returned to his Cabinet in a state of abject despair and indecision, Louis Philippe sat, his head in his hands. He felt beaten. There was a rash of caterwauling hooligans crowding into the Carrousel, just 200 yards from the Palace. He could hear Bugeaud and his officers driving them off with gunfire and violent struggle. Fighting now skirted the entire Tuileries walls. On the East side, facing the Place du Palais Royal, a desperate detachment of the 14th Regiment was barely holding out against an overpowering surge of rebels. A smell of burning straw stole up from the Royal stables; the Palace was set alight. 'The flood is rising,' groaned Thiers to his defeated King whose orders of no bloodshed had concealed his wish that none should die for him. And had Thiers chosen to warn his toppling Monarch with a euphemism? 'Flood' for 'blood'?

The slumped Louis Philippe hardly heeded the gleeful rabble charging brazenly into the emptied Tuileries. Muttering and cries of 'Abdication' reverberated through the seized rooms and galleries. The familiar journalist from *La Presse*, Emile de Girardin, thrust his way through the Ministers. He assured the King that the only solution was his immediate Abdication. 'Don't abdicate!' screeched a bystander. 'It would mean a Republic within an hour.' Louis Philippe faced round to his Maréchals – Soult, Sébastiani and Gérard. They all now intimated he could no longer be defended. With a heavy step he stumped over to the maplewood desk, which had been Napoleon's before him. He began to write out, laboriously, his abdication, as a crowd of unknown onlookers pressed around, chivvying him 'Faster! Faster!' His youngest son, Montpensier, urged him to write more quickly. Louis Philippe, who resented such prompting for this undeniably important document, impressed upon the room that he had always written slowly and did not intend to change his habits. The King's Cabinet was now alive with anxious shouts and there was a crush of foul bodies. Again Montpensier urged his father, 'For God's sake hurry; we shall all be murdered.'

As Louis Philippe bent over his words, the rumour of the cast-off crown had swirled through the Palace surrounds and beyond. The screams and shouting came closer and a rising pall of smoke spread voluminously from the stables. Louis Philippe's letter of Abdication, signed in his flowing and elegant hand, dated February 24th, 1848, is stored in the Archives of the Empire Français. It was torn unceremoniously from his hand by the eager Girardin. '*Je le tiens enfin!*' In vain had the author pleaded for a copy, before it was besmirched with blots.

'I abdicate this Crown which the will of the nation called me to wear, in favour of my grandson the Comte de Paris. May he succeed in the great task which falls to him today.'

Marie-Amélie, an incomparable heroine in scenes of crisis and panic, had been opposed to the Abdication: 'The King and his family must await their fate at the Tuileries and die together if need be.' As she had watched her King sign the dread document, she cried out: 'They are not worthy of such a good King, and soon they will be sorry.'

There were screams of savage joy from the Tuileries courts and terraces. A frenzied rush through the salons was clearly imminent. The Palace cry went up: 'The people are coming ... they will be here in minutes ... Sire, you must go.' They must all go: the family, the household retinue, the remaining Ministers and the Military. Louis Philippe flung off his uniform. Where were his keys? He needed a frock-coat and a plain citizen's round hat. His keys? 'Forget your keys!' His valet found his keys. Marie-Amélie, turning to the Comte de Rumigny, in her supreme *de haut on bas*, afforded him the peremptory command: 'Go and take off your uniform and accompany the King!' Rumigny rushed up to his room to change into a Bourgeois coat.

It was noon when Louis Philippe, in a final gesture of gallantry in the eye of death, bowed to his Queen and offered her his arm. As they trod the long and empty corridors and a succession of salons, their sons and daughters and grandchildren, with the courtiers and military attendants, pressed up hard behind them. 'Quick! Quick! They're coming! They're in!' With rapacious screams and shrieks, the people set up a stampede through the Palace. Sounds of firing came from the Place du Carrousel. The bellicose

Bugeaud, confronted with Louis Philippe's oft-repeated 'Spill no blood! I am a peaceful King', had withdrawn all troops, with a ceasefire everywhere. He had seen fit to hand over his command to the elderly Maréchal Gérard. The Carrousel was now awash with insurgents, aiding the excited mobsters to crash through the Tuileries doors and windows. Bugeaud knew that all was now lost. The gallant, half-blind Maréchal Gérard was now persuaded to mount a horse and proclaim the King's Abdication. It was hoped the rabble would be calmed by their sensational victory.

Twelve escape carriages had been prepared in the Carrousel stables; the first to be released had been fired on, killing a groom and two horses. Nemours had quickly renegotiated for a hooded one-horse cabriolet and two closed carriages to convene in the Place de la Concorde. The Royal party walked under a Cavalry escort of the Garde Nationale through the Great Walk of the Tuileries Gardens to the deserted Place. The forlorn family waited a few minutes at the foot of the obelisk ... Where was the Comtesse de Montjoie? Aunt Adélaïde's dearly loved companion?

A strong lady and once apportioned 'the body of a Grenadier', she would be safe and sure to follow... Mélanie de Montjoie had succumbed to a raging migraine as the King wrested with his Abdication; she had retired up to her room. An unfamiliar man had soon entered. He advised her to scoop up her valuables into her handbag. As the rabble rushed up the stairs, she was helped out of the Palace by her timely intruder. A gaggle of hostile women had now collected around the Orléans; after some awkward minutes, the three carriages mercifully arrived. Marie-Amélie and Louis Philippe, with three grandchildren, climbed into the first carriage; the Duchesse de Nemours and her children, the Duc and Duchesse de Montpensier, Clémentine and Gusti, and their son Ferdinand, future King of Bulgaria, and the Princesse de Joinville, were all joined by the recovered Comtesse de Montjoie. The modest cavalcade, under the command of Général Dumas, set off rapidly to Versailles where the fugitives separated to cover their escape.

Louis Philippe, in an attempt at disguise, had removed his toupee and rammed on a black cap down to his eyes, which in turn he masked with thick spectacles. Marie-Amélie, jogging beside him in the mean carriage, assured him that he looked 100 years. She had dissuaded him from pushing on to the Château d'Eu; she had sensed an imperative need to stay overnight at Dreux;

to pray by the tombs of their beloved dead children and family siblings. At five o'clock they had gained Dreux. The Royal Chapel with its dome and pinnacles was etched against the darkening sky. Louis Philippe, gazing on the vast rotunda, remembered how hard his mother had worked to restore this Royal Chapel of St Louis. A man stepped out of the dark. It was Monsieur Maréchal, the *sous-préfet*. Amazed at their unannounced arrival, he busied himself with food and bedding. The Royal fugitives slept deeply in the unaccustomed peace. Louis Philippe had even allowed himself the belief and satisfaction that his ten-year-old grandson would succeed to the throne.

At seven o'clock, on the morning of February 25th, they were woken suddenly by the Comte de Rumigny; the *sous-préfet* had disturbing news from Paris. He was asked to enter their room. It was a shock for him – a painful dénouement – to see his King dishevelled from sleep and unshaven. 'Sire! France is now a Republic. The Paris crowds are in tumult: "No Bourbons! *Vive la République*!" ' The news was sweeping through the country. The King and Queen should escape to England immediately. Their young family was on its way even now, making for Boulogne. Precipitate plans were made. The Royal couple was to be named Monsieur and Madame Lebrun. They were to set off for Honfleur in a race against time to beat the news before they were stopped and recognised. The Comte de Rumigny, the King's valet, Thuret, the Queen's maid of honour, Mademoiselle Müser, and Monsieur Maréchal, the *sous-préfet*, should travel with them in a single berline.

They sped through the quiet Normandy morning, with Monsieur Maréchal at the wheel. Past Anet, Pacy-sur-Eure and through La Roche-Saint-André, where it was market day. The King was recognised. '*Arrête*! *Arrêtez*!' However, the highly esteemed Monsieur Maréchal was not questioned. It was possible that these market folk were still basking in a misconceived allegiance to their Monarch. On the outskirts of Evreux, still fifty miles from the coast, the couple were offered a good meal by Monsieur Renard, the resident Keeper of the Royal Forests. Nearing midnight, it was decided they should travel in two separate carriages. Evreux was not a friendly town. It was a filthy wet night. With Renard driving, Louis Philippe sat between him and Thuret, in the small cabriolet. Taking leave of his Marie-Amélie, who would travel with Rumigny and Monsieur Maréchal, they set off on their respective ways. Louis Philippe bundled in his hard seat, his collar turned up and his cap down, kept still and silent. Thuret even wondered if he was still alive. They were passing through Evreux. As they trotted past the last straggling house, they were barred exit. A man with an official bearing strode out to them and seized a bridle. '*Halte-là!*' He had heard the King was taking this route. A lantern was shoved under Louis Philippe's nose. 'It's old Renard – I know him,' cried their detective. Lowering his voice, he urged Thuret: 'Go quickly.' He had recognised the King.

The blizzard conditions worsened as they neared the sea. The flapping hood on the cabriolet threatened to blow off in the wild wind, and the ice-cold rain pierced every crack. They stopped at two tavern yards to feed the horses, Renard talking companionably to the King to offset any suspicion. By dawn on February 26th they had reached Honfleur. It had been arranged for them to spend the night at a private house in the picturesque Val de Grâce quarter, high above the town. Owned by Monsieur de Perthuis, a kinsman of Général Dumas, it appeared deserted; its gabled, hooded windows were smothered around in ivy. A thick surround of yew added to the mournful seclusion. Thuret rang the bell in vain. There was no sign of life until the gardener ambled up. He had been alerted by Monsieur de Perthuis that relations might be calling. The house was damp, he warned them, and cold. Thuret lit a fire, while Louis Philippe sat beside it, befuddled and exhausted. Marie-Amélie! Rumigny! Had something happened to them? He had waited two hours! They had a desperate story. Due to stops and searches, they had to continually change course. Rumigny reported that news of the King's plan to escape to England had spread up the coast. Trouville was on full alert – where was the King?

That same evening, Rumigny, fearful of the King's discovery, left for Trouville. He tried, unsuccessfully to negotiate with the skipper of the English Channel mail-boat, the *Express*, to take passengers aboard. However, the Captain informed the Admiralty of the request, who in turn commanded the Consul in Le Havre to effect immediate rescue plans. For a week the fugitives lay low and crouched in the modest Perthuis house, the rain and wind batting on the windows of their first-floor rooms. The wild waves and mountainous sea made torturous viewing from their steep cliff top. They sensed the net was closing round them; that Honfleur was now rife with rumour of the King in their midst; poised for escape, his intention, made impossible by the pounding sea.

By March 1st, the storms were subsiding. The following morning there was an unexpected and ominous knock on the door. It was the British Consul, William Jones. He had an immediate plan for their crossing to England. They should cross the Seine estuary on the public ferry, from Honfleur to Le Havre, that very evening. He, Mr Jones, would accompany them. The King should travel as William Smith. Mr Featherstonhaugh, the British Consul at Le Havre, would be waiting at the quayside at 7.30pm, for Mr and Mrs Smith. The King would be posing as Mr Featherstonhaugh's uncle and should be holding a white handkerchief. Mr Jones's instructions continued; rarely had Louis Philippe listened to another so attentively. He should shave his side-whiskers and wear thick goggles. Most importantly, he should talk English to his nephew and *not too loudly*. It will have been market day; there would be a good, bustling crowd, to include piglets and poultry. On that very evening, March 2nd at seven o'clock, the King and Queen, nursing their deception, were detailed to be on the quayside estuary of Honfleur.

In the event, Mr Featherstonhaugh had an awkward wait on the quayside at Le Havre. Sightings of the King were rumoured. He himself let it be known that he had read reports of the King escaping in a fishing boat from Tréport. Mr Featherstonhaugh had also taken the precaution of alerting Captain Paul of the *Express* to be ready at 7.30pm; his boat's steam should be hot and it must be moored to the quay with just one rope. It was essential, he warned Captain Paul, that when the two distinguished passengers boarded at eight o'clock, the boat must 'push off' immediately. The percipient Mr Featherstonhaugh next staged a fake fight on the quay between two persons to thus waylay the attention of the *Gendarmes*.

The Honfleur ferry boat docked on time; the trembling Queen was clearly bemused and unsure of her new identity. Featherstonhaugh took her hand and then the King came stumbling, being unused to his goggles. They greeted each other in English as planned. Louis Philippe was so relieved and garrulous with their escape so near at hand that his voice had to be quietened down by his 'nephew'. The 'uncle' and 'aunt' were seen on board the *Express* by their 'nephew'. Featherstonhaugh was thanked effusively and with tears by his 'aunt', as he left the couple installed in their cabin. He slipped hurriedly ashore and urged Captain Paul to 'let go'.

In minutes a port official came aboard and demanded to inspect the cabins. 'On my next voyage,' replied the wily Captain, 'unless you want to make the trip with us.' The boat moved slowly from the quayside; the official leapt for his life. Who was the man he'd put on board? he asked the British Consul. 'My uncle,' replied Featherstonhaugh. 'Oh, Consul, what have you done?' 'What you would have done in my place.' The *Express* steamed off for England with no further recall. Featherstonhaugh wrote a full report from 'Havre' on 3rd March, 1848, to his Foreign Secretary: 'My dear Lord Palmerston, it was a hair-trigger affair altogether, but thanks be to God everything has gone off admirably.' Lord Palmerston afterwards remarked that ... 'It equalled the best of Walter Scott's tales.' It later transpired that as the fugitives embarked at Le Havre, three *Gendarmes*, sent by the new Republican prefect, arrived at the Perthuis house to arrest them.

As they were shunted in limbo over the rough passage to Newhaven, Louis Philippe noted in his head the letter he would write to Queen Victoria; to recall her former kindnesses, to inveigle her help for some peaceful retreat. Had he known that she and Albert had followed details of his downfall, he would have been greatly heartened. The young Queen had set down in her diary on February 25th, 1848:

> Albert has just come in with terrible news from France. The King has abdicated and has left Paris. His grandson Paris has been proclaimed King, Nemours having not accepted the Regency. This is all too unbelievable, too surprising, too frightful. We are terribly upset and full of anguish for the fate of the poor dear family.

On February 26th, Albert and Victoria saw Palmerston. He had more news from Paris. Victoria summed up the scene concisely:

> A blundered command of troops, with the Garde Nationale made powerless by the King's dictum of no fighting and no blood-letting. The Government had lost its head, and now a Republic installed. The Tuileries and Palais Royal are burnt and pillaged. The entire city is in an abominable state.

After an appalling overnight crossing, 'Mr and Mrs William Smith' docked at Newhaven on March 3rd at seven o'clock. As the exhausted old couple stepped ashore, Louis Philippe cried out: 'Thank God! I am on British ground!' He and Marie-Amélie were taken up the hill to the seventeenth-century Bridge Hotel where they were given a room with a bow window. As they considered their position, slumped and aching with fatigue, the landlady offered them breakfast. Louis Philippe sent a letter post-haste to Queen Victoria, which was delivered with *her* breakfast. Later in the day the Queen's messenger arrived with the offer of Claremont House. Her Majesty had been touched by his letter. It had struck a chord from their once close friendship.

I impress upon you, Madame, that I can only underline my old attachment for you, your Majesty, with the greatest affection.

Louis Philippe

'But,' exclaimed Victoria ruefully, 'he does not call me "*Ma chère Soeur*" and he does not sign himself "*votre cher Frère*".'

Early next day Louis Philippe, the first and the last King of the French, and his Queen Marie-Amélie, left Newhaven for their final home in exile. On March 5th, they were featured in *The Illustrated London News*, lunching at Claremont, with members of their family. Louis Philippe is shown in the Great Gallery, at the head of the long table with his back to the fine fireplace, paired by its female caryatids. The Royal exiles were described in good health and not outwardly affected by their terrible ordeals. A decimated ham is seen in the foreground, swathed in crumpled napkins. Louis Philippe was inordinately proud of his carving. It was said that a newspaper could be read through his astonishingly thin slices.

On the previous day, the angelic Louise, Queen of the Belgians, had been handed a small envelope; marked 'Pour Louise', it had been sent to Laeken from Newhaven on March 3rd at 1.30pm.

Chère ange de mon cœur,

After nine days of agony I am here with your venerable and unhappy father and I bless God for having preserved this precious treasure. He is well – I am half-dead and know nothing of the children...

Louise had read all the news. Paris – a Republic! What a catastrophe! A calamity without equal! She sent an urgent consignment of money and warm clothes to the family, now collecting at Claremont; the Nemours, the Montpensiers, Princesse Joinville, Clémentine and Gusti. Marie-Amélie, who had been shamefully bandaged in the same black dress for nine days, wept with relief.* Lord Aberdeen had also slipped a thousand pounds to the household on their arrival. His generous gesture saved the family acute embarrassment.

Louise, '*their queen and Mediatrix*', also suggested alternative exiles. Why not Sicily? A lovely climate – the island where their happiness had begun … Queen Isabella sent an offer from Spain. Aumale, who found the idea of establishing themselves under any English Government repugnant, suggested the United States for an obscure and tranquil life. Berlin? Vienna? Salzburg? There was everywhere blood and fighting. Louise finally condemned her idea, with the words: '*Un vertige universel a saisi le monde*'. The chance of some contagious revolution galloping through the peaceful Continent had ruled it out. The Orléans were agreeably resigned to their dependable mansion on the mount.

---

* According to the Marquis de Flers, she always kept it and, at her express wish, it clothed her in her coffin.

31

Claremont, set upon the hill in four-square grandeur, with its porticos of Corinthian columns and its balustrades, proved a peaceful retreat. Marie-Amélie was thankful to be free of fear, of riots and suspected assassination. She could now relish time spent with her adored husband and enjoy their lively grandchildren. Aumale and Joinville relinquished their dashing careers in Algeria; Claremont had become the family's chosen exile. The large rooms with elaborately plastered high ceilings were not especially convivial; although the entrance hall, with its scarlet scagliola columns, suggested promise.

The Orléans were soon equipped with a Court Household of tutors and governesses and the domestic servants. Marie-Amélie ruled the roost and prescribed early morning cold baths for the children; riding and swimming and plenty of gymnastic exercises designed to make them brave. Louis Philippe's financial agent, André-Marie Dupin, managed to recover funds for their marginal needs. Table silver from Eu was procured and there were horses in the stable.

The inflicted Louis Philippe read cursory reports on his remarkable life's trajectory. His rating was set to be dichotomous. The scoffers with their snivelling derision, he particularly noted. The reviews of wise and sympathetic hearts, he brushed aside. The prosaic opinion that he should rest in the bosom of his family, after the ups and downs of a staggering life, he was ready to accept.

The Spectator, a radical critic of the great and the good, was quick to sharpen its claws: 'He comes for shelter with his cajoling tongue in his cheek . . .; he shakes hands all round.' Queen Victoria, writing on March 15th to her long-treasured Melbourne, blamed the 'poor King's' tumble on the last two years of his reign. 'For *sixteen* years he did a great deal to maintain peace and made France prosperous, which should *not* be forgotten.' The connivance over the Spanish marriages still clearly grated. The young Queen even suggested that if the 'dear King' had died in 1844, after his stay at Windsor, he would have been revered as a great Monarch.

There was more catastrophe in store for the ill-fated Orléans. In the late autumn of 1848, a wave of chronic diarrhoea surged through the household. Defective lead pipes in the old Claremont plumbing had poisoned the drinking water. The resulting deaths of the two much-loved ladies-in-waiting – Madame de Montjoie and her sister, Madame de Dolomieu, together with Louis Philippe's librarian and confidant, Jean Vatout – spread gloom and alarm. The family made a temporary move to the Star and Garter Hotel in Richmond, their old haunt, high on the hill overlooking the Thames. Louis Philippe, ambling one day along the Twickenham tow path, was surprised by an effusive man who shook his hand. It transpired he had been the publican who 'kept the Crown'. 'That's more than I did,' replied his former patron.

In March 1849, Louis Philippe and Marie-Amélie visited St Leonards, on the Sussex coast, to finally restore their health. The grand sea-front terraces, with a phalanx of cream Ionic columns, recalling Regent's Park, made an imposing backdrop. The elderly couple walked purposefully along the shore, breathing in the prescribed sea air. By May they felt considerably invigorated and had a surprise visit in early June from the Duchesse d'Orléans, with their grandsons, the Comte de Paris and the Duc de Chartres. Hélène had made the journey from their chosen home at Eisenach, a German city of culture, set in the forest and lush valleys of Thuringia.

This impromptu family meeting gave great joy to Louis Philippe and Marie-Amélie; promises were made to all meet again the following summer, in London; notably on July 20th, for the first Communion of the twelve-year-old Comte de Paris.

Visits from his old confederates livened Louis Philippe's autumn at Claremont. Guizot, de Broglie and Thiers were especially welcomed. It was even mooted that the Republic would soon disappear. Retorted the old King: 'All is possible in France but nothing will last, because the respect exists no more.' Guizot would nod sagely and repeat his time-worn views: of the French's dislike of happiness and their endemic ennui. Louis Philippe, who had always loved to talk, now preferred to listen. Thiers' blood-soaked summary of the Revolution that had erupted in Paris the previous June (a mere four months after the flight of the Orléans), was astounding. The people, well aware of their new-found strength, were fiercely opposed. Yet Général Cavaignac, the newly elected Minister of War, had lost five of his

Générals – and his effective repute with Louis-Napoléon. Louis Philippe listened intently to this bloody account and felt justified that his own fall had incurred little carnage.

In the late autumn of 1849, Claremont was wrapped in mists and tranquillity. Marie-Amélie attended Louis Philippe's every need. The old King's mind and memory were clear, his conversation full of the familiar humour and charm. He was eating well and still reading *The Times* with vigour. He felt boosted by his old supporters and their assurances that his reign of peace and prosperity through eighteen years would be his unique, historic legacy. His young executor, Comte de Montalivet, openly revered the July Monarchy. Whenever Louis Philippe's record was subsequently denigrated by Napoleon III, the Comte would publicly repudiate him. The Duke of Wellington, the ultimate hero, finally assured him that the 1848 Revolution of February 24th could not have been avoided; that bread and boredom were always at the root of French Revolution; the want of one and excess of the other.

The curt profiles in the *Illustrated London News* were in stark contrast: 'Coldly correct', 'deficient of genial warmth', 'the good son of a bad father', 'moral and decorous in a most immoral and indecorous age', 'self-reliant in adversity', 'selfish, mean', 'he thought the French, a nation of knaves and fools, to be ruled for his purposes'. One particularly fatuous observation could only reflect the author's crass ignorance of his subject. 'As a man he had one great error, or one great misfortune – perhaps it was a combination of them both. He was never thrown into the society of good and great men and he had no faith in human nature.'

On December 18th, Louis Philippe made his way to Drayton Manor, in Staffordshire, for a long and enjoyable lunch with Sir Robert Peel. The retired Prime Minister, still handsome and commanding, was also nearing the end of his life; fifteen years younger than the King, he was destined to be thrown from his horse, on Constitution Hill, beside Buckingham Palace, in 1850. Released from the exigencies of their past positions, the two men talked long and freely. Louis Philippe looked on Peel with admiration and envy; twice a Prime Minister and revered more than reviled. Like all acclaimed men on the brink of death, Louis Philippe was pondering his posthumous record; his portrayal through the annals of time, his ultimate failures. Peel could have no such qualms; with his powerful performance laced with admirable detail, 'no one was a more refined master of persuasion than Sir Robert Peel ...' As if sensing his guest's thoughts, Peel turned to Louis Philippe with every assurance: 'Sire, to you we owe the peace of the world; as head of a Nation justly sensitive and justly proud of its military glory, you were able to attain the great end of peace, without sacrificing any of France's interests; without ever losing any of her honour, of which you were more zealous than any person. Above all, it is the concern of all those in the seat of Government, for the British Crown, to proclaim this.'

The winter of 1850 was exceptionally rough and Louis Philippe's health was noticeably sinking. In May, a change of air at St Leonards was again advised. Guizot, hearing rumours of his master's health rapidly deteriorating, arrived in June to see him. He found him 'horribly changed, thin as a sheet of paper, his face fallen in'; yet his eye was still bright and his voice unimpaired, with all the natural force of his intelligence to prompt it.

Louis Philippe now believed he had a liver complaint and walked the sea front assiduously in an attempt to cure it. He attended the first Communion of the Comte de Paris, in London, at the French Chapel, on July 20th. The effort entailed had exhausted him; he returned the next day to Claremont. The summer breezes wafted over the groves and green vistas spread all before him.

On Saturday August 24th, 1850, Louis Philippe joined the family for lunch on the portico terrace. The sun blazed down as he was demonstrably failing. He ate nothing. After a feverish night, his doctor, Gueneau de Mussy, diagnosed pleurisy. 'You come to give me my leave,' Louis Philippe commented cheerfully, and sent immediately for Général Dumas; there were details in his will to settle and a page in his memoirs, on Maréchal Macdonald, that he had still to complete ... He signed his papers with a hand already frozen from approaching death. At three o'clock the Abbé Guelle entered the cabinet room next to the King's bedroom. 'My dear Abbé,' greeted Louis Philippe, as he sat quietly in his armchair. 'Do not hesitate to give me Communion, I feel that I am going ...' The Princes and Princesses entered and were blessed by the King, one by one. He took Communion and was given unction.

Turning to Marie-Amélie, he murmured, 'You are happy? Good! So am I.' 'Yes and I hope to join you soon!' A fleeting joy lit up her face. Their twelve grandchildren were brought for him to kiss and to bless. Towards evening, the fever gave him fresh impetus. He repeated to Marie-Amélie: 'I am content; I feel a well-being in my approach to God . . .' The night passed free of crisis; by morning the fever had dropped but his febrile body was slipping away.

On August 26th the Abbé found him in his bed; his face serene and free from pain. Louis Philippe told him he felt better; that he hoped for many more hours of life. He would like to pray again ... but his lips could now barely move and no sound came. It was eight o'clock; the family and the faithful household convened hurriedly to kneel at the foot of his bed. At 8.15am, without suffering, Louis Philippe gave his last sigh.

In May 1849, Louis Philippe had written a simple testament, to include these words:

'Let the light of truth come to enlighten my country on its true interests; to dissipate the illusions that so often falsify its aim, leading it to resulting opposition to what it wants to achieve. May it bring back to its ways, equity, sagacity, public morale and respect of all beliefs, that only are able to give its Government the necessary strength to repress hostile passions – and to establish confidence of its stability. Such wishes have always been most dear to me, and the misfortunes experienced with all my family, will do nothing but render them more fervent in our hearts.'

On Louis Philippe's death, there was a flurry of comment in the European press. Perhaps his close acquaintance, Victor Hugo, wrote the most concisely. He had followed the dramatic vicissitudes of his life; the testing circumstances and his ways with compromise: 'There was freedom of the Press, freedom of Parliamentary debate, freedom of conscience and of speech.'

Henri, 2ème Comte de Paris (1908–1999), also emphasised the freedom issue. In his brilliant Foreword to his great, great grandfather's *Memoirs*, he concluded: 'It is to Louis Philippe that France owes its freedom. It would be only fair to remember this.'

Post Script

On Tuesday October 14th of the year 2008, as the trees quivered gold on Avenue Matignon, the doors to Christie's, Paris, were thrown wide. The fine façade with its Corinthian columns and tall arched windows opened on marble salons and a grand bifurcating flight of stairs. But the scene of action was below stairs, where an auctioneer in the rostrum wielded his gavel. The last emotive souvenirs of two centuries of the Bourbons and d'Orléans were on offer from the recently deceased Comte and Comtesse de Paris. The poignant miniature of the imprisoned Dauphin, the ten-year-old Louis XVII, reading his book; the ivory silk pochettes, embroidered with roses and garlands of leaves, by his mother, as she too languished in the Temple prison; Marie-Amélie awash with lace and blonde curls under a wide red hat where white ostrich feathers nestled in the brim; Louis Philippe's enviable blue-tinted sunglasses, made in England.

As the illustrious effects were swept one by one from the screen, reserve upon reserve was exceeded. The 500 lots drew 2,000 reviewers and an estimated 800 buyers. The sale totalled 2.38 million Euros.

The present Henri, Comte de Paris, Duc de France had anticipated certain portraits and pieces would be added to museum collections where such symbols of history and heritage would be cherished by all. In the dimly lit side aisle, his heroic ancestor – Louis Philippe, First and Last King of the French – appeared to smile enigmatically from a portrait of his benign old age. The deceased hostess of this absorbing show, Isabelle, Comtesse de Paris, glowed from her frame, in a simple scarlet dress, to face the stage.

As I pondered on Louis Philippe's holly walking stick, a handsome young man came up to me and proffered his card: Prince Jean d'Orléans, Duc de Vendôme. We touched on a shared admiration and applause for his underestimated forebear.

Bibliography

Books

Alméras, Henri d', *La Vie Parisienne sous le Règne Louis-Philippe*, Levallois-Perret, 1968

Andress, David, *The Terror – Civil War in the French Revolution*, Little Brown, 2005

Baldick, Robert, *Dinner at Magny's*, Gollancz, 1971

Boigne, Comtesse de, *Mémoires Vol. I*, Librairie Plon, 1907

Carlyle, Thomas, *The French Revolution Vols I, II, III*, Chapman and Hall, 1837

Cashmore, T.M.R., *The Orleans Family in Twickenham 1800–1932*, Borough of Twickenham Local History Society, 1982

Cloake, John, CMG *Cottages and Common Fields of Richmond and Kew*, Phillimore & Co. Ltd, 2011

Cooper, Duff, *Talleyrand*, Jonathan Cape, 1932

Cooper, Phyllis M., *The Story of Claremont*, 9th edition, 2000

Doyle, William, *The French Revolution*, Oxford University Press, 1980

Duhamel, Jean, *Louis Philippe et la Première Entente Cordiale*, Pierre Horay – Editions de Flore, 1951

Dumas, Alexandre, *La Route de Varennes*, Le Livre d'Histoire, Paris, 2004

Dyson, C.C., *Life of Marie-Amélie. Last Queen of the French 1782–1866*, John Long Ltd, Haymarket, London, 1910

Elliott, Mrs, *Journal of My Life During the French Revolution*, Waterlow and Sons Ltd, Constable, 1859 edition

Flers, Le Marquis de, *Le Roi Philippe, Vie Anecdotique 1773–1850*, Librairie de la Société des Gens de Lettres, Palais-Royal, 1891

Gascoigne, Bamber, *Encyclopaedia of Britian*, Macmillan Press, 1993

Goethe, J.W., *Italian Journey 1786–1788*, W.M. Collins, 1962

Green, James & Greenwood, Silvia, *Ham & Petersham as it Was*, Hendon Publishing, 1980

Greville, Charles, *The Greville Diary, Vol. I*, Wilson, Philip Whitwell Wilson (ed.), William Heinmann, 1927

Guérard, Albert Léon, *French Civilisation in the Nineteenth Century*, T F Unwin, 1914

Hall, Major John, *England and the Orléans Monarchy*, Smith, Elder & Co., London, 1912

Horne, Alistair, *Seven Ages of Paris*, Macmillan, 2002

Howarth, T.E.B., *Citizen King*, Eyre & Spottiswoode, 1961

Jardin, André & Tudesq, André-Jean, *Restoration and Reaction 1815–1848*, Editions du Seuil, 1973

Joinville, Prince de, *Vieux Souvenirs 1818–1848, avec illustrations de l'auteur*, Calmann-Lévy, Paris, 1894

Lassère, Madeleine, *Louise, Reine des Belges 1812–1850*, Perrin, 2006

Lejeune, Anthony, *White's – The First 300 Years*, A & C Black, 1993

Lenôtre, G., *Les Fils de Philippe – Egalité Pendant La Terreur*, Librairie Académique, 1907

Loomis, Stanley, *A Crime of Passion*, Hodder & Stoughton, 1968

Louis Philippe, *Mémoires 1773–1793*, Librairie Plon, 1971/74

Lucas-Dubreton, J., *Restoration and the July Monarchy*, Lucas-Dubreton, 1929

Maricourt, Baron André de, *La Duchesse d'Orléans, Mère du Roi Louis-Philippe*, Emile-Paul Frères, 1914

McCarthy, Justin H., *The French Revolution Vols I, II*, Chatto & Windus, 1890

Montpensier, Duke of, *Autobiography*, Baudouin Frères, 1824

Morison, Elizabeth & Lamont, Frances, *An Adventure*, Macmillan & Co. Ltd

Orléans, Duchesse d', *Journal de Marie-Amélie de Bourbon des Deux-Siciles, Duchesse d'Orléans (Volume II), 1814–1822*, (ed.) S.A.R., Duchesse de Vendôme, Librairie Plon, 1938

Orléans, Louis Philippe d', *Correspondance, Mémoires et Discours Inédits de Louis Philippe d'Orléans*, Librairie de la Société des Gens de Lettres, Palais-Royal, 1863

Price, Munro, *The Fall of the French Monarchy*, Macmillan, 2002

Price, Munro, *The Perilous Crown*, Macmillan, 2007

Recouly, Raymond, *Louis Philippe, Roi des Français*, Editions de Paris, 1936

Ritchie, Leitch, Versailles, Longman & Co, 1839

Rousseau, Jean-Jacques, *The Confessions*, Penguin Books, 1953

Rudé, George, *The Crowd in the French Revolution*, The Clarendon Press, Oxford, 1959

Rumigny, Général Comte de, *Souvenirs 1789–1860*, Emile-Paul Frères, 1921

Seward, Desmond, *Prince of the Renaissance – The Life of François I*, Constable, 1973

Stoeckl, Baroness de (Agnes), *King of the French – A Portrait of Louis Philippe 1773–1850*, John Murray, 1957

Thiers, M.A., *History of the French Revolution* (5 Volumes), Richard Bentley, "Publisher in Ordinary to Her Majesty", London

Tour du Pin, Madame de la, *Memoirs*, Harvill, 1969

Trognon, M. Auguste, *Vie de Marie-Amélie, Reine des Français*, Editions Michel Lévy Frères, Paris, 1871

Verlet, Pierre, *French Furniture and Interior Decoration of the 18th Century*, Barrie Books Ltd, 1957

Vigée le Brun, Elisabeth, *Memoirs*, (trans. Siân Evans), Camden Press, 1989

Washington, George, *Rules of Civility & Decent Behaviour*, Applewood Books Inc.

Wright, Rev. G.N., *Life and Times of Louis Philippe, Vol I*, Fisher Son & Co., London, 1842

Newspapers, Magazines and Other Sources

Christie's, Paris, Catalogue *Succession de Feus Monseigneur le Comte de Paris et Madame la Comtesse de Paris* (October 14th, 2008)

Journal des Débats, December 20th, 1917

Moniteur Universel, July 30th, 1835

La Grande Encyclopédie, Libraire Larousse, Paris, 1971

Louis Philippe at Windsor, Parts I and II, Scott, Barbara. *Country Life*, November 10th and 17th, 1983

Orleans House – The Octagon, Hussey, Christopher. *Country Life*, September 15th, 1944

The History of Orleans House, Twickenham (Compilation), London Borough of Richmond upon Thames

"The King of the French at Windsor", *Illustrated London News*, October 12th, 1844

"The Late Louis-Philippe, ex-King of the French", *Illustrated London News*, August 31st, 1850

Château de Balleroy, Bayeux

Eton College Library

London Library

Musée Louis-Philippe du Château d'Eu

Redwood Library, Newport, Rhode Island

State Library of New South Wales, Sydney

Index

265